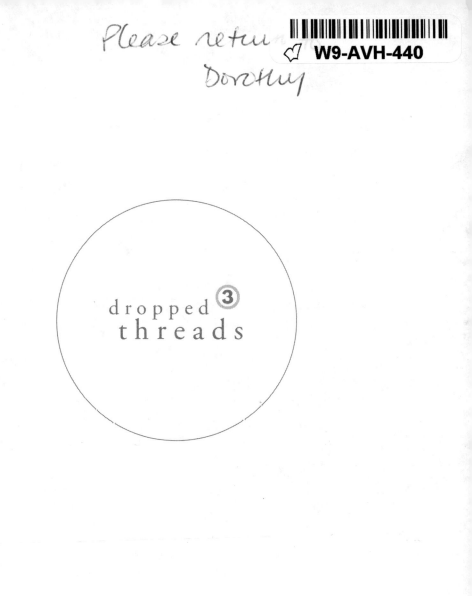

dropped ③
threads

dropped ③ threads

BEYOND THE SMALL CIRCLE

edited by **MARJORIE ANDERSON**

introduction by **ANN-MARIE MacDONALD**

VINTAGE CANADA

Pages 385–86 constitute an extension of this copyright page.

www.randomhouse.ca

The phrase "beyond the small circle" is from the poem "To See Clearly,"
in the book *Whetstone* by Lorna Crozier. Used by permission of
McClelland & Stewart Ltd.

National Library of Canada Cataloguing in Publication

Dropped threads 3 : beyond the small circle / edited by
Marjorie Anderson.

ISBN-13: 978-0-679-31385-4
ISBN-10: 0-679-31385-0

1. Canadian essays (English)—Women authors. 2. Canadian essays
(English)—21st century. 3. Women—Literary collections.
I. Anderson, Marjorie May, 1944–

PS8235.W7B49 2006   C814'.60803522   C2005-905105-1

Text design: Kelly Hill

Printed and bound in Canada

10 9 8 7 6 5 4 3 2 1

For Gary, with love

CONTENTS

FOREWORD

MARJORIE ANDERSON

My first discovery of the universe a word can hold happened on a December night in rural Manitoba, where I lived with my seven siblings and our parents. I had been at a sleepover with a cousin who lived a half mile down a bush trail. In the middle of the night I was struck by a wave of loneliness so powerful it forced me out of bed, into my clothes and, stealthily, out the door of my cousin's house. The path home, familiar in the daytime, had been transformed into foreign territory with its alternate strips of moonlight and tree shadow stretching over mounds of snow. I felt as though I had never been on that trail before and, moreover, that no one knew I was there. At that moment, I was outside every known person's awareness—and I was *inside* the word *alone*. I knew it intimately and totally.

The next week in school I learned that a classmate, an only child, had lost both parents in a boating accident. Immediately I understood that she too had crossed over to the interior of the word *alone* but, with a start, I recognized that her invisible landscape was vastly different from mine. My eight-year-old mind did the transference, and I was left unsure and wobbly where earlier I'd been certain I had discovered the absolute, shining truth about aloneness.

These two experiences strongly shaped my relationship with language, and with what language builds—knowledge.

Never again could I feel the charmed security of knowing something totally. Truth and meaning became provisional, someone's small claim on a vast landscape of possibilities, one dot in a pointillist painting. My initial sense of loss was replaced by a fascination with the personal stories of others and their claims on what a word signified or an experience held. I sensed that if I listened closely and gathered in as many "dots" of meaning as I could, I might, just might, come close to the marvel of that mid-winter epiphany of 1952, when the gap between language and complete understanding vanished.

I've come to understand the force of women's interest in personal narratives as a collective version of that impulse born in me when I was eight. We need to know how to read the world beyond our experience of it, and we trust first-person accounts, perhaps more so because of the lack of faith in political and corporate declarations of truth and meaning. Personal stories are one means of getting a trusted inside view—*This is how wisdom, love, joy, betrayal, fear, regret have been for us.* No assertions of absolute truth, no earth-shaking revelations or attempts to manipulate another's belief, just individual voices making individual claims on the discovery of meaning.

Several years ago Carol Shields and I had the privilege of tapping into this passion for an inside view of women's experiences when we collaborated on editing the first two *Dropped Threads* anthologies. These collections of intimate stories on surprise and silence in women's lives have been embraced by readers with an enthusiasm that left all of us—contributors, editors and publishers—amazed at the size of the community of shared interest we found. The fact that Carol's wisdom and generous spirit were central to that community gives those paired books an especially treasured quality.

And yet there has been an ongoing insistence for more, from both readers and writers. In the three years since the publication of the second *Dropped Threads* anthology, personal essays have continued to come in "just in case," and in every women's gathering or discussion group I've attended, inevitably there was the question "Will there be another collection?" The decision to go ahead with a new anthology was a way of honouring the creative fervour swirling around me and, happily, keeping connected to it. The idea for the new theme came easily when I thought again of how varied our encounters inside language can be. Instead of having women focus on what they *haven't been told*, I wanted them to write about their significant discoveries of meaning, to pass on what they *have to tell* all us enthusiastic dot collectors.

In direct invitations to established writers and in a cross-Canada call for proposals placed on the *dropped threads* website and in the *Globe and Mail*, the publishers and I asked women to consider the topic "This I Know." The responses were immediate, as women released their well-earned wisdoms into stories, which rose up from across the country like happy vapours too long confined. The only hesitancy was with absolute truth-telling, with the ring of certainty that "know" suggests. Many writers obviously felt far more comfortable with a stance one of them referred to as "this I suspect." Advice-giving too came in on a slant, delivered with humour and a clear-eyed view of the limited benefits of unsolicited counsel, no matter how well intended.

There also seemed to be limits on the kind of stories women wanted to tell. None of the three hundred proposals and submissions dealt with what women have learned about long-standing love relationships with men, and only a few were about their experiences of professional work in the traditional haunts of men. As if . . . well, as if these topics have had adequate coverage, or verge on dangerous territory.

What women did want to write about was the importance of other connections—to nature, to animals, to dance, to lives beyond the familiar, and above all to the varied choices and experiences of motherhood, a topic central to a third of the submissions. Another common theme was a sense of place: discovering it within families and in the world, but also asserting it by showing the unique experiences behind common terms such as victim, addict, rebel, celebrity. Women's remarkable affinity for endurance and peace surfaced in all these accounts. Whether they shared intimate moments of grace and beauty or charted paths through minefields of personal pain, these writers left blueprints for ways of being that others could follow.

The thirty-five pieces I've selected from this rich array of stories stood out for me because of the particularly fresh, engaging ways they provide the sustenance we tend to look for in narratives. Each story either places us in a landscape we can experience anew—*Ah, yes, I recognize that feeling, that thought, that phase*—or takes us to new territory where we're left altered in understanding and empathy—*So that's what it's like inside an experience I've never had*. Either way, we're enriched.

An eighty-two-year old friend of my sister commented when she heard I was working on this collection of women's personal essays, "Tell her to lighten things up a bit for us." Well, Rose, I hope you and all others come away from reading this book buoyed up by the courage and creative wisdom of the contributors. And by the fresh glimpses they offer of what might otherwise lie just beyond our own small circles of meaning and sight.

ANN-MARIE MACDONALD

When I was in elementary school, teachers would commonly assign to the class the task of writing a piece of fiction—a "composition"—with the advice "Write what you know." This directive always gave me a sinking feeling, as if the teacher were attaching concrete blocks to my imagination. "What do I know?" I'd think. "I'm nine years old!" Leaving aside the fact that a writer's point of view is pretty much forged by the age of five, and the templates for most of experience are cut by the time one is nine, I was not in a position, at that tender age, to mine my own experience and shape it in a way that might speak to others. What I understood from the teacher was that she or he was advising a concrete, literal approach: "Write about what you did on your summer vacation."

While, as a much younger person, I didn't know what I knew, I did know what I could imagine, and I had no trouble authorizing myself to travel infinite distances from the concrete "known." I didn't have the words to describe it, but I know now that metaphor—with all its bright trappings of myth, fairy tale and fable—was my native clime, the universe in which I felt at home; and of course my stories about headless horsemen, nine-year-old spies and daring rescues at knifepoint said far more about the concrete facts of my life than any forensic description could have. As I matured as a writer, my stories became more and more rooted in the "here and now." I didn't need such elaborate masks to convey my meanings and I strove for a deceptive realism: a layer of what looks like solid ground that, in fact, is afloat on a sea of metaphor—the inverse of magic realism. In a sense, I started way outside of the "small circle" and worked my way back in. Or perhaps I dove down, spiralling into the centre of it, toward the vanishing point that suddenly opens up, like a wormhole, onto a strange new world.

How can we know what we don't know? What is it like to be someone else? Does cinnamon taste the same to you as it does to me? When I see a round red fruit and call it an apple, are you seeing the same shape and colour? As a child, these were the questions that took my mind out to wander during long sermons at Sunday mass (along with fantasies of rappelling with rope and harness up the inside walls of the church) or at bedtime just after the lights went out, when thoughts of infinity (more circles) made me feel carsick. And in adolescence: how big are our individual circles? Are we doomed to be utterly alone in them? My skull is a circle: the ultimate prison. (See June Callwood's piece for a wise antidote to adoloescent angst.) Now I take solace in a paradox: each of us is indeed alone, and it's our awareness of this, along with our ability to empathize with the isolation of others, that allows us to become less so. Empathy is the raw material of compassion. Compassion is an act of imagination; a leap of faith into another's closed circle.

This ability to extrapolate from one's own limited experience to that of many unrelated others is a type of magic, no less than the transformation of a scarf into a bouquet of flowers. Compassion is the power to transform the base metal of mundane experience into a kind of universal gold, recognizable—valuable—to all; compassion is the ability to see deeply enough into our own souls and memories that we glimpse a kind of *prima materia*, that elusive substance sought by alchemists, physicists and mystics from which all matter—including all life—is formed; that irreducible stuff or force (noun or verb) that we share with the merest parti- cle in the farthest reaches of the universe. Surely we are all working with the same basic materials even when it comes to those carbon-based emanations we call thoughts and feel- ings. This means that, across great gulfs of time, experience, class, culture and gender, and more, we not only can, but must imagine ourselves into one another's points of view. Not because "to understand all is to pardon all." But because without understanding there can be no "fellow feeling," which is what compassion is. And without compassion there can be no wisdom. No peace. Compassion implies humility. What could be humbler than the act of listening, of placing one's imagination at the service of another's point of view; even if on occasion we conclude that we must fight what we have heard and seen, or abandon someone we have put our heart and soul into understanding.

In this book there are grab bags stuffed with toothsome pearls of wisdom; there are cautionary tales by turns humor- ous and harrowing; there are finely distilled stories of loss and letting go, of redemption through contact with unlikely others (including and, at times especially, other animals); there are accounts of the struggle to balance personal fulfill- ment with the needs of others, of the mortal combat that precedes forgiveness. Epiphanies are shared in the bracing and irreverent tones of a kitchen-table conversation, and mundane moments are lit with lyricism such that the famil- iar is revealed as fleeting, and terribly precious. And there are striking contradictions. A piece by a mother of sons mourning the absence of daughters sits cheek by jowl with a daughter's account of the painful necessity of cutting her mother out of her life. Most of the pieces, however, inhabit the border zones: those uncertain territories where peace and strife are in constant negotiation.

The writers themselves are a diverse group: journalists, authors, athletes, homemakers, teachers, artists, office workers and entertainers, many of whom combine several of the above. Some inhabit very large social and professional circles, others trace a shorter radius of home and family, but these differences are, I believe, far from definitive when it comes to a highly evolved world view: the Brontës and Emily Dickinson are evidence of that, just as an adventurer like Jane Goodall makes of her journey, far from human culture, an illumination of what connects us most intimately. And, indeed, this book is concerned with relationships— personal, political, environmental. Some of the pieces are funny, others are angry, many are both; some are poetic, others are barbed with satire. All are earnest, even the ironic ones. Each writer has done her utmost to share a scrap of wisdom—something torn from experience and saved against the day when it will find its place in the quilt—along with her doubts, in a way that is unmediated by ego or apology (that false humility which is really a disguise for fear). At the centre of this collection is each writer's struggle to articulate a unique point of view in such a way that it can be launched like a message in a bottle to innumerable other "islands"; or, more aptly, to cause a ripple that dilates and intersects with other circles until the circles disappear and we are left with something that resembles more of a web: interdependent, inextricable. The result is thirty-five acts of compassion and little leaps of faith.

In this book, confidences are shared that might not even be whispered otherwise, certainly not to a stranger in a bookstore. But the page is different. When I write fiction, I imagine that I am speaking to one person: I can't see the face, which is indistinct in any case, hovering just outside my peripheral vision; but I am aware of a benevolently inclined stranger, a tender ghost, politely yet eagerly haunting my left shoulder, trying for a glimpse of the page. I have compassion for this hopeful ghost. She or he is craving something true, something nourishing. Reading is among the few truly private and intimate acts left to us. As such, it has the paradoxical power to bring us closer to one another than any of our high-tech amenities. This book assumes complicity and understanding. It assumes imagination in its highest form: compassion. This book makes of the reader, a friend.

part one

A KIND OF BENEDICTION

POLONIA

MARGARET ATWOOD

In response to
"What advice would
you give the young?"

What advice would I give the young? That is the question put to me by the editor of this book, and it's one I have trouble answering. Here's why.

Just before Christmas I was in a cheese store, purchasing some cheese, when a very young man of—oh, say between forty and fifty—entered, manifesting bewilderment. His wife had sent him out to get something called "meringue sugar," with strict instructions to buy no other kind, and he didn't know what the stuff was and couldn't find it, and nobody in any of the shops he'd so far wandered into had any idea either.

He didn't say this to me. He said it to the cheese shop person. She too appeared to be without a clue as to the meringue sugar mystery.

None of this was any concern of mine. I could have— should have—simply pursued my own personal goal of cheese acquisition. Instead I found myself saying, "Don't buy icing sugar, that isn't what your wife wants. What she probably wants is something like fruit sugar or berry sugar, which is sometimes called powdered sugar but it isn't really powdered, it's a finer grind than ordinary white sugar, though you'll have a hard time finding it at this time of year. But really, ordinary white sugar works just fine for meringues as long as you beat it in very slowly. I use it all the time myself, and it helps if you add just a tiny bit of cream of tartar and maybe a half teaspoon of white vinegar, and . . ."

At this point my daughter—who'd succeeded in identifying the required cheese—got me in a hammerlock and dragged me over to the cash register, where a lineup was building. "The white vinegar, not the brown," I called in closing. But I was already appalled at myself. Why had I spewed out all this unasked-for advice to a complete stranger, albeit a helpless and confused one?

It's an age thing. There's a hormone in the brain that kicks in when you see a younger person in a state of shell shock over meringue sugar, or how to get the lids off jars or the beet stains out of tablecloths, or the right way of dumping the bad boyfriend who should be disposed of immediately because as anyone with half a wit can see the man is a psychopath, or which candidate is the best bet in the local election, or any number of other things on which you appear to yourself to have an overflowing fund of useful knowledge that may vanish from the planet unless you dish it out right and left, on the spot, to those in need. This hormone automatically takes over—like the hormone in a mother robin that forces her to cram worms and grubs down the gaping maws of plaintively cheeping nestlings—and reams of helpful hints unscroll out of your mouth like a runaway roll of toilet paper falling down the stairs. You have no way of stopping this process. It just happens.

It's been happening for centuries; no, for millennia. Ever since we developed what is loosely called human culture, the young have been on the receiving end of instruction from their elders whether they liked it or not. Where are the best roots and berries? How do you make an arrowhead? What fish are plentiful, where and when? Which mushrooms are poisonous? The instruction must have taken pleasant forms

("Great arrowhead! Now try it this way!") or unpleasant ones ("You idiot! That's no way to skin a mastodon! Do it like this!") Since we've still got the same hardware as Cro-Magnon man, or so we're told, it's merely the details that have changed, not the process. (Hands up, everyone who's ever taped laundry instructions to the washer-dryer for the benefit of their teenaged kids.)

There are mountains of self-help books testifying to the fact that the young—and not only the young—are fond of securing advice on every possible subject, from how to get rid of pimples, to the suave way of manoeuvring some youth with commitment issues into marriage, to the management of colic in infants, to the making of the perfect waffle, to the negotiation of an improved salary, to the purchase of a rewarding retirement property, to the planning of a really knock-out funeral. The cookbook is one of the earliest forms of self-help book. Mrs. Beeton's enormous nineteenth-century tome, *The Book of Household Management*, expands the tradition, and includes not only recipes but advice on everything, from how to tell a real fainting fit from a sham one, to the proper colour choices for blondes and brunettes, to which topics of conversation are safe for afternoon visits. (Stay away from religious controversy. The weather is always acceptable.) Martha Stewart, Ann Landers and Miss Manners are Mrs. Beeton's great-granddaughters, as is Mrs. Rombauer-Becker of *Joy of Cooking* fame and every home handywoman, interior decorator and sex expert you've ever watched on television. Look at the shows and read the books and authors quickly, in sequence, and you'll feel the need of some cotton wool to stuff in your ears as a defence against the endless stream of what would sound like relentless finger-waving, hectoring and nagging if you hadn't chosen to let these folks in the door yourself.

With how-to books and self-help shows you can absorb the advice if and when you want it, but relatives or friends or acquaintances or mothers cannot be so easily opened and then closed and put back on the shelf. Over the centuries, novels and plays have given us a stock character: the older female—or male, both versions exist—who's a voluble interfering busybody, deluging the young folk with unasked-for tips on how to conduct their lives, coupled with sharp-tongued criticisms when the advice is not heeded. Mrs. Rachel Lynde in *Anne of Green Gables* is a case in point. Sometimes this type of person will have a good heart—Mrs. Lynde does—although, just as often, he or she will be a sinister control freak like the Queen of the Night in Mozart's *Magic Flute*. But good or bad, the meddlesome busybody is seldom entirely sympathetic. Why? Because we like other people—well-meaning or not—to mind their own business, not ours. Even helpful advice can be indistinguishable from bossiness when you're on the receiving end.

My own mother was of the non-interference school unless it was a matter of life and death. If we children were doing something truly dangerous and she knew about it, she would stop us. Otherwise she let us learn by experience. Less work for her, come to think about it, though there was of course the work of self-restraint. She later said that she had to leave the kitchen when I was making my first pie crust, the sight was so painful to her. I've come to appreciate these silences of my mother's, though she could always produce a condensed pill of sensible advice when asked for it. All the more puzzling, then, that I have taken to blurting out instructions to strangers in cheese stores. Perhaps I take after my father, who was relentlessly informative, though he always tempered the force of his utterances by beginning, "As I'm sure you know . . ."

I went to high school at a time when students were required to learn things off by heart. This work formed part of the exam: you were expected not only to recite the set pieces out loud but to regurgitate them onto the page, with marks off for faults in spelling. One standard item was the speech made in *Hamlet* by the old court counsellor, Polonius, to his son, Laertes, who is departing for a trip to France. Here's the speech, in case you may have forgotten it, as I found I had when I tried for total recall.

> Yet here, Laertes! Aboard, aboard, for shame!
> The wind sits in the shoulder of your sail,
> And you are stay'd for. There,—my blessing with thee!
> And these few precepts in thy memory
> See thou character. Give thy thoughts no tongue,
> Nor any unproportion'd thought his act.
> Be thou familiar, but by no means vulgar.
> Those friends thou hast, and their adoption tried,
> Grapple them to thy soul with hoops of steel;
> But do not dull thy palm with entertainment
> Of each new-hatch'd, unfledged comrade. Beware
> Of entrance to a quarrel; but, being in,
> Bear't that the opposed may beware of thee.
> Give every man thy ear, but few thy voice:
> Take each man's censure, but reserve thy judgment.
> Costly thy habit as thy purse can buy,
> But not express'd in fancy; rich, not gaudy:
> For the apparel oft proclaims the man;
> And they in France of the best rank and station
> Are of a most select and generous chief in that.

Neither a borrower nor a lender be:
For loan oft loses both itself and friend,
And borrowing dulls the edge of husbandry.
This above all, to thine own self be true,
And it must follow, as the night the day,
Thou canst not then be false to any man.
Farewell: my blessing season this in thee!

The method is aggressive—Polonius scolds Laertes because he isn't on the ship yet, then holds him back with a long list of do's and don'ts—but it's all very good advice. A rational person can't disagree with any of it. Yet in every performance of *Hamlet* I've ever seen, Polonius is played as a comical but tedious old pedant and Laertes listens to him with barely concealed impatience, although he himself has just dished out a heaping plateful of his own advice to his younger sister, Ophelia. Looked at objectively, Polonius can't really have been the boring idiot we're usually shown: he's chief adviser to Claudius, who's a villain but no fool. Claudius wouldn't have kept Polonius around if the latter had really been several bricks short of a load. Why then is the scene always played this way?

One reason is that it would be boring if done straight, because advice you haven't asked for is always boring, and it's especially boring if the person giving the advice is old and you yourself are young. It's like the cartoon with the caption "What people say, what cats hear": over the head of the cat is a voice balloon with nothing in it. The advice to the cat may be perfectly good—"Don't mess with that big tomcat down the street"—but the cat isn't receptive. It will follow its own counsel, because that's what cats do. And that's what young people do as well, unless there's something specific they want you to tell them.

Which is my way of ducking the question. What advice would I give the young? None, unless they asked for it. Or that's what would happen in an ideal world. In the world I actually inhabit, I break this virtuous rule daily, since at the slightest excuse I find myself blathering on about all kinds of things, due to the mother-robin hormone I've already mentioned. Thus:

As I'm sure you know, the most eco-friendly toilet is the Caroma. You can state your position and stick to your guns without being rude. Awnings cut down on summer heat through your windows by 70 percent or more. If you want to be a novelist, do back exercises daily—you'll need them later. Don't phone him, let him phone you. Think globally, act locally. After having a baby you lose your brain and some of your hair, but they both grow back. A stitch in time saves nine. There's a new kind of crampon you can strap onto your boots, handy on icy sidewalks. Don't stick a fork into a wall socket. If you don't clean the lint trap on the dryer it may burst into flames. If the hair on your arms stands up in a thunderstorm, jump. Don't step into a canoe when it's pulled up on the beach. Never let anyone pour you a drink in a bar. Sometimes the only way out is through. In the northern forest, hang your food from a tree some distance from your sleeping area and don't wear perfume. This above all, to thine own self be true. Eyebrow tweezers are handy for getting big wads of glop out of bathroom sink drains. Every household should contain a wind-up flashlight. And don't forget about the little touch of vinegar, for the meringues. That's the white vinegar, not the brown.

However, here's the best piece of advice of all: *Sometimes young people don't want advice from their elders.* They don't wish you to turn into Polonia, not as such. They can do without the main body of the speech—the long checklist of instructions. But they welcome the part at the end, which is a kind of benediction:

Farewell. My blessing season this in thee!

They want you to see them off on their voyage, which is—after all—a voyage they have to make on their own. Maybe it will be a dangerous voyage, maybe you'd be able to handle the danger better than they will, but you can't do it for them. You've got to stay behind, waving encouragingly, anxiously, a little plaintively: *Farewell! Fare well!*

But they do want the goodwill from you. They want the blessing.

CREATURE
COMFORT

MARIE-LYNN HAMMOND

Picture this: a four-year-old girl sees a horse in the flesh for the first time. The creature looms above her, enormous, like something from a fairy tale or dream. The copper-coloured beast is tied up to a corral railing, somewhere on the Alberta prairie, circa 1952. The sky is a blue inverted bowl, the August sun almost at its zenith. The heat is unreal. Everyone's sweating.

The child's mother stands several yards away on the veranda of the ranch house, not just because of the shade, but because she's scared silly of horses. The child's father is not, although horses don't interest him much. He rode a few times as a child, then fell hard for airplanes and the sky. But he can see his daughter is mesmerized. A man in chaps and a dented cowboy hat asks the child if she'd like to sit on the horse. The child nods, so he scoops her up into the western saddle that feels as broad as a couch. The horse, its head low in the heat, doesn't move. A few feet away, the father and the cowboy chat desultorily, but the child barely hears them. She leans down to touch the bright shining neck of the horse, she inhales its scent of sweet grass and warm earth and dust. No one offers to lead the horse around—perhaps they think she's too small to stay on, even at a walk—but she doesn't care. She's in some kind of swooning ecstasy.

A few minutes later, her father reaches up to take her off

the horse. The child makes a face. "Noooo," she whines. "It's time to go now," says the father sternly, and begins to pull her out of the saddle. A much decorated World War II pilot, he won't have a four-year-old defying him, no sir, especially in front of another man. The child stubbornly grabs the high pommel and hangs on with all her tiny might. The father pulls, she begins to wail: "No! No! No!" Her mother comes rushing over, but slows down uncertainly several feet from the horse as her maternal instinct collides with her terror of the beast.

The child is screaming now, but it's no use—the father yanks his flailing daughter off the horse and unceremoniously carries her to the car. The child's screams pierce the summer afternoon as the family drives off, the parents embarrassed as hell over the mystifying behaviour of their child.

• • •

That child was me, and I can still hear my own screams from that day. Of course, at the time I couldn't explain what had happened. All this over a horse? Well, yes. I had just found my primary totem animal, my spirit guide, my religion. And they had torn us apart.

Horse crazy, they call girls and women like me. It's a sex thing, snicker the boys and men. They are *so* wrong.

What makes a small child know so strongly, so deeply, that she has connected with something vital to her soul and heart and body, something that seems to come out of nowhere, with no immediate precedent? Do we humans have genes for our passions? Researchers are beginning to think there's a gene for religious faith or belief. That might explain why some people find God so fervently and defini- tively, and others, like me—despite fifteen years of rigorous

Catholic brainwashing—thoroughly lose God as soon as they're old enough to think for themselves.

But animals . . . go figure. My father's mother loved animals, horses and dogs in particular. Did I somehow inherit my passion from her? Or are past lives operating here? I don't know, but I do know this: I'm not alone.

Whether it's horses or dogs or cats (if the horse is my main totem, then the cat ranks just below it), there are legions of women (and some men) who love animals. I'm not talking about celebrities who dye their poodles pink to match their wardrobes, or stuff their chihuahuas in Vuitton handbags as though a dog were just one more accessory. And while I know some of us are guilty of infantilizing our kitties or turning our pooches into human-companion surrogates, I also know that many more of us have made deep soul connections with animals that are mystical, mysterious and profoundly healing.

But this is a passion that until recently we've been somewhat embarrassed to acknowledge. It's a passion that gets ridiculed. With homosexuality now out in the open in Western culture, *this* is the new love that dare not speak its name, especially in our patriarchal world, where it's seen as somehow soft to love animals. Animals are for hunting down and eating, for God's sake. And if you're a woman, you're soft already, so better shut up about critters.

Picture this: I'm visiting a ramshackle house in the Southern Ontario countryside. I walk in through the screened-in deck, where thirty-odd cats laze in the sun. At least ten eagerly rush over to me, like a horde of feline Wal-Mart greeters. I enter the kitchen, where another twenty or so drape themselves over every flat surface. The living room is wall-to-wall felines, the bedrooms too. About two hundred rescued or abandoned cats live in the house, and the big workshop building outside holds another two hundred. One human lives on the property. Do I hear you thinking "crazy cat lady"? You'd be wrong. The person who runs this rescue shelter is a man named Larry, but who ever heard of a crazy cat gentleman? We have no such phrase in our culture.

Same with "horse crazy." It's only girls and women who get labelled that. Was Roy Rogers, despite his singular devotion to Trigger (he even had him stuffed after the animal died), ever called "horse crazy"? Is Ian Millar, Canadian Olympian, World Cup show jumping champion and partner to the illustrious Big Ben? I think not. And that's telling.

But never mind, ladies. Whatever they call us, science is on our side, proving through countless studies what we already know: that the human-animal bond is good medicine. Nobody is sure why contact with animals reduces stress, lowers blood pressure, banishes depression, increases longevity and just makes us goofily happy. But it does. I own a horse now (are you surprised?) and where I board him, there are twenty-nine other horses—all owned by other contented women. Why, you can practically smell the endorphins when you walk past as we groom our steeds. And I know that for many of those women, their horses function as Beau does for me: part buddy, part fitness coach, part entertainer, part therapist, part teacher, part priest.

Yes, priest. The researchers don't seem to talk about animals and spiritual health, but for me, that's part of the bond too. Lacking that religion gene, I have tried but failed over the years to find a faith or philosophy that spoke to me. Of all the paths I explored, Buddhism was the most compelling, but though my head was intrigued, my heart and soul remained unmoved. Besides, every time I tried to meditate, I fell asleep.

Still, I longed for inner peace. Throughout my twenties and most of my thirties I spent hours in therapy dissecting my drearily unoriginal dysfunctional family. I constantly struggled with depression and rage. The world seemed a dark, chaotic and terrible place, and contentment largely evaded me—except when I was either writing (songs, plays, anything), happily in love (a stage that rarely lasted more than ten weeks) or when I was around animals. Then I felt calm and whole and—*right*.

And it's always been like that. Not surprising then that, regardless of circumstances, I gravitate toward non-human species. I'm the six-year-old kid who bawls for days when her turtle dies. I'm the teenager at a convent school on Lake Nipissing who spends lunch hour alone by the water luring seagulls with sandwich crusts, because she loves to watch them wheel and dip around her. I'm the woman at the sparkling soirée in a Rosedale mansion who's ignoring the famous guests in order to crouch down in a corner and commune with the family hound.

And shadowing me through all my years are horses, horses, horses—those creatures so magnificent in the flesh and blood, so rich in mythic dimensions. I had a pony for two years as a kid, and a horse for three years as a teenager. I rode on and off until I moved to Toronto at age twenty-three to follow my creative muse. When I discovered how broke the muse was, I was forced to repress my equine passions for over twenty years. But every time I saw a police officer ride by on one of those splendid mounts, my breath stopped and I felt a yearning so powerful it was like mourning a lost soul mate.

●　　●　　●

I think now I finally understand what's going on with me: animals are my conduit to the natural world. In their presence I get out of my frenetic, neurotic human brain, out of my messy, bewildering emotions, and I connect with my animal self. I stop thinking, and start to just be. As meditation is supposed to do (but I wouldn't know . . . *yawn* . . . *snore* . . .) animals keep me in the present, because that's where they live, inhabiting fully each ticking second of time. Around animals, I stop fixating on the past. I stop fearing the future. I'm in the moment, where I'm able to somehow transcend ego, self and all my petty problems; I'm even able to stop obsessing over the human condition with its incomprehensible pain and evil. And that's as close as I get to being spiritual. Animals lead the way.

And animals will save my life.

Picture this: my sister is dying. My sweet, kind, beautiful, gentle sister, the person I love most in the world. Her imminent death, at forty-seven, will be the last in a chain of major losses. First, the man I'm living with, despite having declared commitment, walks out. Four months later, I lose my beloved mother; eight weeks later, my father dies. Four weeks after that, my sister is diagnosed with brain cancer. Five months later one of my aunts, who is also my godmother, dies. I feel as though I'm in a slow war, loved ones dying or going missing all around me. By now, everything that has ever given me joy—friends, books, good food, my music, my writing—is powerless to budge me even an inch out of my wild grief and suicidal depression.

Except animals.

As my sister's illness progressed, as hope of her survival faded, animals became my lifeline. I had started riding again in my forties, so once a week I'd leave the city for the surrounding farmland. I didn't have my own horse yet, so I rode other people's—skittish young creatures that liked to buck and shy and bolt. In order to stay on I had to stop thinking about my grief. I had to stop thinking, period, and focus, through my body, on each nuance of the horse's mood, each twitch of muscle or sudden movement. At the same time, in that heightened Zen state of awareness, I experienced the world in stunning, sharp relief: the shapes of clouds scudding over the hills; the scent of fresh-cut hay; the sudden surprise of deer popping out from green shadows.

The horses also gave me physical comfort. During that whole time of loss, except for the occasional hug or massage, no one touched me. I came to crave contact with the horses and their massive, gentle warmth. I loved the feel of their satiny bodies, their sweet, warm smell—the same smell I first inhaled in that dusty corral—and the way I could lean against them, surrendering my weight to their broad, breathing flanks. I loved that I could climb on and they would literally support me and carry me away.

But I always had to return—home to dread and trying to imagine how I would live without my sister. When I entered my house, though, my other totem animal came to minister. My cats had no clue anyone had died or was dying, and it was business as usual on the feline planet. Even if I lay sobbing on the floor, they insisted I feed them, play with them, admire their elegant posturing. During that time I also fostered kittens for a rescue group, and sometimes I'd bring my sister over to the house for what I called kitten therapy. She was having seizures by then, we both knew it was hopeless, and yet, as a bunch of striped fluffballs tumbled about and slammed into each other like tiny furry bumper cars, we'd be oohing and aahing and giggling like fools.

●   ●   ●

After my sister died, my doctor wanted to put me on antidepressants. I resisted for two years, knowing my body chemistry tended to react in weird ways to mood-altering substances. And then I bought Beau—a purebred Canadian horse, or *cheval canadien*, a rare and amazing breed that few people know about. He's what they call a black bay, the colour of bittersweet chocolate. Compact and curvy, with a voluminous mane that falls to his chest, he's handsome and sassy and too damn smart—an equine rake if ever there was one. Financially, I'm now beyond broke, but I'm no longer wishing I were dead, and my doctor agrees he can now stop pushing Prozac.

The loss of my sister has changed me forever, no question. I was never an optimist, but what shred of faith I might have once had that good could triumph has vaporized forever. If Pinochet is alive, if Osama bin Laden is alive, hell, if Bush is alive, and my sweet sister dead, then there is no order, no justice, no reason in the cosmos. And I *miss* her. God, I miss her. Five years later, her loss is a wound that still hasn't closed. I will always move in a darker space now, but if there's still some light in my world, it's because of animals. I love my cats, I love their liquid grace that alternates with Chaplinesque comedy, and their selfless commitment to sensuality. I love my Burmese's soulful, doglike devotion, his unfailing radar that sends him to my side whenever I'm especially blue. But it's Beau, my black Pegasus, who transports me up and out of myself, who gallops me out of thought and sorrow. And, if only for brief moments, it's like bursting through tangled, swampy underbrush into the open, blue-gold dazzle of a perfect August afternoon.

BELIEVE YOU ME

LORRI NEILSEN GLENN

Annie's survival tips
for late bloomers

Sit yourself down, she says. Take the comfortable chair. You're excited, I can tell. I hope I can help. Let me just put the kettle on.

Books in piles around her desk. Plants spilling from the window.

Glad you called, she says, smiling. Amazing, isn't it? After years of broken snowsuit zippers, midnight feedings and car payments you look up one day and there it is: that glowing, fragile egg of a thing—the future you want to have. All along you wanted something like it, but it was hiding under a security blanket or the telephone bill.

And now here it sits, as if it had one eye cocked, challenging you: I'm yours if you want me, it says. It's now or never, it says. Believe you me, I know what that's like. I was fifty when I woke up and said, Annie—time to grab the future. Red Rose okay? I have decaf, too, she says.

Oh, let's see: Hildegard of Bingen. Rachel Carson. Grandma Moses—seventy-eight when she got serious. Virginia Hamilton Adair. Mary Lawson. All late bloomers. Ah, yes, there are more talented women around than bus tours to Peggy's Cove. Her laugh is like her voice: deep, seasoned.

Just tell that cat to get down, she says; just wants the body heat. Coyote, we call him. You're not allergic, are you?

And don't let him do that—rude thing. Taking your picture, I call it.

You're wondering: am I too late? Her eyes narrow. Can I write that novel, learn to sing, open a retreat centre for adolescents? Well, you can. Let me guess: the mirror is looking more like your mother and the years are disappearing like summer fog. Am I right? Her eyebrows are up, waiting for an answer. So, what's stopping you?

Yes, I hear you. I thought that too. But, you know—oh, for goodness' sake. Coyote, that's enough of your tricks. Outside you go. He's hungry, all right, but for attention.

Where were we? Would you like honey? Milk? Well, grab a pencil from over there. Now that I'm retired, I have more time for a good chat. My friend Marce calls this a chinwag. Ah yes, women: after thirty years of working in the academy, I am still struck by how little we believe in our own understanding.

Elizabeth. Susan. Seemeen. Frances. She puts down her cup, looks somewhere out the window. A woman—her name changes with the semester, the years—who has accomplished amazing feats, scaled emotional mountains, been lost in a dead-end marriage. A fiercely intelligent mother or sister or wife who can negotiate the rocky landscape of childraising or minimum-wage work or chemotherapy or the death of a parent with wisdom, grace and the efficiency of a Swiss train. A wizard. Yet she appears on campus eyes down, racked with anxiety, apologizing for everything. Doesn't know just how much she knows.

Have one of these crispy squares. Low fat. Easy. Remember the ad, the woman slaving over a hot stove to make them? Reminds me of my first year of marriage; I'd make the bed just before my husband came home. He was dazzled. "Wow," he'd say. "You've been housecleaning!" Bless him.

So, here we go.

She looks to the ceiling, holds up a finger. This is the rest of your life we're talking about here. You've decided what you want, now how can you make the most of it? Oh, my dear, my dear, where to start?

Red shoes. That's my first thought. Red to stand out in a crowd, with good support to move quickly without hurting yourself. Find out what your red shoes are—your distinctive feature or talent that sets you apart from others. Shine them up.

Travel light. What's that rather crude saying— "It's not the ups and downs in life, it's the jerks"? You'll be surprised by the characters you have to dodge. So the less you carry, the better. I mean, of course, grudges, your own demons, unfinished business, all that.

Be smart. I don't mean careful, strategic, shrewd—those go without saying. I mean let yourself be smart, don't hide your intelligence. Can't tell you the number of students I had who didn't know they were smarter than their own professors sometimes. Yes, smart. Smart with a smile is disarming, you know. She dabs a drop of tea off her chin, curls a slow grin.

Yes, please, help yourself to another. Was that the phone? I'll let it ring. And that's another point. This fragile egg— this goal you have. Give it room and time and space. Helps you focus. You know the old Maria Muldaur song—*I can wash out forty-four pairs of socks, feed the baby, grease the car, starch shirts, give my man the shiverin' fits?* The woman was a magician, all right, but for whom?

Send signals that this is important. Put a sign on the door of your room—you have a room, or at least a corner, don't you? Claim the part of the day when you are fresh. You'll teach your family self-sufficiency, inspire your friends. Sleep better, too, knowing you spent that time. My friend Joan unplugs her phone. I used to mark half-day appointments with myself. Told people they were for dental surgery.

She stands up. Can you hear anything? Is that the cat?

Where was I? Oh, yes—choose good travelling companions, she says. Read. Make phone calls. Have tea, like we are. Get the backstories and horror stories. Don't spread the negative; just make a note of it; there could be trolls under the bridge. Look around—find out who has integrity. Find your tribe, as Margaret Laurence said. Mary Meigs found one—did you see *The Company of Strangers?* You have family you don't even know yet. She reaches for the box of tissues.

Look at you, she says. Full of mother wit and female wisdom. You can organize a birthday party for an explosion of nine-year-old boys; navigate a Stonehenge field of bureaucrats to find your father an assisted-care home; you know ten ways to nip a hot flash in the bud. You think those things didn't prepare you? Listen, my dear, late bloomers are street-smart, savvy and generous. Every grey hair holds a truth, I always say—of course, I have to, look at this head—and every wrinkle a line of wisdom. Please—finish this last square. That cat is crying to get in and you need some hot in that. I'll be right back.

No cat, she says and pours more tea. Yes, you're right, of course. It's gender. It's about whose knowledge matters. Wit, common sense, intuition, embodied knowledge—put any words around it you want. What you know is valuable. The Wife of Bath—now, what was it she said? Here it is: "All these tales were written by men and scholars—now if women wrote them very different they would be." Then she ripped out the pages of the book her husband was reading and threw them in the fire. Isn't that a stitch?

She shakes her head, leans forward:

You see, here's the thing. Official knowledge: rules, reg-
ulations—those are stories too. We tell ourselves stories in
order to live, Joan Didion says. And theories and rules are
just stories people tell themselves about how the world
works. Or how they think it should. Stories change. Some
are abandoned—take the flat earth theory, for example, or
chastity belts. Some last longer than they should: funda-
mentalism, Colonialism, that a second X chromosome
is needed for housecleaning and finding the mustard in
the fridge.

But the unofficial stories—hard-earned wisdom—are just
as credible, you see. Yet we're taught to look outside. I grew
up—Edson, The Pas, Saskatoon—certain that culture's
prime meridian was a street in Manhattan, or—in a pinch—
Toronto. Answers were at the back of the book. Poems and
stories and radio news had essential meanings that rose up
like morning mist from a valley called Truth.

Oh, I've let my tea get cold, she says. I get so worked up!
Dick and Jane and Sally would never have lasted a day in the
real world. We jumped off the coal shed, played tag until
dark, yet on Monday mornings, there they were in all their
primer glory, writing Life for us. Illusions.

Think of Dorothy. When she pulled back the curtain, she
found not a wizard but a funny little guy pushing buttons.
That's it in a nutshell.

We've got to push our own buttons, change the old patterns. Too often I see women seeking out rules, even if there
aren't any, looking for the *right* way, even when there isn't
one; and believing in the hierarchy, even when it is specious.
You know, my dear, women believe the treasure—answer,
solution, workable theory—is "out there" and seldom realize
that we bring it with us; it's been there all along.

So throw that book in the fire. Use your wits and . . .

You said it—trust your gut. How's our time? she asks. Oh good. We'll have a bite of supper soon.

Listen, you're bound to step into alien territory, cross a line, get someone's knickers in a knot. Don't worry about it. Enjoy it! Late bloomers have little to lose except time. Use your moxie. Besides, middle-aged women are invisible to most people, so use that to your advantage.

Let me see—what else. Ah, yes: send postcards. I mean— tell everyone where you're headed. Sister, partner, favourite grocery store clerk—let them know when you've published an article, earned an A, written a song. That way, when you're slogging through sloughs of despond or up to your kneecaps in a pothole, they'll be like water bearers at a marathon. And—you know this—you're more likely to per- severe because they're with you.

Good grief. The sun goes down early, doesn't it? Over there, she says; the switch is at the base.

Start now. One of my students cared for her autistic son, held three part-time jobs, gave palliative care to her mother, and still managed to finish a master's degree and enroll in a doctoral program. Paula didn't wait—things weren't going to get easier. Take whatever small steps you can. Funny, though; as Paula persevered, doors opened—to scholarships, work that served her goals.

Pat's another example. We wore Cowichan sweaters in high school, became stage rats at Aden Bowman Collegiate. We loved poetry. Three years ago doctors removed every- thing cancerous they could find, and then some. Bald and gut-empty, Pat began to write poetry, to rethink those hundred-hour workweeks. She saw a shaman, Buddhist monks, inhaled poetry books. And wrote. Full, she says, I've never felt so full and whole.

Finally, candles—celebration, faith, ritual, all rolled in

one. I wrote a novel, someone will say, but it wasn't nomi-
nated for the Giller. Yes, I wrote a song, but I'm not Connie
Kaldor. Forget the yes-buts. Get out a journal—write down
all you've done; turn around, see how far you travelled. Kick
up the heels of those bright red shoes.

And never forget that little girl writing chalk lines along
the sidewalk to jump into and over, an arc at the turn-around
end. Pedestrians scuffed it. Rain came. Every night the girl
slept hard, dreamed. And every morning she went out again
with her chalk, writing herself into the landscape.

Now, she says, rising, reaching out her arm. That's
enough from me. Let's put some soup on. I want to hear all
about you.

NOTES ON A COUNTERREVOLUTION

PATRICIA PEARSON

"Promise me this," I urge my nieces, as we sit around a bonfire on the edge of the lake we all love. My family has traded secrets and elicited promises here in the late-summer twilight for five generations.

"In the next few years," I venture, from my vantage point on an upended stump of wood beside the flames, "you're going to try some grown-up stuff." I glance toward the cottage a few hundred feet away. Their mother, my elder sister, has retired there to read after dinner. Her two girls, their lips smeared pink and their shorts too short, wave marshmallow sticks at the fire and giggle.

"No. I know you are," I say. "We all do. I got loaded on Kahlúa at your age, thirteen or fourteen, and did a face-plant in the snow in my friend's backyard." They whoop with laughter. Their hilarity seems fuelled less by the fact that I've ever been drunk than by the exuberant notion that I, their aunt, should be telling them so.

"It's true," I go on, smiling. "It's crap, Kahlúa. Haven't touched it ever since." I lean in too close to the fire, wincing at the heat as I wedge in another pine log. "I'm just saying that this goes with the territory of being teenaged. You're going to try booze. You're going to find pot. And I fully expect that you'll be asked by some good-looking guy in your high school to . . ." I try to think of the current slang for casual sex, "to hook up." I gesture vaguely. "Or whatever."

They stare at me, their firelit faces bright with expectation, awaiting a punch line. I am the irreverent Elder in their lives, I suppose. The one who quips, and blithely smokes and wears fashionable shoes from Berlin. My adolescent nieces and nephews have read passages in my books about one-night stands and characters who drop LSD. Of course, it pleases and surprises me that they go to the trouble to read my books, but sometimes I worry that my writing is like the in-house, familial version of the purloined *Playboy*. A treasure trove of outré adult behaviour just for them.

"Listen to me, girls," I say, hoping like hell that my sister wouldn't strangle me for this, "experiment with alcohol! I'll give you some tips. And go for the pot, it can be incredibly fun, as long as you only take one puff of a joint. One puff. No more." The girls trade looks of wide-eyed glee. "Just confine your experiments to those things," I say, "and only with your girlfriends. Okay? Promise me that you won't hook up."

I study their faces. "Promise me that you won't experiment with sex."

They nod, their smiles fading, their mood suspended by my unexpectedly adamant plea. The fire crackles, and somewhere a loon calls.

•   •   •

Make Love, Not War

I grew up with that mantra. It permeated the air as a gleeful command—one that echoed through the years and across the miles, until its connection to Vietnam and the Sexual Revolution grew faint and it reached my late '70s high school in St. John, New Brunswick, as a vague cultural prerogative to have tons of sex.

War, certainly, no longer had anything to do with it. When I came of age *Make love, not war* simply meant that guys in wide-leg Wranglers with peach-fuzz moustaches could plunge their hands into my bra as we lounged in a basement rec room listening to the Cars, and feel no sense of obligation to date me.

It meant going all the way as soon as I was "legal," and accumulating more than a dozen lovers by the time I was twenty-one.

There was the Summer of Love, 1967, when sexual freedom fairly vibrated with political and cultural purpose. And then there was the Summer of Graduate School, 1987, by which time *Make love, not war* meant spending a given Sunday sipping coffee whilst idly jotting down a list of "Men I've Slept With," as if engaged in an obscure sort of moral or emotional math.

I only ever wrote their first names: Rod, Jonathan, Oliver, Glen. As if the addition of last names rendered the list too impersonal. A list of invitees to a ball, a list of grant applicants. A list of airplane passengers, or war dead. There was one fellow whose name I could never remember at all. I vividly recalled being with him, for his presence in my bed felt particularly strange. We hadn't sparked through flirtation, or laughter. There hadn't been any preamble to our intimacy, which came about after meeting in a bar. He was solemn, largely silent, pursuing something private for himself that nevertheless involved my body. I registered his emotional absence as an alien scent, a hard mouth, an unknowable face in the half-light. On my list, in referencing him, I usually just wrote: "Guy from Windsor."

Why "Guy from Windsor" was more important in my

mathematical exercise than the friendly men I merely kissed, or rolled around with on the moonlit grass confounds me a little now. In my emotional innocence, sex meant intercourse. Other encounters, including oral sex, didn't count. They were something else, matters of hazier significance.

I can't imagine now, what I was trying to calculate. There was nothing to conclude from my tallied account. What about the men who loved me, truly, whose sexual touch was confined to a gaze. I had no list for them. And my husband is the last name jotted down, which means what—about our relationship, our friendship, our shared parenting and entwined life history—beyond nothing at all.

Incredibly, my nieces are practising this aimless old math of mine in the corridors of their high school. Sex = intercourse, or so they hear. Hook-ups don't count, nor do kisses. Nor does love.

How do I explain the folly? How do I show them, in advance of their own scarring experience, how they need to guard a different, less tangible door to themselves than the singular orifice that lies between the legs?

Alas, for all I've been through, with more than thirty lovers on the list, I fear I'm just another grown-up now, going "wah, wah, wah" like the adults in the *Peanuts* comic strips. The generations reinvent themselves. They clap their hands to their ears.

I remember sneaking home with a friend from high school at some impermissible hour, and being duly confronted by her mother. "In my day," she would say, and then expound upon the rules for young ladies and their suitors, while we rolled our eyes in a magnificent display of indifference.

"In my day," she would persist, "young men would escort young ladies home at this hour."

How would the phrase sound now, to my nieces? "In my day," I can hear myself saying at the next intimate sharing around a campfire, "we screwed everything that moved."

"Well, girls," I want to say to them, assuming I have their attention. "Let me tell you about my twenties. I was healthy, young, attractive, energetic and enthused. And I cried all the time. Have another marshmallow."

I want to imagine them listening earnestly, all ears, like Luke Skywalker to Yoda: "Understand, my daughters," I might say in a grave and wise voice, "I cried when I found myself pregnant, and plodded off to Women's College Hospital in Toronto for an abortion, because this was a transgression that I was expected to attend to, *pro forma*, after my boyfriend had dumped me. I cried when men said 'Oh, actually, this is just sex,' and I wept when they said 'It might have been more than sex, but I've changed my mind, you don't object, do you?'"

So what if I did? Object. The next thing I'd know I would be the spooky witch in *Fatal Attraction*, wielding knives and boiling bunnies.

It is one thing to be a mother, as I am now, anchored in family and strengthened by accomplishment, desirous of erotic adventure. Another thing entirely to be young, wishing, without faith or discernible rules, for life to take hold and begin.

"Ah, nieces, you will find your hopes crushed throughout your most fertile years, as you find love and then watch in astonishment as it passes through your hands as swiftly and ephemerally as sand. Sometimes, you'll think you're about to go stark raving mad as men with whom you have everything in common—laughs, sparks, intellect, attraction—nonetheless find themselves intoxicated by the infinite prospects unleashed by the mantra *Make love, not war.*"

Or, at least that was the case in my day.

One lover dumped me during his lunch hour, even though we were living together. He invited me to join him for Chinese food during his one-hour break and then assured me that I would "make somebody a wonderful wife and mother one day." Just . . . not him. Another future life partner dropped me scant months after I had miscarried his unborn child—when I was still reeling around in the echoing hell of that ill-defined experience. His reasoning—and theirs, the other men—was preposterous, if judged against the ages of human experience. There might be other women out there! They might be better! More perfect! There could be a woman somewhere who was perfection incarnate! Who knows, there might be a goddess awaiting him.

A goddess, good lord. And who did these men, who were so fired up by romantic possibility that they left me, sobbing and effectively widowed without access to a dignified black wardrobe, wind up marrying? Ordinary women like me, with tempers and big noses and garden-variety insecurities, that's who. Regular Janes, who merely happened to happen along, to turn that corner of the street or show up at that party, exactly when the men I loved had tired of conquering the High Seas and were more amenable to settling down.

"Of course," one ex-lover told me a couple of years ago, as we spent an afternoon together drinking beer on the patio of my hotel in the shadow of a Mexican volcano, an hour's drive from where he now lives with his wife and two daughters. "It was all in the timing," he said. We took a walk, then, along the steep, cobblestoned streets of the village, and I found myself falling behind him, pulling away in a state of melancholic revelation so profound that it physically slowed me, as I recalled our unborn baby. Our son, or daughter, our thrown-away child.

Please, I want to say to my nieces, please, understand! The hours and hours I spent examining my own personality for the critical flaw that made me lose this man in Mexico, and that child. The scrutiny of my body in the mirror. The raging at my lack of perfection, the unsent letters. And all it turned out to be was timing? Only that. The impersonal calculus of a convenient time.

Now and then, I read Jane Austen, or catch one of the many films and TV shows based on her work—for we are captivated by her world of romantic restraint now, are we not? And I note that twenty-something men are no different, now, than they were in the nineteenth century. Why should they be? A man of "five and twenty" is a creature fuelled by ego and testosterone. In Austen's era, such men felt compelled to join Wellington's campaign in the Peninsular War, or do a stint with the East India Company. Their spirit of adventure didn't include turning all of the women of their acquaintance into unpaid strumpets. But it might have. They were simply not allowed.

Looking back, it seems to me that the social restraints placed upon women needed to be loosened, but perhaps . . . perhaps . . . less so the overthrow of honourable behaviour in men. Adultery without stoning, yes, and freedom from Scarlet Letters. Rape without social ruin. Premarital passion without banishment from the realm of the marriageable female. Enlightenment on the subject of feminine sexuality. All yes. The overthrow of powerlessness, with its gendered double standards, and the condemnation of sex as a means of control, yes, yes.

But what did we do wrong, here? When did we send out the invitations that made us forget ourselves? From Regency culture to the rec room: a revolution gone a wee bit far? That sounds good and academic. I could present that as a paper somewhere. But how do I translate my meaning to my nieces?

You make the rules, I must say to them, as I reconsider the achievement of Gloria Steinem and her peers. You have the power, now, to decide which boy or man has honoured you enough to gain the privilege of seeing you vulnerable. Because you will be vulnerable, when you are naked and shy and uncertain in someone's bed. You decide what you need from the encounter. And I will help you to learn how to get it. This is how you drink beer, this is how you smoke pot, and this is how you explore romance. Not sex. But romance: in tentative, curious steps.

If it is love that you need, then understand you will not win it through your body. The intimacy is false, and it is dangerous. And it doesn't matter, my beloved, bright and vibrant girls, if you break it down by orifice. The math is misleading. Cross it out, I plead with you. Let's start again.

THE GOSPEL ACCORDING TO ELSIE

M. A. C. FARRANT

There's a cartoon that I've come to love in recent years. It's by the American cartoonist Robert Crumb, and is nothing more than a large bowl of bean soup, drawn cartoonishly, of course. The beans near the surface of the soup are distinctly drawn—bean after bean nuzzling one another like . . . well, like so many beans in a soup. Only one of the beans has a face, though, and this face bears an astonished look. A big white arrow points down at this single bean, and there's a caption alongside it that reads: *He thinks he's the only bean in the soup!*

    •   •   •

Long before I realized that I was not the only bean in the soup, I was a teenager. This was in the early sixties. My world and the worlds of my family and girlfriends were the only worlds that mattered. The fact that I was growing up in an oddly configured household didn't trouble me, either. I was being raised by my aunt Elsie, her husband, Ernie, and my father, Billy, who was Elsie's younger brother. Billy visited us every other weekend from his job in Vancouver where he worked on the docks. My mother, Nancy, had flown the coop when I was five; packed her bags for greener pastures, as the saying went, and caught the last ocean liner out of Vancouver for Australia in 1952. She had done all of these things, Elsie claimed, because she was a gold digger.

"Women like Nancy give the rest of us a bad name," Elsie frequently sniffed. By the "rest of us" she meant herself and the other stolid housewives of Vancouver Island.

By all accounts Nancy's gold-digging exploits were successful. By the time I was fifteen she was on her fifth marriage, having hopscotched from man to man, getting wealthier along the way.

Not that her success was of any use to me

Nancy seldom wrote or sent gifts. By the time I started dating, I hardly thought about her any more, other than as an exotic character I could use for spinning tales—My mother is fabulously rich, has beautiful clothes, can play the piano like a concert pianist, travels the world on cruise ships like a pirate in search of wealthy men.

It was Elsie who provided me with steady information about the world of men: the Gospel According to Elsie, as I came to call it. We never sat down and discussed these things. Rather, it was me watching and listening. Elsie wore her opinions about men like a battle shield, and her opinions were so clear and definite that I didn't doubt them.

I had a boyfriend by then. Martin Defolio, a guy from Victoria who had a car. I didn't particularly like him, but he was the first one who seemed interested enough to ask me out. And at fifteen it was crucial to be asked out. All my friends had boyfriends and if I didn't have one, too, I could kiss popularity goodbye. I'd be lumped with the wall-flowers—a certified cretin.

It wasn't enough to *get* a boyfriend, though. Somehow you had to *keep* him. Keep him without getting knocked up and ruining your reputation, or losing him to a rival. It was difficult work. My friends and I talked of nothing else.

So I was Elsie's gung-ho apprentice. When she'd spit out things like "Men! There's no pleasing them!" or "Men! Who do they think they are?" I'd lap it up. My friends and I would feast on these tidbits. Apparently there was a war going on in the murky world of romance that we hadn't known about. The war was called the Battle of the Sexes, and if you played your cards right, it was a war you could win.

I cut my teeth about men via the living proof that was Elsie and Ernie's marriage. Theirs was the only marriage in the soup. And Ernie became the singular bean, the stand-in for every man in the Universe. Poor old Ernie.

•   •   •

Back then, I bought into what Elsie had to say about men, bought into it heart and soul. In 1962 I wanted guidebooks, diagrams, maps, and Elsie provided them. I became convinced by what she had to say. Being in charge sounded good to me. Better than good. A huge and wonderful relief. I liked the idea of power, of being dominant, of pushing puny Martin Defolio around when he whined that no sex made a guy go blind. Up on Mount Tolmie on a Friday night, I could roar with confidence, "So go blind, ya big ape!"

With men, the main thing, apparently, was to never give in—to anything.

Elsie never gave in, particularly to Ernie. With him, she acted like he was another household chore, someone she had to clean up after. It didn't help that he was fat and bald and worked as a janitor at the public library and watched *Fun-O-Rama* cartoons after work every weekday at four. She'd be standing beside the TV set with a lighted cigarette in her hand and snarling, "Why do you watch that junk? Sometimes I wonder what I've married."

Ernie would pretend he was deaf, especially if he was watching the *Popeye* cartoon where Brutus was being whacked all the way to the moon.

Elsie used her unalterable opinion about the opposite sex to achieve a different kind of whacking: all men, according to her gospel, were a necessary evil. Necessary because you needed a husband in order to have a house and a family, and they were okay—meaning a woman could stand them—as long as they were kept busy with a hobby or fixing things around the house or digging in the garden. The evil part was that they were prone to laziness and sex. If they started lying around the house doing nothing then one of their eyes would go funny. They'd get that look—"a bedroom look," Elsie called it—and start slobbering and leering. Then it was, watch out! A perfectly good afternoon could be flushed down the toilet.

"Because, after all," Elsie would snort, "the only thing a man's interested in is sex and his supper." Her statement was irrefutable. On some days, "What's for supper?" was the longest sentence Ernie delivered to his wife.

·   ·   ·

Around this time we were learning about the Greek myths in English class, and in particular, the Amazons. Miss Hewitt, our young, brown-suited teacher, told us that the Amazons were a tribe of giant women warriors, so fierce that they had a law decreeing that only girl children could live. "They drowned the boys like rats," Miss Hewitt said.

The brains in the front rows—the science club guys—cringed when they heard this.

She also said, with evident zeal, "The Amazon women were in charge! Think about that!"

I passed a note to my friend Dana: "My aunt is an Amazon."

There was no disputing the fact that Elsie was in charge—of Ernie, me, the entire known world.

Dana passed the note back: "Ha, ha. What are you wearing Friday night?"

But the Amazon idea stuck.

*   *   *

I thought I would write an essay about the Amazons for Miss Hewitt. We had to pick one of the myths. I chased the idea further. I would describe Elsie as an Amazon queen. The women in my family were Elsie; Maudie, her sister, a widow; my crinkly old grandma, who sang nursery rhymes and lived with Maudie; and Elsie's married daughters, Doreen and Shirley. Even though they were all short, I didn't consider this a hindrance. They could be Amazons in disguise. Being a housewife, I decided, could be a clever ploy that had allowed the Amazons to survive to present-day times.

The idea delighted me. Home life might not be a prison sentence after all. Seen in this light, Elsie and the others were confident women, possessed of a sure clarity about the purpose of our lives. Within their homes, they miraculously enlarged, like Alice with the pill, and became giants, enormous in influence, compelling in control, the huge hearts at the centre of the family fortress.

I didn't know the word *anthropologist* at the time, but all this was about discovering a tribe, one whose existence I had been blind to. Housewives! Not to be found, shockingly, within the pages of *National Geographic* like those bare-breasted native women whose lips were made monstrous by inserted plates. But no-nonsense, rolling-pin-wielding women existing right under my nose. I started looking at Elsie with new-found interest.

I called the tribe the Amazon Housewives.

When Miss Hewitt told us that Amazons had fought in the Battle of Troy with the help of the goddess Artemis, I decided the Amazon Housewives needed a patron saint. I chose Blondie, from the comic strip of the same name. Blondie was the boss of her family, like Elsie was of ours, though Elsie was dumpy and wore glasses, while Blondie was something of a glamourpuss.

Ernie played out as Dagwood, Blondie's husband, a sub-servient, henpecked weakling.

Once again, poor old Ernie.

All men, according to the housewife followers of Blondie, were Dagwoods: mid-day couch sleepers, sneaky avoiders of chores, destroyers of housework, and foulers of clean sinks and towels. They left grimy fingerprints everywhere, slopped mud onto shining kitchen floors, and snored and farted with abandon.

No wonder women had to be like Blondie. They were forced to it. Forced to use "every trick in the book" to keep their husbands in line. Blondie used rolling pins and frying pans to keep Dagwood in line. The Amazon Housewives used sharp tongues, guilt, sarcasm, and withheld sex. Only a woman's steady vigilance kept a man civilized. Otherwise the man she had married would gain the upper hand and she'd wake up to find she'd married a slob.

This was the Gospel According to Elsie and the Amazon Housewives

Whew!

I never wrote that essay for Miss Hewitt. I wasn't up to it. I couldn't reconcile the man-hating meanness of the Amazons with my own dimly realized yearnings for love and romance. And where was tenderness? And the rumoured gallantry of men? Where was their care and kindness, qualities I had often seen in Ernie, and in my father, Billy? So instead, I handed in a dry little book report: "The Amazons were an ancient tribe . . ."

57

•   •   •

Now and then Elsie and I would watch a late-night movie together. A musical, or a romantic comedy. She would be on one side of the den, in Ernie's recliner (he'd have gone to bed), and I'd be on the couch wrapped in a blanket. The Fred and Ginger movies. And *Mrs. Miniver, How Green Was My Valley.* We smiled at the spunky portrayals of women with spirit who stood up to a man, who were independent and cutely petulant. No man could ever "get to first base" with them, not until they were "churched," as Elsie called it. Enchanted, we watched the men in these movies. They were so remote from us, so clean and handsome in their tuxedos. They could dance and sing and had "hearts of gold" and went gallantly about the intricate business of winning a woman's heart. Entire films were given over to the tug and pull, the sexless sophistication that was the fantasy of romantic comedy. There was not a man in our known world who could reach the elevated level of Cary Grant or Fred Astaire, though in my heart—and I believe in Elsie's, too—we knew we were equal to them, knew we could turn into Ginger Rogers at the drop of a top hat.

Elsie never had much to say about these movies, other than to sigh, "Too bad life's not like *that!*"

Once, during a musical, Ernie shuffled out in his flannel pyjamas; the fringe around his bald head was ruffled like Einstein's. He told us to turn down the TV. All that tap-dancing was giving him a headache.

Watching him return to their bedroom, Elsie snorted. "There goes the man of my dreams."

Poor old Ernie, I thought, feeling hopeless for him yet again. There seemed no escape from the Amazon Housewives. He'd lost the Battle of the Sexes.

I wished Ernie could be on a TV show where he'd be given his most-wished-for things. Like *Queen for a Day*, the show for hard-up women. Ernie could be *King for a Day*. He'd turn into Cary Grant, be tall and handsome, have thick black hair. He'd be given a year's supply of chocolate bars. A new truck. He'd drive off in the new truck, with a new wife, a dish he'd call "baby". . . .

* * *

If "The Gospel According to Elsie" didn't stick with me, and I went searching for other bowls of soup, it was because of Ernie.

IN PRAISE OF MISFITS

NATALIE FINGERHUT

For Rob

Dear Raphael Max Winters, a.k.a. my son,

You know that woman who likes to drive through Forest Hill with the sunroof open to titillate the teetotallers and tipplers with the sounds of Joe Strummer? You think she's pretty cool, don't you. Well, she wasn't always. In fact, that woman was beaten up by a horrific pipsqueak half her size in grade four while the rest of her classmates laughed. In fact, she was taunted from her first day of school until she ran screaming to New York when she was eighteen. Yes, I can see by the way you are tossing your macaroni that you feel my pain, you feel the injustice. Why was she so maligned? Well . . . because your mama was different. She couldn't cut it. She was a misfit.

Where is it written that the ability to recite the Maple Leafs lineup at the age of eight relegates you to the Land of the Losers, or that the entry into the in crowd (and all their birthday parties) is barred to you? Who decides that you are the untouchable who has to sit alone at lunch, that you don't fit in, that you are different? Is it self-selection or are you selected? Who knows? Do I look like the Philosopher Queen with my hair coated with your raspberry Yoplait? OK, OK, stop flinging your arrowroots, here's the story.

I'll admit, I was a weird kid. Once when I was seven my father gave me money to buy a book of fairy tales, and instead I bought Gerald Green's *Holocaust* and read it all night in my walk-in closet. Other kids in my 'hood bought *Owl* magazine; I had a subscription to *Pro Wrestling Illustrated*. The girls had long beautiful brown hair and were cute and petite. I had short curly red hair and was all legs. "Please God," I'd pray at night, "please let me be like THEM." But, my son, God didn't listen.

Your now so-hip-it-hurts mommy used to be a serious dork—a geek of the highest order. Rejected by the in crowd (or any crowd, now that I think about it), I buried myself in my books. From grade nine to grade twelve, I never saw a mark lower than A. My teachers loved me because I was smart; my classmates loathed me for the same reason. What's this? You want to give me a hug? Such a good son you are. But wait, I have to tell you something else first. When I used to cry on the toilet in my mother's (your baba's) bathroom before school she would say, "Fuck 'em. Get good marks then get outta town." Your baba also didn't fit in. At twenty-one, she ran screaming from the *shtetl* of Winnipeg to the Promised Land of Toronto and there she met my father, your zaida.

Charming and totally bonkers, your zaida would put on his fur coat, red Chuck Taylors and a black Russian fur hat, and drive Shabbat morning carpool to Holy Blossom Temple in a green army jeep. After he dropped the other kids off at religious school, explaining to them that he and I had "important business" to attend to, we would go watch the fights at Maple Leaf Gardens. When I should have been practising my *aleph bet*, I would spend glorious hours screaming at the Wildman from Syria while he broke his opponents in two. My beloved father, as you might have guessed, also didn't fit in.

Tragically, his time in my life was short. His sudden death

when I was twelve really did me in. In a minute, my childhood and its innocence were over. The ground beneath my
feet was gone. The taunting bestowed upon me by my classmates was replaced for a time by an embarrassed silence, and
my different-ness magnified.

Sounds brutal, doesn't it? It was. But you see, my son, I
learned very early in my life what hell looked like. Knowing
that, I became a lot stronger than the other kids, and I used
that strength as a shield. Their continued rejection of me
bounced off. What did their childishness mean to me? I,
who had seen my father smash his head on a rock and float
lifelessly down the Don River—the consequences of a canoe
trip gone terribly wrong—became tougher, harder. I stopped
caring about being an outcast. Hell, I stopped caring about
most things.

I stepped away from my past. I threw out all my shirts
with the alligators on the left breast and purchased a used
trench coat at Kensington Market. Not content with little
diamond studs, I pierced my ears eight times and put safety
pins through them. I found new friends who took the subway to have lunch at the Hare Krishna Temple cafeteria or
to eat scrambled eggs at the Mars on College St., rather than
drive their fathers' spare BMWs to the local mall. We threw
pillows at boom boxes playing the Top 40 and refused to go
to big-name concerts like the Boss or Madonna. Instead, we
would put on our gloves with the fingers cut out, paint our
faces white, our lips red and enter the late great Concert
Hall to hear Echo and the Bunnymen, snatching a few tokes
off the older punk rockers. We refused to do the Toronto
two-step: the pathetic excuse for dancing common in the
suburbs. Instead we would slink around the hall and, in
moments of sheer ecstasy, lie down on the cigarette-covered
floor—an indication that we had shut the world out and had

become one with the music. My new friends had introduced me to a cooler world and I loved it.

Instead of my classmates rejecting me, I started rejecting them and their stunted upper- middle-class values. The more I rejected them, the happier I became and the more I embraced my new, trench-coat-wearing, purple-haired self. I had found new meaning and new places to go. And once I had a taste of that more accepting outside world, I just kept running toward it.

Wow . . . I sound like one of those women who run with the wolves . . . I sound like someone who watches too much Oprah. Oy and vey . . . we had better continue this monologue while we watch the Leafs game. I need some testosterone.

.   .   .

Where was I? Oh yes . . . so, being different sucked rocks the size of Stonehenge at first, but then it provided your mother with the courage to go exploring and to apply to university at a left-wing loony bin in Bronxville, N.Y., which her teachers and classmates had never heard of. "Sara Lee," they would say. "Isn't that a type of frozen dessert?" "No, it's Sarah Lawrence . . . you know. . . . that hotbed of radical feminism, an institution where women are encouraged to think beyond marrying the boy next door and settling in Thornhill."

Being on the outs with the in crowd also gave your mother the freedom to question the Establishment and its confining elitism. Let me give you an example. As a visiting student at Oxford, your mother learned that among the learned, there was a subculture of single mothers who could afford to pay babysitters only in hashish. And she knew this because she was free to question privileged worlds, to see that what lies below the surface is often more real than what lies above. And freedom, my boy, also means never getting bored. If you take anything from this maternal treatise, let it be this: boredom = death.

Now, sweetness, I want you to understand that when your brain refuses to think à la mainstream, you will be able to straddle many kinds of worlds. But you should also know that you probably won't fit into any of them. You'll go to business meetings and want to throw fastballs at the CEO for rejecting any idea that might be, *God forbid*, creative, or for dismissing a solution that came from someone without an MBA. You'll go to poetry readings and roll your eyes at the poets who just seconds before going to the microphone had ended their sentences with the oh-so-comfortably-Canuck *eh* and then read their poems in affected, attitude-filled voices as though they had just graduated from Eton.

You will feel equally out of place at the fanciest restaurant or the dingiest bar. In your many moments of frustration, just remember this: being different is a real pain in the ass, but ultimately you'll have better stories to tell at cocktail parties.

Seeing things differently allowed your mother to start a PhD in genocide studies, but it also gave her the instinct to know when to walk away from it. So after meeting the love of her life—also known as your father—she tossed her notes on the Khmer Rouge into the garbage and followed him to Winnipeg, where she worked as a receptionist—all in the pursuit of love and a regular sex life.

But be forewarned, my son: different-thinking people often don't have a straight career path like those with LLBs, PhDs or degrees in accounting. This can be a good thing since you won't get stuck teaching Genocide 101 at the University of Yahoopitzville to a bunch of bored students who have better things to do. Nor will you have to have professional hair. However, should you choose a winding career path and quit high-income jobs to find your calling, make sure that your partner is both gainfully employed and highly sympathetic. Because you are going to spend many angst-ridden moments on your marital bed fretting to your spouse about what you are going to do when you grow up.

And speaking of that marital bed . . . being different has its advantages. When you accept that you stick out (sometime after puberty), you lose your self-consciousness. You become a little freer with yourself and with others. Now let me give you a piece of non-motherly advice: we chicks who lost our inhibitions because we had no one to impress, we are great in bed. Those chickies with the long nails, high-maintenance hair and wacky weight obsessions . . . bad lays. Every single manicured one of them. I know that you're still young and sex is not on your eighteen-month-old radar screen, but trust me, it will be. And when it shows up, remember what I have said. Still, I have a few years to distract you with other topics, so let's talk love for a second.

When you allow yourself to be different from others, you love differently and I would argue, more successfully. You and your partner (is that politically correct enough for you?) don't have to spend your precious time together keeping up with the Ginsburgs because, hey, they've already rejected you. Instead, you can love each other completely and gratefully because you can distinguish between the baubles of love and the love itself. That's a bit heavy-duty for a toddler . . . let me explain. I remember sitting in *shul* one Yom Kippur and watching the couple in front of me. She with her multi-string pearl necklace and large ruby ring displayed for all to see. Her husband, a "big-time Bay Street lawyer," beside her. "He's been sleeping with his junior—a blonde *shiksa* with big tits," my father whispered to my mother. I knew then that I didn't want to end up like the ruby-ringed woman or the blonde shiksa with big tits. And I know now that I wouldn't want you to end up like the "big-time lawyer" either.

So what does all this ranting mean for you? Wait, let me wipe your nose. Here's the deal—parents who are different are able to resist much of how parents are supposed to be. You look confused. OK. You know that awful smell that arose from our kitchen stove when you were about six months old? That was the aroma of my frying the baby development books. The ones that said you were supposed to do something at some specific time. Do you recall that wacko lady who made you bang on a drum to "Mary Had a Little Lamb"? That experience was called a "program." A program is something that parents insist that their children do "to socialize them," a.k.a. make sure that they fit in. Because, after all, our kids must fit in, they must get it. No square pegs allowed. Kids, in case you haven't figured it out, are the unsuspecting beneficiaries of their parents' insecurities. And you know who the worst offenders are? The square pegs who still try to pound themselves into round holes! If they can't fit in, then their kids damn well better. The more these parents fall outside the in-circle, the more they push their kids toward it: shop at the most expensive stores, enroll at the best schools, play with the kid whose parent is a big *macher* in the entertainment world. I could go on and on . . . By the way, in case you are wondering why we haven't been to that music class for a while, I thought it would be more fun to crank up a little Bob Marley and teach you the lyrics from *Songs of Freedom*.

Do you mind if I preach a little bit? I think I've been pretty restrained so far. Here goes: if squirts like you can both accept the differences that lie within you and respect

67

the differences among you; if you can open up your ears to voices that sound different from your own, that come from places you have not yet seen, then you will learn that tolerance is more than just a word on a spelling test. Once you learn tolerance, you will understand empathy. And if you and all your little boy buds and gal pals become more tolerant and more empathetic, there might just be a hope in hell for a little peace in our tired world.

Hey . . . why are you looking at me like that? Are you nodding your head in agreement? I'm not surprised. After all—you are my son.

Love you,
Mom

TINY TOMATOES

GILLIAN KERR

When I was eleven or twelve, I began to spend my Saturday afternoons in my mother's kitchen, taking instructions on pounding meat, whipping cream and grinding graham crackers into crumbs. *Where's the chef's helper?* my mother would call up the stairs until I dragged myself into the kitchen. *It's good for you to learn these things,* she would tell me. And then, most often, she'd say, *Now put on your apron, put your hair up and get started. You're going to make Tiny Tomatoes.*

Tiny Tomatoes was a time-consuming, messy recipe and a favourite on my mother's menus. *Now, no arguments—you know everyone always enjoys these. Get the boxes out of the fridge—the cherry tomatoes. There's a few dozen in there. Set aside the ones that are too big or too small and make sure they're all decent. Remember that you have to wash them really well. Really, really well. Take your time.*

Weekdays our routine was much like other families' in suburban North Toronto: in the morning I would get a quick glimpse of my father as he gulped down his coffee, grabbed his briefcase and fled out the door to catch the subway downtown. My mother rushed us through breakfast, thrust lunches into our school bags, and banged the dishes into the dishwasher before she put on her nursing uniform and drove to her job at a local day clinic. Many women who managed this life—a full-time job and a family—would have welcomed a rest at the end of a week, but not her. Though we were not wealthy, my mother liked to have dinner parties, almost every weekend. *I'm going to need your help today,* she would say most Saturday mornings, and after the house was cleaned from corner to corner she would call me into the kitchen and announce who was coming to dinner. Then we would start to cook.

My sister Julie was older by eighteen months, and it was long understood that she would not be in the kitchen. In her bedroom, with its walls covered in pictures of Cat Stevens and long strands of wooden beads draped over the mirrors, Julie and her friends spent Saturdays listening to music behind a closed door. *She doesn't have your interest,* my mother would say, with pursed lips. I wondered when it was exactly that I had expressed my interest.

Are you ready to slice the tomatoes? Make sure you don't take too much off the top; otherwise it's a waste. Get a sharper knife than that one. Hull them out, completely, all the tomato meat, the seeds and the juice. Lay them out upside down on paper towels, so that they dry perfectly. No, absolutely dry. If they're not dry inside then use the paper towel to dry each of them. I know—but they have to be dry. If you don't do it right, the filling won't stick and you'll still be at it when the guests arrive.

"All this for what?" I asked myself, hands full of the stinging tomato juice. It wasn't as if my parents knew enormous numbers of people or needed to entertain them. My mother didn't really expect invitations to other people's houses; she just kept inviting them to ours. And sometimes it was only our family who came, like Grandma, who had grown up in rural Newfoundland. When she saw all the activity in the kitchen, she'd say it was "a lot of fuss for no reason." I sensed that my mother wanted Grandma to understand that things were very different in her house; that there was more to a meal than Grandma's standard boiled beef and cabbage.

While you're waiting for the tomato hulls to dry and every single drop of moisture to disappear, you can make the filling. Get the blender out—be careful, it's heavy—and put in the cottage cheese, whipping cream, lemon juice, Tabasco and chopped onion. Well, that's the way chopped onion is—it stings—don't rub your eyes— now you're going to have to wash your hands. Quickly! Quickly! That's better. Puree until smooth, Really smooth, absolutely no lumps, No. Do it again, it's still not smooth enough.

Tiny Tomatoes could never be made quickly, but I knew it was pointless to try and convince my mother that something easier would be just as good. I mentioned to her that at our aunt Elizabeth's house they only put out cheese and crackers for appetizers and asked her why we didn't do that. *People appreciate it when you make things special*, she told me, but I wasn't sure that was the whole answer.

When the tomatoes are ready to be filled, you need a tiny spoon or preferably the melon baller. It's in the bottom drawer. When you start filling the tomatoes, there are two things to watch out for. I know you've done it before but listen anyway. First, because the bottoms of the tomatoes are round, once you've filled them they tend to topple over. Ooh—watch it—like that one there. So it's best to try and get the first three done quickly, stand them up against each other in the middle of the tray, and then have all the others lean against them. Second, try to keep the sides of the tomato clean. The filling is gooey and sticks everywhere. You've got to pay attention because the opening is not as wide as the tomato bottom being filled. Go slowly. OK—you're almost finished. Cut up chives and you're going to sprinkle them over each one. No, don't toss. Try and get three or four chive pieces on each tomato. Why? Because it looks nice. There—that looks lovely. Now wrap the tray with Saran and put it in the fridge. Be careful. No—I still need you in the kitchen.

I was always needed in the kitchen. *We only have a few hours to put this party together,* my mother would declare if she was running behind schedule. I sometimes wished she could be more like Aunt Elizabeth, who never got behind schedule because she didn't put exhausting things like Tiny Tomatoes on her menu. Or like the mother of my friend Ginny Buckle. When Mrs. Buckle had guests for dinner, she simply pulled out her extra yellow TV tables, and placed them around the room so that everyone had the good view of the set. On the same TV tables where they had dinner, Mrs. Buckle would sometimes help Ginny with her "fashion scrapbook," cutting out pictures from magazines of clothes that Ginny might try on at the mall. I wanted a fashion scrapbook and shopping trips to the mall too, but my mother and I were both too busy with her weekend dinner parties to think about those things. If I wanted my mother to spend time with me, I had to join her in the kitchen. She wasn't like Mrs. Buckle, or Aunt Elizabeth or even her own mother, and proved it Saturday after Saturday, one recipe at a time.

The quiet, purposeful preparation of the tomatoes and the rest of the cooking went on all afternoon, quickened only by my mother's occasional announcements—*One hour left!* or, *Twenty minutes and this has to be in the oven!* By day's end, we had completed half a dozen dishes. By the time the guests arrived, the kitchen was packed away and clean and my mother's table set: the crisp linen cloth and napkins squared perfectly and the good cutlery and glasses glowing. My father was told to put on his best pullover and my sister and I were sent to get into our dresses. My mother took the last half hour to transform herself into a glamorous hostess; she had a bath, curled her hair and put on makeup, her dress, brand new pantyhose, high-heeled shoes and special ruby and emerald rings that she pulled from a velvet box in her top drawer. From her bedroom, over the noise of the blow-dryer, she shouted last-minute instructions to me. *Bite-size pieces—tear the lettuce into bite-size pieces. If it won't fit in your mouth, it's too big!*

When the guests had arrived and were seated in the living room with their cocktails, my mother set the tray of the appetizer Tiny Tomatoes in my arms. *Pass them around, make sure everyone gets a little blue napkin.* "They look precious," a guest would say. *Gillian made them,* my mother would answer proudly. And always, I was proud too. I watched our guests pop them into their mouths and kept passing the tray until they were all gone. At the dinner table, the meal delivered *oohs* and *aahs,* and my mother beamed as the conversation and laughter bubbled, the wine flowed and second helpings were served. Even my grandmother, if she was there, enjoyed the "fuss" and scraped her plate clean. Afterwards, as my mother and I did the dishes, she went over everything, giving a little critique or comment here or there. *The potatoes were a little dry, I should have served them a bit earlier* or, *I think we could have had even more toasted coconut on the cake, don't you?* And always: *Those Tiny Tomatoes are always such a big hit.*

I know that a different mother might have treated me more like a daughter and less like a sous-chef. While I was helping her in her kitchen she spoke to me as if I wasn't so much her child, but someone who worked for her and knew just as well as she did when the coconut was toasted or the cream whipped to perfect peaks. Maybe my mother was selfish, for I know it cost me other experiences to be the supporting act in the show of her life. Other mothers, like Mrs. Buckle, spent more time presenting options and helping their daughters discover their own pleasures. Mine did not. I lived in the full-force wind of my mother's passion—there was no escaping it. I would know it intimately.

"Why does your mother make you work in the kitchen so much?" Ginny asked me one Saturday, after I had to turn down an invitation to join her shopping for a new, blue mascara. Then, I had no answer. I really didn't know.

But I do know now. I realize how much I'm like my mother, and I am grateful for all those days of cooking lessons. Because of them, I would rather be in my kitchen than almost anywhere else. There, the demands of my life fade away, and I get lost in the experience that yields a soup pureed to a silky cream or a salmon poached a few seconds past pink.

I also know that she gave me a gift far greater than my competence in front of a stove. My mother insisted on bringing her own art and beauty to the few spaces she found in busy family life. By her example, I was able to learn to reach past what I was given and beyond what I know: to "make things special" for the simple joy of it. This, perhaps, was the "interest" she saw in me long ago.

Now in spaces not taken up by my home and full-time marketing career, I continue to teach myself new recipes and endeavour to write down the stories of my life. And when my mother and I cook together, we take turns as sous-chef, share recipes we discovered while apart and challenge ourselves to perfect and reinvent the ones we know well: my lemon chicken, her hazelnut cheesecake and one that belongs to both of us—the classic and beautiful Tiny Tomatoes.

PITCH: A
DANCER'S JOURNAL

JODI LUNDGREN

This morning as I run down porch steps to load the car, I shiver and my mind clears. Victoria air: not even July can dispel its salt chill. I absorb coastal crispness before my cross-country flight.

The minute I disembark, past midnight, Toronto air licks me, resists me like water. An oily sweat pools at the base of my throat. Skin bare and glistening, muscles spongy, I have come here to dance.

THE SCHOOL OF TORONTO DANCE THEATRE

In Cabbagetown, on a narrow street of tall, peaked-roof houses with bay windows and vine-hung porches, the Toronto Dance Theatre (TDT) occupies a one-hundred-year-old church of warm red brick. A stained glass window filters sunlight into the main studio, where the choir loft has been converted into a sound booth, the pews into raked theatre seats and the chancel into a dance floor that doubles as a stage. St. Enoch's is an apt setting for a four-week intensive course in the modern dance technique developed by Martha Graham.

We dancers rise when the teacher enters the studio and then, at a word from her, sit on the floor and draw the soles of our bare feet together. The torso contracts to initiate sixteen bounces. As the back rounds, nose points to navel, and crown aims for crotch. After the pulses, spine straightens in a diagonal; legs lengthen, then open to a wide V. Arms curve, wrists face the floor, abdomen hollows, and, again, sixteen bounces. We expel our breath as if sighing.

The Latin word *spiritus* means "a sigh, the breath of life, inspiration, spirit." As I move through the floor work, my centre of consciousness drops into my core. Why was this hidden from me? Why do worldly pressures crush vitality and force us all into nine-to-five ruts? When we could dance first thing in the morning, dance all day . . .

I know it is a privilege to be here. One of my dear friends who loves to dance is now raising a son alone. For my brother, who suffers from severe arthritis, even walking hurts too much. I am dancing, not only for my own sake, but because they can't. I can, so I must. Passion demands to be followed, it demands risk and change. By the end of the first class I am already burning to commit myself to a year of the full-time TDT program.

SCHEDULE

9:30 a.m. Technique class. The musician's hands tap brisk rhythms on the skin of a drum to guide our "bounces," "openings" and "long leans": set floor work that limbers the body sequentially. Fibres loosen and lengthen as we spiral and stretch: sudden suppleness.

11:15 a.m. Barre class. In a continual about-face, we stand with first the right hand on the barre, then the left, as we execute demanding, balletic exercises. Legs warm, we clear the barres away for *adage:* the "working leg" quivers to support an extension while the "standing leg" bores the ground.

At last we can travel. We race across the floor with runs, triplets and hops, then progress to difficult combinations.

Direction changes and intricate footwork complicate the diagonal journey from corner to corner of the studio. Drumbeats propel the dance—the percussionist inspires and pushes us, sets our hearts racing.

1:00 p.m. Lunch. We pull on shorts and line the sidewalk, backs to sun-warmed brick, legs bent into triangles, knees to the sky. Chestnut trees in full leaf cast shade. We eat sandwiches from brown bags or visit the old-fashioned corner deli to spoon lentil soup from thick, white bowls.

1:45 p.m. Back to the studio. Repertory class demands both spontaneity—we sometimes improvise to find movement—and persistence, as we repeat phrases over and over to polish them for presentation. The choreographer, a tiny woman with birdlike alertness, encourages wildness yet insists on precision. When we wilt in the heat, she urges us not to succumb. "Don't sink into the floor. Find it in yourselves to pull up and push through it, and you'll feel much better." I respect her words: she knows what it means to be rehearsing tired, into your sixth hour in the studio.

3:15 p.m. The end of the day. Many head off to their waitressing jobs; I can barely exit the building. Today I hobble to Carlton and collapse on a park bench to drink iced tea. Riding home afterwards strains me. Although I believe in gritting my teeth through repertory, what am I trying to prove by cycling home? Tomorrow I'll treat myself to the streetcar.

RAIN

I leave the Free Times Café on College and catch the High Park streetcar back to Roncesvalles, where I sublet a long, narrow apartment that overlooks Queen Street. Rather than transfer, I walk, so that I can buy Epsom salts, fruit and bread. The sky has clouded over, and I slip on an extra shirt. When I emerge from the drugstore, it's drizzling. At the bakery a few doors down, braided clerks address customers in Polish. I point to a loaf of sourdough rye and raise my eyebrows hopefully.

As I continue south with my bread, the downpour redoubles. Eaves are dripping, puddles collecting, umbrellas mushrooming. When I stop for bananas and nectarines, the proprietor suggests waiting in the store. I decline the invitation and pursue my path, pack on my back, shopping bag swinging in my hand. With every step my shoes become more waterlogged. They squelch and the dye starts to run. Rain flattens the hair to my head, plasters shirt and shorts to my body with form-hugging transparency. Pedestrians have gathered under awnings and in doorways. Arms folded, they watch the storm—and me.

Nobody stops for rain on the West Coast, where the showers aren't fierce and momentary but steady and relentless: you would wait all day. Unaccustomed to rain that halts the community, that draws people into neighbourly clusters, I resist when it would be wiser to conform. The price of my initiation: a soaking and a ruined pair of shoes.

REPERCUSSIONS

Body being worked so hard I'm pushed to some verge, of breakdown or breakthrough, exhaustion, despair, tears, exaltation.

Today in barre class, I couldn't master the combination so I threw myself into it, channelled my frustration into intensity. A good way to cope, but it means that my body ricochets with aggression. My muscles rip and rebuild daily, an industry at the cellular level. Irritated flesh resents change, and I experience its mood: pugnacious.

"Injury comes to those who go for it," I overheard in the change room. There was an odour of menthol.

Pinched hip and inflamed hamstring sear my left leg, and this wooden chair aggravates them. I shift in vain, much like my brother at family meals. His joints swell; his bones disintegrate. His habitual expression, a wince. Pain has come to him uninvited; some would say I asked for it. Still, my desire to train persists.

Later: Feeling better, no thanks to the Epsom-salts bath or the tiger balm or the cold pack or the tennis ball massage or the mild bike ride to High Park, or even the cathartic effects of writing—though I have done all these naturopathic things, have assiduously cared for myself tonight. No, I attribute it to the Tylenol I took half an hour ago. I don't regret it. I can't justify dancing full-time if it means I have to suffer like this.

PERSPECTIVE

Our technique teacher, Lynn, stresses that parts of the body oppose each other. When you draw in a leg in the openings, for instance, the torso does not simply turn toward it. There must be a fight. Lynn herself looks tough and sinewy as an animal that has been fighting for survival all its life. Her body resists itself to such an extent that it can express only private struggle. Never ease or pure affirmation.

But today she reminds us that the high lift in the floor work expresses ecstasy, and that at our level, everything we do should look like or, more importantly, *feel* like dancing. "You're past the stage of forming letters of the alphabet between the dotted lines. Now you've got to write beautiful poems!"

She has us repeat a combination on single counts, fast, so that we're forced to abandon ourselves to instinct. She keeps up a stream of exclamations: "Yes! Oh! Now *that's* a different story!"

Lynn has danced professionally for twenty years—no one would dance that long without love. What appeared to be severity I now recognize as the capacity for *work* that sustains any intense endeavour. The Graham technique arrives at emotion through discipline, for even the desire to dance wildly cannot be realized without a vocabulary of movement and a strong, flexible body. Depth of feeling does not suffice: impulses need painstaking artistry in order to be rendered with power.

PROGRESS

Unseasonably cool weather means that early air stirs fresh against a moving form. Most mornings I cycle up the alley, turn on Sorauren, then follow College straight across town. As a cyclist I join the urban groove in a way bus passengers don't. I thrill with danger when I signal a left turn and cross streetcar tracks in the rain.

Pain in my left hamstring and hip has diminished. And today I make a breakthrough in the floor work: as I rotate out of contraction, I feel my spine spiralling, twisting in segments like something you manipulate with your hands. Achieving the positions requires so much effort that when their logic infiltrates my body, I am gratified. On almost everyone in class, I see the elegance and beauty of the neck long, the shoulders dropped, the chest and back wide and open, the head turning on top of the spine, energy rising up the torso and pouring into the ground behind. I can now understand those who maintain a daily practice for years. It is devotional. For dancers in this converted church, the ritual of Graham floor work serves as prayer, or meditation.

ZEST

A guest teacher, Viv, arrives to teach technique class ten minutes late and sets the clock back by five. She announces her age—sixty—with an irascible slur. Her demeanour unnerves me and my progress is lost. She torques my ribcage painfully on the spiral in second, preceding the long leans: "Take the ribs with you!" Such pulling and twisting make this technique feel taut and strained. My pelvis often hurts as the bones press the floor. Is this the kind of pain my brother feels as he attempts a normal range of motion? Is it worth harming the body to celebrate movement?

By the end of class, we are fifteen minutes over. I feel hot, tired, dehydrated and annoyed that we will have no break. Viv beckons to me and says, "You've got to shift your weight. You're just stepping." She demonstrates. To shift the weight, it turns out, is a good synecdoche for zest, urgency, emotional engagement—for making the sequence come alive as dance. When I repeat the combination, she says, "What a difference!" and raises a fist in tribute, elbow tucked to her side.

Last Christmas, after witnessing my brother's rigidity, I had to throw it off in an exultant jog to the waterfront. To compensate for his loss of mobility, to claim motion for both of us, I swung from the gnarled branches of Garry oaks, leapt from benches, flew across grass into handsprings.

In my family, we've denied ourselves sensory pleasure— a Protestant legacy. We've rejected experience, restrained ourselves, wasted years severed from joy. My brother once chose to hold back; now incapacity stills him. He can no more ripple his limbs than can the Garry oaks, stunted trees that recoil from coastal wind. I can't bear what has happened to him.

85

Refusal to follow suit has fuelled my commitment: to move, to thrive, to live. I've rerouted asceticism into dance—a discipline that remembers bliss.

COUNTERBALANCE

As the program draws to a close, my spirits falter. Familiar sentiments nag me: dancing this much is self-indulgent. I must hold myself in reserve for more important, serious things in the Real World. I must earn a living, advance in a profession, save for retirement. My shoulders slump as I enter the studio.

In class, we pitch in contraction over a bent front leg, the back leg in attitude. The move feels reckless and abandoned, but safely held by the tight abdomen. It yokes those two opposing human impulses: to risk and to be secure. Pitch yourself over the edge *and* hold on. It expresses my longing to dance full-time, yet maintain a teaching career. This wonderful move demonstrates that paradox does not paralyze. In fact, the Graham technique depends on such tension. As we reach and resist, our gestures gain definition. We don't simply live with contradiction: it provides meaning.

CULMINATION

Last day at TDT. Barre class ends with leaping from the corner, and even after the signal to stop, people circle back to repeat. At the final moment I too race back, breaking a threesome into two pairs, so my partner and I cross last. The percussionist spurs us to jump higher and longer and to sharpen head and arms. We mirror his swell on the final jeté. The summer concludes with a drumbeat and us in the air.

THE ROAD TO
KIHANDE VILLAGE

MELANIE D. JANZEN

In the early afternoon, in the oppressive heat of June, I begin my walk to Kihande—a small village outside of the town of Masindi in Uganda. The red dirt road from my house, barely wide enough for a vehicle, is lined with elephant grass that towers over my head and hushes in the breeze. After the bend, the road gradually widens and joins up with the main road leading from town to Kihande village. The roads are not marked, and I can take a number of different trails and paths; as long as I walk in the same general direction, I always arrive at my destination. I smile as I trek to the village—anticipating my afternoon and wondering what might be revealed on this day with the women of Agabagaya.

Agabagaya is a group of women I meet with for the purpose of a small research study I'm conducting for my master's degree in women's studies and education. I'm interested in exploring the ways in which women share knowledge to support their families and communities, and in examining the types of power—although often unrecognized in the public sphere—women hold within society.

My interest stems, in part, from my own childhood experiences. My mother had a strong network of women neighbours when I was growing up in the suburbs of Winnipeg in the 1970s. These women collaborated to share insights, to save money and to reduce their workloads.

They owned kitchen appliances collectively: my mom had the only canner on the block, midnight blue with white speckles; Joyce had the only meat grinder, used for making fancy ham fillings for Christmas hors d'oeuvres. When my mom's raspberries were ripe, she picked them, froze some and then invited the neighbour women to help themselves. Joyce shared her herbs and Trish snipped plant cuttings from a new variety of geranium she had acquired. The women shared sewing patterns, sauce recipes and apple-preserving techniques.

When the three neighbouring women returned to the work force on a part-time basis, they worked on alternate days so that we kids could still come home for lunch. On Mondays, we all arrived at Joyce's for homemade chicken soup with noodles as wide as our fingers. At Trish's on Tuesdays, we'd have ravioli, from a can, no less—unheard of in our house. And in our kitchen, on Wednesdays, the neighbourhood favourite was served: tuna melts, creatively turned into *high wires* as we stretched the cheesy bites across the table between us, letting the melted mozzarella hang and swing in the air. For many years these women, my mother and her two friends, cooked for us, cared for us, scolded us and taught us. And now in Kihande, a village twelve thousand kilometres from home, I witness this same collaborative spirit among the women of Agabagaya.

By the time I reach Kihande, forty minutes after starting out, my shirt is wet where my backpack rests. Sweat trickles down my inner thigh under my skirt, my head is hot under my hat and my sandalled feet are red with dust. Although weary, I am genuinely happy to see the smiling face of Shakillah, the chairperson of the group, as she comes down the path to meet me. She tilts her head as a broad smile crosses her beautiful brown face, as though she is sharing a secret with me. As I approach, she gently embraces my hand with hers and the lengthy greeting begins.

"How are you?" she asks slowly and intently.

"I am fine, Shakillah. How are you?"

"I am good. How is Masindi?" she asks, as part of the greeting is to ask about the place from where you have just arrived.

"Masindi is good," I answer.

"And how is your friend Dominique?" she inquires about the Canadian friend I'm staying with while living here in Uganda.

"She is fine," I reply. "She is at work today but she sends her greetings." All this time the handholding continues and we stay comfortably connected as we begin our walk up the narrow path. When we arrive at the meeting place, each woman greets me in much the same way, shakes my hand and then adds, "You are most welcome here."

Today we gather in a cool grassy spot in the schoolyard on Harriet's large straw mat. Jamiila and Shakillah are sitting side by side, singing the Agabagaya song as Shakillah records the lyrics in my notebook. Although there is a mild breeze, the women occasionally dab their faces and necks with handkerchiefs. They sit with their legs outstretched in front of them, barefoot and relaxed. Jamiila's baby plays contentedly with the grass that tickles her chubby legs. Occasionally, a chicken clucks by, inspecting and stabbing the ground intently, and when the hen does not move on, it is subtly shooed away by one of the women.

I greatly admire these women and their commitment to each other and to their group, which began informally and then gained official recognition from the Masindi District Office three years ago. Their purpose is clear and simple:

they want to eradicate poverty in their village. And the women work vigorously in a multitude of ways in an effort to achieve this goal. Being members of Agabagaya means that the women contribute to a cash cooperative every other Sunday. The bulk of the funds they collect is given to a different woman each meeting and so, over a six-month period, each member of the group receives a lump sum payment once. How the women use the money is up to their individual discretion. Harriet paid for materials to add a room onto her home; Epiphania used the money to pay the school fees for her children; and Joy purchased clothes in Kampala and then sold them to the villagers in her front yard.

The surplus funds collected at each meeting remain in the group pot and are used to make purchases that benefit the group or to generate an income for them. Currently, the women have purchased and are raising one hundred chicks to be sold once they have matured. They own a cow for milking and they grow mushrooms, which they plan to dry and sell at the market. The women do not own land as a group, so each "project" is housed at one of the members' homes: the chickens at Shakillah's, the piglets at Dorcas's and the organic compost at Epiphania's.

The women of Agabagaya, all of whom have some formal education, continue to further educate themselves in areas such as farm management, first aid and organic gardening techniques; therefore, sometimes the group spends its surplus money to pay for the women to attend workshops or courses. The women ensure that their children attend school, and they have organized Runyoro literacy classes on Saturdays for villagers who are interested in learning how to read and write in their local language. One of the members of the group, sixty-seven-year-old Aidah, who cares for six of her orphaned grandchildren, runs a nursery school in a simple brick building in her backyard for the villagers' preschoolers.

The women of Agabagaya labour endlessly within their homes and communities and yet many of them are also employed: Harriet is a waitress at a local guest house, Lois is a high school teacher, Dorcas is a controller, and Shakillah owns a small sewing shop.

The children of Kihande attend school, run and play with other children and help out with chores and housework. They delight in knocking mangoes out of the trees, singing songs to each other and playing with simple, often home-made, toys. After school they come home and work alongside their mothers, preparing meals and fetching water. The children often gather near us when we meet, curious about my presence. It took days for me to figure out whose children were whose—the Kihande women allow their children to be cared for, monitored and disciplined by the collective. The children, in a sense, belong to all of the women.

I understand that these women's and children's lives are not perfect. They are faced with issues that are not prevalent in my world: the devastating effects of AIDS, the ongoing threat and treatment of malaria, inequitable access to education and an unsettling and sometimes brutal political situation. But what impresses me the most is not just the way in which the group cares for their children, but also the strong commitment to collaboration that these women have established in so many aspects of their lives. Collectively, they provide emotional, financial and educational support for each other. In Kihande, as in many other parts of the world, the burden of household responsibilities—child rearing, food production and preparation—rests with the women, and these women have found a way to share the load, to prosper not just individually but also in ways that benefit their greater community. Undoubtedly, they could not achieve alone what they are able to do as a group.

I recognize the worth of the bond the women of Agabagaya have created because I experienced similar benefits from my mother's relationships with the other neighbourhood mothers. Their focus, like that of the women in Agabagaya, was their children and their families. And as children we had space to roam and unscheduled time to play. There was joy in our simplicity: coming home after school, eating carrots that we pillaged from the garden or snacking on buns still warm from the oven. And yet these women, my other mothers, also made time for each other emotionally and socially.

●   ●   ●

I can't help but reflect on my own life as a grown woman in light of these two collectives. I too have a circle of supportive women in my life—women who give me strength, courage and support. However, the relationships I have with my women friends have little to do with daily survival—with actually bettering our families and enhancing our communities. In contrast to the women of Agabagaya, our relationships are an embarrassing privilege of middle class—we golf nine holes, eat at Thai restaurants and meet on the occasional Wednesday evening in the middle of winter to enjoy a latte and share a slice of cheesecake. We go out with our own cars and our own bank cards, leaving our partners—and for some, our children—at home.

Our survival and our children's well-being do not depend on our collaboration. Like the women of Agabagaya, we socialize, laugh and share daily problems, but we are careful not to overstep certain boundaries—like those of parenting.

We don't generally share our resources, work collaboratively for the betterment of our communities or openly consider the long-term possibilities of our friendship. Although I value and am grateful for what we have (and I know my women friends are too), in our increasingly individualistic society, there are boundaries to our friendship, territories that we do not enter and ground that we do not tread. Our focus is often on the sharing of our personal successes, struggles and career and family milestones, not on a concern for the wider community.

And yet, as I go on with my routine life in Winnipeg, having completed my studies and returned to work. I hold on to Agabagaya's story carefully, not wanting the memories to fade, and greatly aware of the possibilities that the women of Kihande village have allowed me to imagine.

•   •   •

I prepare to leave Kihande just before sunset in an effort to get home before it grows so dark that I can no longer see my way on the unlit roads and paths. Tradition dictates that one or more of the women will walk me partway home, sometimes holding my hand as we proceed. In the beginning, the women insisted that most of the group walk with me, often taking me on different roads and pointing out important landmarks. As time went on, however, fewer women came along. I took this as a sign of acceptance, of no longer being perceived as a guest. Now, only one or two women accompany me each time, and I silently celebrate feeling less like a visitor who needs formal hosting and more like an equal, a friend, a member of their group.

Tonight, after sharing a huge traditional meal that some of the women prepared, we talk about an incident at one of the local schools where a girl had been reprimanded for not complying with the dress code. After debating the different sides of the issue, the topic of conversation naturally shifts, as conversations do, and Lois sings for us a song she wrote. Eventually we are all singing and laughing and dancing. There is always a lot of laughter with these women and being with them gives me great comfort and a sense of familiarity. I feel overwhelmed and in awe of their kindness, their generosity—and their ambition. I dread leaving, but the room is growing dim as the sun begins to set, and I know it is time to go.

Sally walks me from her house across the road and then stops. "You know the rest of the way from here." She encloses my hand in both of hers and smiles. We can hear the faint voices of the women singing, interrupted by splashes of their laughter. Sally begins to step backwards, eager to get back to the house to join them.

"Greet Dominique when you see her," Sally calls to me over her shoulder. "I will," I call back, waving. As I meander down the road past the barefooted school children walking to the pump with jerry cans to fill with water, I watch the sky change colour, from azure to shades of indigo near the horizon. Birds are calling and a boy on a bicycle speeds past me ringing his bell, signalling the children to move off the road. I am aware of the smile that I wear and of the feelings of contentment that rise within me as I continue to walk on, the rest of the way home—alone.

part two

A CLARITY OF VISION

BAREFOOT
IN THE SNOW

BETH POWNING

My husband and I take our three-and-a-half-year-old granddaughter, Maeve, for a walk. It's cold and we're bundled up: toques, neck warmers, felt-lined boots. The ground is frozen. There's no snow and a bitter wind, so we head up along the edge of the field, duck into the shelter of the woods and visit a stone firepit we made last summer. We squat by it, pretending to be camping. She loves this.

"Pretend we're the Gypsy family," I say.

"We're cooking rabbits," she says. "We caught one, and smacked him till he was dead, and then we put him on a stick, and now we're cooking him."

Later, we go up to the highest field. Our feet crunch frozen reindeer moss. There's a pale sun, presaging snow. Maeve is stumping gamely uphill, holding Peter's hand. We stop to admire the view: far below is our farmhouse with its cluster of barns, beyond the meadow is the church, and across the road from the church is an old one-room schoolhouse. It's been converted into a home, and Maeve lives there with her parents and little sister, Bridget.

I kneel beside her to point out these landmarks. She's ripping off her mittens, stuffing them in her pockets.

"Maeve! What are you doing? You can't take off your mittens!"

"My hands are having hot flashes," she insists indignantly.

She waves her hands back and forth, fingers spread. I feel her hands. Indeed, they are sweaty hot.

. . .

When she has hot flashes for real, I'm happy to think, they won't be a shock to her, as they were to me. "Why didn't anyone ever tell me?" I said, constantly, to my friends, at the onset of menopause, feeling as if I'd entered the strangest territory, having crossed a boundary I never knew existed. My mother told me nothing, since she says she wasn't aware of menopause, although she may not have realized what it was that was affecting her. I remember how, when I was twenty-two, she'd spend a day in bed for no discernible reason. Or fly into sudden trembling rages—once, even, hurling a bowl of mashed potatoes at my father. (It wasn't the best china, she explained later.) My mother-in-law told me about the time that *her* daughter asked for information on menopause, having chosen it as a subject for a school project.

"I was mortified," my mother-in-law told me, in a lowered voice, distressed by the memory. "I don't think I'd ever spoken that word out loud."

Women still lower their voices when voicing the word *menopause*. Over the years, I've heard older women say, "She's going through her change," looking at each other significantly, their words reverberant with hushed momentousness, like so much else to do with women's lives. And I realize that within myself is a voice that whispers, even now: *Shame, embarrassment, weakness, mortification.*

This time in my life began, like secrecy, with the presence of absence. Nothing happened; and then, one day, I realized that I had passed a few months with no period. I was as shocked by the lack of blood as I was when I was fourteen and found my underpants stained with brilliant red. Both events elicited confusion. At fourteen I thought—where is my tomboy self? The girl who could beat boys at arm-wrestling, jump off roofs, ride bareback? Furious, I lay on my bed curled around the clutching pain of cramps. And for the next thirty years, I struggled with a slippery sense of identity. I felt continuously at odds with my body, the one thing in my life I was enraged at being unable to control. I was not glad to be a woman.

In the 1950s, there were almost no successful female role models. I was deeply imbued, not by my parents but by the culture of the times, with a sense of inferiority. Women had intuition rather than intellect. Dick and Jane's father went to work, and their mother was waiting at the door at the end of the day, in wasp-waisted dress and red lipstick, fresh and cheery, having spent all day readying the house for his return. This enraged me, once I was old enough to think about it; yet by then the damage was done. I'd absorbed the insecurities of my generation. Museums celebrated the accomplishments of men, in both the arts and the sciences. Men were explorers, athletes, musicians, physicians, lawyers, engineers. Women were bad drivers, incompetent, helpless, destined for blowsy, bosomy middle age.

I spent the middle years of my life—from first period to menopause—battling this early self-image, and creating the person I wanted to be. It was a time of marriage, mother-hood, homemaking, career-building, enthusiasms, despair, perfectionism, and above all, busyness. Too busy to dwell in the present, I lived the moments of my life with increasing despair since I tried, endlessly and without success, to con-trol my circumstances. Trying to be strong and whole, I bat-tled a sense of inadequacy that made me both furious and fearful; I held a created image of myself up like a paper with a high grade so that I could safely say, "See? This is me."

When I was in my mid-forties, depression did its work, broke me down as rain batters a dead leaf, until I found qualities within myself never before acknowledged. I learned to listen, but also to speak. I learned to be quiet in a group of people and not feel I had said nothing. The many sides of my personality blended, and I learned to be one person, the same person, always. It was a wondrous process, as satisfying as planting tulip bulbs, learning to sing or recovering a lost sense.

Then, at the age of fifty-two, just when I feel more often happy than not, capable, tender, at peace with my strong body, it begins: the great pause, the death of fertility. Strangely, and fittingly, it *burns* away. My body blazes— flushed, sweating—as if fertility, like any dead thing, is most thoroughly cleansed and transformed by fire.

•   •   •

On a February night, it's freezing cold in the unheated bedroom of our old house. Peter and I are snuggled together under three blankets and a quilt. I've got a hot water bottle between my knees. When I went to bed, my nose was so icy that I pulled the blankets over my head and made a breathing-cave.

The instant I begin to drift off to sleep, I feel the subtlest touch, like a fingertip pressed on the skin, or a mouthed message. *Here I come.* My body responds with a flight reaction. Panic, starting in my legs; the need to run. Then my mind catches up. It fills with despairing thoughts, and is suffused with doom. *Oh, God.* I kick off the blankets, heap them between me and the silent mound of my husband. I roll onto my back, haul up my nightgown. I am being consumed by an intolerable heat. My heart races, sweat prickles between my breasts. I slide my legs restlessly, seeking coolness. Beneath my shoulder blades, the sheets begin to dampen. I imagine flames coming from the soles of my feet, and lay them against the bed's wooden footboard.

Did I think this room was cold? I wait for the inner furnace to subside, for my sweat to dry. Sometimes I let myself get too cold. Then I cling to Peter, shivering.

On and on it goes, sometimes every hour on the hour. I wake, in the morning, tired. I face going to bed like a chore.

I sense the same bewildered ache I had when I was fourteen and felt I'd lost my tomboy self. Now I wonder what will become of the strong, youthful woman I sought for so long, worked to create, and finally found? For I'm at the start of another passage, and this one ends in death.

* * *

I'm feeling a sense of sadness about the woman I no longer am, and yet she is the one who enables me to have the good sense to accept what is happening. I develop humility, humour and perspective, new tools I recognize as blessings, since I'll have them well entrenched when, in the next stage of my life, I may face far more debilitating losses.

I've chosen not to take hormone replacement therapy—my woman doctor has never recommended it. At first I think, "I can deal with this, it's only discomfort, and won't last long." After a few years, however, I see that the process needs my attention and respect. But I have to go about it the way I tamed a wild pony who could not be touched. I spent an entire winter singing to her, my head bent, never attempting to pat her. One day, I slowly raised my arm to stroke her neck and she lowered her head to my breast. She changed me; I changed her. Finally, I slid onto her back and we moved as one.

I decide it is time to systematically try vitamins and herbs—ginseng, vitamin E, black cohosh, dong quai—until I find something that calms the daily and nightly waves of roaring heat, and the insomnia or anxiety accompanying them. I've learned that menopause is far more than the absence of a period. It is an enormous change—emotional, physical, spiritual—and is as irresistible as the contractions of birth. Day after day, night after night, year after year, I'm faced with the evidence of how I'm like the sea, or the moon, or the seasons. Heat rises within me, my blood vessels enlarge, my skin sweats. When this happens, I have no choice but to stop what I'm doing, wait patiently, and endure, since resisting, like fighting contractions, makes everything worse.

Lack of resistance, like singing to a pony, is not passivity but wisdom.

* * *

My granddaughters and my mother pull me beyond the narrow circle of my own perspective and teach me about what I think of as "the authority of the self."

Bridget, eight months old, spies a blue-eyed stuffed dog on a shelf. She crawls toward it, making imperious barking sounds. "Ha. Ha." She reaches up. Reaches, reaches. Her tiny, strong hand grasps the edge of the shelf and she pulls herself onto her feet. She stands, wobbling, picking up the dog with delight, entirely unaware of her precariousness. And Maeve, in the tub, declares, "I'm dog/fish/woman." And she's absolutely right. Her perfect female body is fully stretched, fish-like, in the dappled water. She reaches her arms forward, swimming, while her feet *kick kick kick*, with puppy-like abandon.

My mother, at eighty-one, thinks of death as a beginning,

and is certain that something amazing will occur when she goes forward into her next life. She wears sneakers and jeans; works out with a personal trainer. "Punch, punch!" the trainer shouts, and my mother jabs body blows at a leather bag. She and my father still live in their drafty old farmhouse, and she breaks from our phone conversation to tell me what she is seeing at that moment: the blood-red amaryllis on her desk, glowing in sudden sun; a cloud of pink-speckled blossoms on the crab-apple tree.

They persist, and insist, both tiny girls and elderly woman—embracing life, discovering it, delighting in it. This is what I am going to do, they declare. They accept the conditions of their life.

And they also see more clearly. Time confers clarity. There is so much time, for the little girls, that it's like an ocean. There is so much less, for my mother, that it's like an exquisite wine, drunk in smaller and smaller sips and held longer on the tongue. Yet in both cases, the extremity of time's perceived dimensions, either expanding or diminishing, sharpens perception of the present, tipped, as it is, on the lip of either a long future, or a long past.

And I realize that I am beginning to regain a clarity of vision, made necessary both by the incontrovertible facts of my condition, and a sense of time's value.

•   •   •

We make a small campfire next to the driveway, beneath the snowbank left by the plow. We're the Gypsy family again. I'm Zingarella, Maeve is Marshmallow, Bridget is Fire, and Peter is the Pretend Gypsy Dada.

We have some firewood, matches, newspaper, a snowbank, five stale (hard as wood) marshmallows, a toboggan with missing slats. We have sunshine that makes the snow glitter. We have time, all afternoon. Raggedy Ann is wearing a paper diaper that is falling off.

"It doesn't matter," Marshmallow says dismissively. "She's outside, she can poop on the ground."

Fire falls asleep in the Gypsy Dada's arms while I'm pulling Marshmallow on the toboggan and so we wrap Fire in a sleeping bag and lower her into a cradle we've pummelled into the snowbank.

Marshmallow feeds her doll with an invisible spoon. Thin blue smoke rises. A raven, flying overhead, wavers, tips a wing downward, and cocks its eye at us.

Children, old people and birds, I think, know how to make not much into a great deal.

·   ·   ·

I'm three years into menopause, and it's still happening. Every day, struggling out of a sweater, mopping sweat from the back of my neck, I wonder when it's going to end. But I, too, persist and insist, enjoying life with a different kind of delight—it's heavier, richer, like afternoon light. I sense how my patience has grown, like any skill. I see that I've learned how to make do with things as they are.

Sometimes, now, when I'm boiling hot, I slide out of bed with my pillow and lie on the floor. It's lovely: hard and icy cold. Walls and furniture loom, misshapen, like elephant flanks. This, I think, calmly observing the shadow-warped, gigantic bureau, is a new perspective. Or, rather, a deeply familiar one. It's how Maeve and Bridget must see the world.

If this strategy doesn't work to cool me off, I go downstairs in my polypropolene, sweat-wicking, long-winter undershirt. I slide open the sunroom's glass door, go outside and stand barefoot in the snow. I spread my arms, not from ecstasy but to expose every possible bit of skin. The stars glitter, silver, blue-green, smoky red. I feel a bittersweet yearning as I behold the solemn vastness, so seemingly close, so alien. This, I think, is how my mother, sleepless at eighty-one, sees the stars.

FINDING MY WAY

BARBARA MITCHELL

There I am, captured in a black-and-white photograph, posing in my very first formal. But I colour it in with memory—a lush emerald green dress. No dress has ever seemed quite so perfect. Daringly strapless, it was all the rage with its chiffon "balloon skirt." Tucked in snugly at the waist, it fell lightly, then puffed out at the calf-length hemline. I can feel, once again, that anticipatory excitement, though I could not have known then that the High River High School Banquet would be the beginning of something special.

It was 1959, and I was fifteen. I had just been asked to the banquet by Orm Mitchell, whose mother had manoeuvred the matchmaking. My mother, who was the English teacher at my school and knew the backgrounds of all the boys I might date, was always wary. "I don't think you should go out with Doug—his father drinks like a fish." Or "I wouldn't like you to get in a car with Jimmy—he might have a seizure." I never objected to this; I was not rebellious and, critical as my mother was, she was often right. So, when Orm asked me out, I waited apprehensively for the assessment. Nothing. That was hopeful.

As I cast back over this evening, my parents are not in the scene. Did they say, "You look beautiful," or "I hope you have a good time"? Perhaps my mother was going over her reply to the toast to the teachers, or perhaps, she, too, was thinking how she looked in her fitted black satin dress with the shimmery green stripe through it—one of the yearly presents my father bought for her.

Orm's parents had asked him to bring me by the house before the banquet. I had never met his father, and didn't know that he was W. O. Mitchell, a famous writer. To me, he was simply Bill Mitchell who didn't work regular hours and couldn't pay his bills, including one at my father's store, Way's Grocery. Orm led the way down the steep basement stairs and, as I tottered after him in my unfamiliar pumps, I heard loud "hurrays" and "Judas Priests" overtop the TV hockey commentator. Petite, dark-haired Merna was curled up on the couch, cigarette in hand. W. O., in scruffy sweater and jeans, smelling of pipe tobacco, was sprawled out beside her, feet on the coffee table. I stood before them, wondering if I should move aside so they could continue watching the hockey game or sit down—but where? Every chair was cluttered with books, papers and laundry.

"Oh, my dear," Merna burst out, "what a lovely dress!" "You look simply bee-you-tee-ful!" exclaimed W. O. "And your hair—it sparkles!" I had sprinkled it with glitter, which, forever, seemed to him a remarkable thing. I was Cinderella at the Prince's Ball.

W. O. presented me with a flower, "an orchid," he explained, "from my own greenhouse." It was mauve with a frilled velvet magenta throat. "Look," he demonstrated, "if you hold one of these big babies up to the light, there is an internal incandescence as though the petals are all crystal." It was simply stunning. But how was I to wear it? The stem was immersed in water in a discoloured test tube with a red rubber stopper. "Don't take it out of the water," W. O. cautioned me, "and as soon as you get home put it in the fridge. It will keep for ten days, maybe two weeks." At that moment,

I didn't think I could keep my dignity at the dance for even ten minutes with that yellowed tube hanging from my haute couture dress. Somehow Merna attached it with crumpled tinfoil and a pin. I was wrong. All my friends were in awe of such a gift—an *orchid*—right out of Hollywood glamour magazines!

I fell in love with Orm; I fell in love with his family. I was fascinated by the pageant of activity in the Mitchell family— hearing amazing stories, meeting famous visitors, listening to *Jake and the Kid* with the author right there, discussing literature, life. For me it was like going from black-and-white television to Technicolor movies. I was slightly abashed, though, by their emotionalism. Merna and W. O. hugged and kissed and lauded everyone—not just the family (and me—to my surprise), but neighbours, the babysitter, the CBC people who visited, even relative strangers. As a child I had been hugged, but I do not recall my parents' arms around me when I was fifteen—perhaps my father's chapped and roughened hand on my shoulder. Though I never felt unloved or unsupported by my family, displays of emotion— happiness or tears—were uncommon.

The Mitchells would effuse, "We love Barbara." My parents would say, "We like Orm." The Way lexicon was one of taciturn moderation, the Mitchells' one of excess. "Love," "the best," "wonderful," "beautiful" were common words in the Mitchell vocabulary. My family kept those words intact— burdened with a virgin purity. I don't remember saying out loud to my mother or father, "I love you," though I would sign my letters "with love," and I did love them. But Merna and W.O. fell instantly "in love" with people. Later I realized that they sometimes expended a lot of "love" on people who turned out to be unworthy of it—a "brilliant" filmmaker who, in six months, plummeted to a "bastard."

Amazingly, they never felt guilty, or ashamed of having wasted their affections. While I began to understand that the language of love did not need to be bartered out stingily or, worse, avoided, I was bothered by questions of meaningfulness and sincerity.

Soon our families were socializing. A dinner at the Mitchells' was like watching a tennis match—back and forth between the two players at either end of the table while we, the spectators, were left to ooh and aah. Merna would begin a story—perhaps about the evening that the "goddamn horses" escaped from the pasture two blocks over and came trotting down the street, right by their kitchen window where they were having dinner with Bruce Hutchison. W. O. would interrupt, "For Christ's sake, Merna, get the story right. Let me tell it." Merna would give way, interjecting, however, with clarifications. "Shut up, Merna," W. O. would roar, "don't interrupt me." I suspect my parents wondered if this marriage would last.

I was on tenterhooks when my parents were invited to the Mitchells'. My father, who never raised his voice or swore, must have been overwhelmed by the Mitchell bombast. I can visualize him sitting uncomfortably in the living room, waiting for the customary rye and ginger. I nervously wondered how he would fare in the conversation, but there was only one moment of embarrassment that I can recall. One evening he told a joke that so mortified me I blurted out, "That's not funny; that's in bad taste." He said later, at home, having more tact than I, "You are a snob." I recognize now how much I must have hurt him. The Mitchells, at that time, could do no wrong in my eyes. I had dressed them in godlike apparel.

My mother enjoyed the literary talk, and their swearing did not upset her, as she, too, could swear a blue streak (though only at home and at inanimate objects). I enjoy thinking of her cursing "the Christly store" that made my father late for dinners or tossing the unripe tomatoes, just sent up from Way's Grocery, on the counter, saying, "God's teeth! Why can't they send me edible tomatoes?" This, and her other favourite, "Hell's bloody bells," were so antiquated they seemed Shakespearean. In spite of these at-home out-bursts, my mother kept her emotions in check. She had a privateness, a closeness, that mystified me. Her age, finances and health, in that order, were taboo subjects. I see now that it must have been uneasy for her at the Mitchells', as she and W. O. had attended the same university. But she had let me believe that she was younger than he, though, in fact, she was eight years older and fourteen years older than Merna.

My mother was slightly disapproving of the Mitchells. When my relationship with Orm became serious, she was unable to prevent herself from trying to protect me, subtly warning me that Merna and W. O. were unrealistically opti-mistic and self-centred. But her cold truth and their affec-tion for me clashed. Though still hesitant and suspicious, I tried to learn their language of affection. My parents must have felt displaced. Having now experienced this mixing of families as a mother and mother-in-law, I am conscious of the territorial issues involved. But then I was innocently drawn to the Mitchell realm, to the spectacle and drama of their family. My parents could not compete. Who could?

I did not know that my parents and I would have so few years for connecting and for sharing family stories. I moved away to university and, soon after, my mother became ill. I was just twenty, my sister sixteen, when I was called home and told that mother had six months to live. Before univer-sity that fall I married Orm, my mother standing pale and thin beside me. I went off to university while she fought with doctors, insisting on radiation and chemotherapy. She won that fight—and a four-years' grace from death. When I became pregnant with my first child, she said to me how strange it was that she, too, looked pregnant. I knew she meant that mine was life; hers was death.

Four years later I was called home again, this time from England, with two small children. She was in the hospital, sometimes coherent, other times in a morphine-induced schoolroom reverie, murmuring a lesson from the past, inscribing the air with imaginary chalk. In my youth and sadness I asked many useless questions: "What would you like me to bring you?" "Nothing." At least nothing material. I did take her hand, tracing the prominent purple-blue veins, tributaries of the heart. She spoke briefly, pragmatically, of her funeral, "No eulogy," and of her gravestone, "No birth date." We did not say, "I love you." I did not speak of her life, of her mothering. Once she said, "I had a good life. The last five years were important." I hung on to those words, and for many years I thought she simply meant she had had the chance to travel. But now I see that she was giving me a kind of blessing—that she was happy to have seen me married and to have held two grandchildren.

I am haunted by her last night, her black hair on the white pillows. I sat as usual by her side, but there were no words spoken. Finally I took her hand, "I'll be back in the morning." At the door, I turned. I can feel the pull back into the room as strongly now as I did then. I hear her say, "Goodbye"—like the thunk of a stone tossed so high it falls in a single deep-throated sound into dark lake water. There I stand, uncertain and frightened. Then I opened that door and walked down the long hospital corridor.

It is not that I lost my mother traumatically early (I was twenty-four), but I lost the map to my past, to her past.

"What was she like?" I now ask my aunts. I need those emotional co-ordinates. I was startled to discover that she was sixty-two—ten years older than I thought. Before I arrived in her world, she had experienced thirty-eight years of exciting—or boring or difficult or sad—life. She had told me only a few stories from her young adulthood. The one that gives her a glamorous past in my eyes was of a visit in 1939 to "beautiful, beautiful Savory Island." I imagined her steamboating up the coast from Vancouver, landing at the Royal Savory Hotel, settling in the wicker lounges on the veranda overlooking the most golden sand this side of the Pacific. But who were her companions? Were there dances and late-night swims in the sea, sparkling with plankton like underwater fireflies? (I can imagine that scene because my sister and I followed her trail up there nine years after her death.) I want to know some of the passion that must have been in her life—what she laughed about, cried about, loved and hated.

My father died from a massive stroke just five years after my mother's death, although I think he died of loneliness. In the hospital I remember the brief moment of recognition, the flicker of eye contact that, without words, spoke of love. I was able to stay to the end for him. Then I was set adrift from my own past.

I spent almost twice as long with the Mitchells as I did with my own parents. They showed me the joys of expressing emotions, of telling stories, of saying it all out loud. Living in that family was transformative. W. O., very near the end of his days, brought things full circle for me when he spontaneously declared, "I loved your mother and your father, you know." I always did love my parents, but that ease of expression that he possessed never came as naturally to me and my family.

But there was always a gap with the Mitchells—on both sides. From the beginning I could not call them Mum and Dad. Preserving that place for my own parents was an important symbolic gesture. As time went on, the Mitchell standard tarnished somewhat and my parents gained value. I recognized how extraordinarily difficult it was to sustain my own identity in such a powerful family without the balancing factor of my own parents and history. I was always a degree of hyphenation away from the Mitchells—a daughter-in-law. Their own children, quite naturally, but also anyone new and dramatic, registered first on their radar screen. Although W. O.'s exaggerated assertions were sometimes embarrassing to his own children, they conveyed a love and pride that I missed out on. He would say, "I'd like you to meet my son, Orm, the famous Blake scholar, who is writing my biography." When he neglected to mention that I, too, was writing the biography, I felt as if I were being vanished.

I am still finding my way, not to diminish, but to counter-balance the Mitchell luminescence. After twenty years buried in the Mitchell biography that Orm and I have been writing, I have fallen into the role of unofficial memoirist for my own family. My aunts and uncles, now in their eighties and nineties, are, more than they know, bridges to my parents. My father's family has passed on, reminding me more urgently to grab hold of the flesh and blood memories on my mother's side. It's not the statistics I want to gather; it's the physical resemblances, the temperaments, the language, the stories, the intimate memories, the secrets. Now I see that long line stretching back, and I feel the strength and power of belonging. I feel attached; I feel significant, laden with the substance of my family.

Surprisingly, we have discovered a past not known by my mother, not talked about by my grandmother. I find I am descended from Hudson Bay men and their country wives, from Scots (Orkney), from English and Aboriginal ancestry. Now I know the names: Turnor, Harper, Loutit, and the places: Rupert's Land, Moose Factory, Albany Factory, Stromness. My ancestor, Philip Turnor, mapped these places. He taught David Thompson how to survey; he told Alexander MacKenzie, who believed he had discovered the Hyperborean Sea, that he did not know "where he had been."

With such map-making genes surely I, too, will find my way.

REBELLION
AND BEYOND

JUDY REBICK

I was generally well behaved when I was a little girl. The limit of my rebellion then was giggling fits, usually with one or both of my brothers. It drove my father mad. The angrier he got the worse the giggling became. I think it was then that I realized you could push things further than it might appear.

It wasn't until my late teens that my full-fledged rebellion took wing. Whatever I was told I couldn't do was what I wanted to do. "Girls don't go into science," they said. In those days, "they" was the word used whenever anyone in authority was summing up conventional wisdom to limit the desires of a child, most often a girl child. I went into science at McGill University even though my great passion was writing and reading. I would have done much better taking English or general arts, but that was what was expected of me, and I was rebelling against those expectations. I wanted to be a doctor because once again I was told, "Girls can't be doctors."

My rebellion led me into an almost dead end in university. As soon as I understood university science, I realized I had made a mistake. I'm a big-picture kind of gal and the detail of science just didn't suit me. Never one to give up, I looked elsewhere for my passion and found it in the *McGill Daily*. It turned out that the *Daily* was a hotbed of radicalism in those very radical times, and I found other people who didn't like the restrictions that society had placed on us.

I had spent most of my teenage years in pitched battle against my domineering father. My strongest memory from those years is of running up the stairs and slamming my bedroom door. I stayed away from home more and more until finally, in my last year at McGill, I left for good. Even after I was on my own, I made choices to go against what my father expected or tried to insist I do. When that rebellious streak affected my decisions on relationships with men, it was in some ways to my detriment.

In October of that final year at McGill, I met an older man at a party. He came on very strong and ended up coming home with me to my newly occupied first apartment. Those were the days of free love, but the reality of an overweight, insecure middle-class Jewish girl was far from the bohemian appearance that I affected. I had had a few lovers before him, but this man understood female sexuality and provided me with my first experience of an orgasm with a man. He wanted to move in and I agreed, thinking that having an orgasm with him must mean I was in love with him. I was really that naive.

I was twenty-one, Roger was thirty-four—and insistent— and I just let his life wash over me. Montreal in those days was teeming with alternative cultures. Through Roger, I became part of the bohemian scene there, which at the time was probably the most exciting and creative in North America. This was the time of Leonard Cohen, the grand poet, and Roger knew him. All of Roger's friends were fascinating people, like none I had ever known. They were wild sexually and into experimentation with a wide range of drugs, from marijuana to opium to LSD. Roger himself was a kind of dysfunctional Renaissance man. He read and retained a book a day. He was ahead of his time in some ways and very much of his times in others—he was for women's rights at the same time as being an incredible womanizer; he could go months without drinking very much and then descend into frightening binges. Our life was unpredictable and intense.

I stopped being active in campus politics. I excused it by embracing existentialism, which I understood to provide a philosophical framework for living life for the experience alone. And with Roger I was having plenty of experiences. My friends were worried about the *type* of experiences and when my father met Roger by accident, he threatened to disown me if I continued seeing him. That sealed my fate for months to come. If my staying with Roger made my father that angry, it must be a good thing. Ultimately though, Roger's drinking became unbearable, and I realized that my life would be entirely consumed by his if I didn't leave. That's when I moved to Toronto.

I didn't last long in Hogtown, a.k.a. Toronto the Good. I was looking for adventure, and it was a pretty sleepy place in 1967. Not wanting to risk going back to Montreal and falling in with Roger again, I moved to New York City where I had family. As usual I rebelled against restrictions: walking alone at night and refusing to be a prisoner in my apartment in fear of what might happen to me in the (then crime-ridden) city. I was accosted more than once by flashers and by men trying to pick me up, some of whom I had to fight to escape. To protect myself, I stopped wearing makeup, learned how to walk aggressively and make a scene at the slightest provocation. After that hardly anyone bothered me.

I tried just about everything that was going in those crazy days of 1968. Having experienced the open sexuality of

Roger and friends, I gladly participated in the major pickup scene in the Village. I was extremely street-savvy and in one year had five different boyfriends, which I saw as a positive sign of my liberated, independent status.

When the woman upstairs was murdered by her boyfriend and I heard every sound, every word—the shot and the scream still resonate in my head—I woke up to another reality. I didn't have a framework for understanding violence against women in those days. I thought it was just part of life on the streets in New York. Most women stayed off the streets in their own little worlds, but I didn't want to restrict myself like that, so I accepted the risk. The murder made me realize that I was playing with fire. Rather than retreat into a closed world, I decided to leave and move back to boring old Toronto.

That didn't last long. After a month or two I decided to hit the road again. "Girls can't travel alone," they said. Well, I ignored them. I had survived in the Big Apple alone, how much worse could it be in Europe and the Middle East?

Discovering an answer to that question occupied me for the next year, 1969, as I made my way overland from Turkey to India. There is a fine line between courage and stupidity. That was when I crossed it. Travelling on buses from Istanbul to Delhi and then beyond was an insane risk: it damaged my mental and physical health and nearly cost me my life. On the other hand, having had those experiences and survived them put me on the path I would follow for the rest of my life.

The threats were terrifying. In eastern Turkey the bus I was on was surrounded by men who tried to get me off by rocking the bus back and forth, back and forth, while I desperately tried to convince the driver not to make an overnight stop in that town. In Mashad, Iran, where my train stopped for a religious holiday, I was stoned by a crowd. I ran for safety to my hotel and several hours later answered the door to find the instigator of the stoning, beaten black and blue and dropped on my doorstep by way of an apology.

When I arrived in India, a much safer country for women, I developed dysentery and was desperately ill—to the point I thought I might die. In that crisis, I decided that if I survived I would dedicate my life to changing the conditions of terrible poverty that I saw around me. In those days, we didn't have much information about the poverty in the developing world. I knew the rhetoric of American imperialism because of the war in Vietnam, but it wasn't until that trip that I understood the depth of the West's exploitation and oppression of the Third World. At that moment, alone with a high fever in a hotel room, it was more of an epiphany than an understanding. I didn't believe in a god, so it wasn't a prayer but a promise to myself. A promise that I've kept for the rest of my life.

On another level, I also began to understand that my personal rebellion against the restrictions on me as a woman was not going to work. I had foolishly risked my life in order to act out my defiance of those restrictions, and I was paying a big price. In that moment of realization, I had moved from rebellion to resistance.

*   *   *

In her famous book, *Truth or Dare*, the American feminist Starhawk discusses rebellion: "We rebel to save our lives. Rebellion is the desperate assertion of our value in face of all that attacks it, the cry of refusal in the face of control." She goes on to explain, "When we rebel without challenging the framework of reality the system has constructed, we remain trapped. Our choices are predetermined for us."

Until my mid-twenties, my life was all about rebellion. Whatever the cost to me, I was going to do whatever my father or other authority figures told me I couldn't or shouldn't do. That was the nature of my feminism in those days. It was how I made my decisions. I rebelled against all the restrictions of the life set out for a middle-class Jewish girl. In my experimentation with sex and drugs, and in my risk-taking in travelling, I developed a courage that stood me in good stead in my life to come. But I also developed a single-mindedness that narrowed my vision and my choices. And I took too many risks, some of which cost me dearly.

It has been a long journey to where I am now. I don't accept convention any more than I did then; although I understand much better the price of defying it and measure the risk before taking it. I still rail against injustice, but the rage that filled my heart in my youth is mostly gone now. I get angry at injustice and oppression but the anger doesn't take over my life. It no longer stops me from feeling love and joy and appreciation for the lovely things that happen every day, when one is open to them.

Matt Galloway, from CBC radio, asked me, on air, why I was still active well into middle age when so many people gave up activism in their youth. I wasn't sure how to respond then, but I now think the answer is in my passage from rebellion to resistance. If activism comes only from rebellion, only from fighting against what is, it won't last as we age. Resistance is deeper. It is about challenging injustice not just to protest against it, but to end it. You can rebel alone, but resistance ultimately requires collective action. The women's movement was the frame that allowed many of us to move from individual rebellion to collective resistance for social change.

Another thing I had to learn that rebellion couldn't teach me was that each of us, however we despise the culture in which we live, however it oppresses us, have learned a lot of our behaviours from it. In my case, I took on a lot of the behaviours of men, above all my father, who were restricting me. I wanted to be powerful in the world and in my youth the people with power were all men. In my family, although I fought constantly with my father, I saw that he had the power. I constructed myself to be the opposite of my mother. I became aggressive, domineering, single-minded, totally sure of myself and put all of my energy into politics and work and not very much into personal relationships. I almost completely repressed my female side. To this day I'm not much at doing anything domestic. I don't feel that as a loss, but the inability to develop and maintain relationships of trust until I was well into my forties cost me dearly. It wasn't until I got active in the women's movement and realized that through my behaviours I was oppressing other women that I began to change—and it was as if my life went from black and white to Technicolor.

Rebelling against social control is what youth does. The greater the restrictions, whether societal or parental or both, the fiercer the rebellion. Almost my entire generation rebelled against the straitjacket of 1950s middle-class morality. Rebellion is an important step on the road to social change, especially for women. Today the restrictions are different. Due in no small measure to the work of feminists, our choices are much greater. We are permitted and encouraged to do any job that strikes our interest. We are permitted choices in whether to marry and whether to reproduce, and whom to love, whatever their gender, race or religion.

But there are still restrictions: the way we are supposed to look, the expectation that we will be the primary caregiver of

131

children and elders, the assumption that we will do whatever it takes to maintain the home and still give our all in the workplace—and, of course, the fear of male violence.

Resistance is what is required here. Instead of all the individual solutions that young women come up with to make their lives bearable, they could work toward collective solutions to the problems we all share. For example, they could organize women and supportive men at their workplaces to demand job-sharing, care leave and other measures to value caring work in the family and the community. They could join local daycare advocacy groups to work for a national childcare program or for infant childcare in their local areas. They could set up women's groups in their neighbourhoods or workplaces to discuss the issues they face with other women. We have been hoodwinked into believing that we are on our own in solving our problems, but most of the problems we face are social problems and we can solve them better with others.

I return to the wisdom of Starhawk:

Power-over is maintained by the belief that some people are more valuable than others. Its systems reflect distinctions in value. When we refuse to accept those distinctions, refuse to automatically assume our powerlessness, the smooth functioning of the systems of oppressions is interrupted. Each interruption creates a small space, a rip in the fabric of oppression that has the potential to let another power come through.

Rebellion is of necessity an individual act against the rules or mores holding each of us back as individuals. Those of us who have some privilege in our society have a responsibility to go beyond our individual rebellion, to stand up for others, to reject the belief that some people are more valuable than others and act accordingly.

The women's movement in many ways did refuse those distinctions and in so doing opened a rip in the repressive fabric of society that allowed the power of women to come through. My generation and those after have benefited; however, unless young women continue to open up those spaces through resistance to the restrictions placed on all women, those rips could close. While the optimism of my generation is gone, new generations of women have a confidence in themselves, and abilities and access to power that we never had.

Rebelling against the superwoman mythology not by retreating but by organizing with other women and supportive men to create a world in which all work and all people are valued equally—that's where I think rebellion can move to resistance today.

Note

Starhawk, *Truth or Dare: Encounters with Power, Authority and Mystery.* New York: Harper and Row, 1987.

SHE DRINKS

HARRIET HART

"*Who* is that lady?" I asked my mother. Our prairie town was tiny, with a population of just over a thousand, but I had never seen this beautiful creature before, not at the curling rink, in the grocery store or at church—the places where adults spent their spare time. Her auburn hair was wound into a French twist and her milky skin was the perfect canvas for pencilled-in brows, green eye shadow, rouge and vibrant lipstick, the same candy-apple red as her long, manicured nails. It was a look I found fetching at fifteen; indeed, I still do at almost sixty.

"That's Mrs. McTavish. She drinks," my mother said, then added, "Poor Ed." I knew by the tone of my mother's voice what the woman drank—liquor. I wondered why her husband, "Poor Ed," found it necessary to keep her hidden away. Was she violent? Did she shriek and tear her hair, strip off her clothes, run naked through the house? I couldn't believe my eyes. Morris, Manitoba, had a mystery woman of its very own. Just like the mad heiress in *Jane Eyre*, she was kept in a tower, out of sight, a shameful secret. I didn't ask any more questions, sensing that it would be pointless to do so. I never saw Mrs. McTavish again.

Liquor, which everyone called it when I was growing up, was not a forbidden fruit in our household. The minister never preached against it from the pulpit of the United

Church. My schoolteachers didn't warn us of the evils of drink. Although my parents didn't keep a stock in our house, that was more out of parsimony than morality. Once a year, on December 23—his birthday—my father went on a bender. He left the house early in the morning with a case of full bottles. He paid a visit to all his closest friends, pouring them drinks to celebrate his birthday. My older brother was the designated driver whose instructions were to bring father home in time to play Santa Claus at the Silver Plains School Christmas concert. Ours was a very merry Santa. People laughed with him, not at him, and father's carousing was over for another year. My maternal grandfather, who lived with us, apparently had a drink of straight Scotch every morning before breakfast, but this was behind his closed bedroom door and no one ever mentioned it. In fact, I only learned about this unusual habit last year when my older brother was reminiscing.

After my father and grandfather died, my mother started to tipple, though in moderation. It was rye whiskey that seduced her and she often poured herself a solitary nightcap. One night when I was in my teens, I came home and saw her bedroom light still on. *Why does she insist on waiting up for me?* I muttered to myself. When I entered the bedroom to confront her, I found her sound asleep, sitting up in bed, curlers in her hair and an unfinished drink of rye still clasped in her hands. When I touched the drink, her blue eyes flew open and she gripped the glass, daring me to take it away. It became a favourite story, told at family dinners. My mother was a "good" drinker; she became gregarious and was game for anything from poker to arm wrestling, only occasionally crossing that fine line between being the life of the party and the person someone had to see home safely.

I'd like to blame my genetic predisposition to alcoholism on my mother, but that wouldn't be fair.

I have always loved alcohol, from the first cold beer I drank at a party when I was thirteen, to the vats of fine wine I drank in Tuscany and Provence when I became an adult. I loved the taste and I loved the effect. In university in the 1960s I discovered cheap, sweet wine and downed it while my contemporaries experimented with LSD and marijuana. The courtship that led to my first marriage was conducted in the bars of Edmonton, Alberta, while I was attending graduate school there. My betrothed was dead set against drugs, but he plied me with beer and I happily guzzled it down. After we married, we moved to London where I became a connoisseur of British beers. McEwan's Export Ale was my favourite. He drank, she drank, we both drank.

Pregnancy and motherhood slowed me down temporarily, but photo albums from the days of my first marriage reveal a constant round of parties. We danced and sang our way through our twenties. Once I recall hosting a croquet party on the front lawn of our house in the west end of Winnipeg. My husband had to put me to bed, where I promptly threw up on the pillow. He gently cleaned me up with soft reassurances. "It's just like when the baby spits up."

His gentleness didn't last long.

In the mid 1980s I was enrolled in the social work program at the University of Manitoba and elected to take a course in, of all things, deviancy! Our assignment was a research paper on anything we deemed deviant behaviour in Canadian society. I selected alcoholism in women. This was ten years before I qualified personally, but my subconscious must have suspected what lay ahead. There were entire libraries devoted to addictions, but only a handful of articles on women and alcoholism.

I interviewed the program director at a women's treatment centre. "Most women don't seek treatment on their own. They are brought in by the police or their husbands," she told me. *Fix her up and call me when she's sober. Then she can come home.* As we spoke, shadowy figures wafted by the open door. They were alcoholic women in a residential treatment facility. I sat there, the eager university student, asking my questions as an intellectual exercise. I imagined all the mad, drunken heiresses being pulled from their towers and thrown into cruiser cars or family sedans and deposited on the doorstep of the facility.

I got an A plus on my paper and within ten years, I had become an A plus alcoholic. By the time I graduated, I was in the middle of a divorce. My first husband was telling everyone who would listen that I had a drinking problem. Privately I felt hurt and humiliated, but publicly I chalked it up to the ranting of a jilted spouse. A decade of duty had left me exhausted, treading water instead of swimming with strong and sure strokes. I was sinking under the weight of my many roles: breadwinner, wife, mother, stepmother and dutiful daughter.

My second marriage followed a similar pattern. We both drank, but the difference between us was I liked to achieve unconsciousness and my husband knew when to quit. Like my first spouse, he responded by feeling embarrassed by my behaviour at social outings and getting angry when we came home. For the most part, however, he tolerated my drinking without talking about it. When he tried expressing his concern, I became angry and defensive and he fell silent again.

I carefully kept my drinking a secret from my close women friends. I would meet them for breakfast or lunch or line up activities that didn't involve alcohol. If one of them was at a party where I got tipsy, I would wake up the next day feeling uneasy and call her as soon as possible, to take the temperature of the situation. If I pretended my behaviour was okay, and she played along, I felt relieved. Everything was fine . . . until the next time.

That is, until my husband left town on a business trip and I drank the week away. With no one monitoring my intake, even I realized I was losing control. That's when I joined a group called WISE—Women in Sobriety and Empowerment. They were hard to find, an underground, subversive little band of women who believed in the sixteen-step approach to recovery developed by Dr. Charlotte Davis Kasl, a savvy woman whose personal wrestle with addiction showed her that the AA twelve-step model, which was developed for men, was less effective for women. Recognizing the difference in women's motives for drinking and in their need for support in quitting, she encouraged them to find their own way to recover from their addictions, by thinking for themselves, using a process of trial and error, not strict adherence to a rigid external model.

WISE met in a church basement. I attended faithfully. Before I knew it, I was chairing the meetings. I was skilled at group facilitation. The only problem was I never stopped drinking.

You see, I became beautifully adept at hiding my habit. I held down a good job in the social services, where I was surrounded by doctors, nurses, psychologists and social workers. I either fooled them all or they just kept quiet. *Why speak up? It's her business.* I ran a household, raised a son and stayed married. I made and kept friends, volunteered on boards and belonged to a service club. I was a model citizen. I kept my problem well hidden most of the time; after all, I am a white, middle-class girl who knows how to match the china teacups with the proper saucers. I appreciate the importance of a thank-you note. I dressed in little business suits and went off to work every day to help others.

Then, regrettably, I took to falling down. I fell down staircases, off the front steps of friends' houses after parties, into ditches and even off our boat. The last time I fell down, it was dark. We were navigating the steep path from dock to cottage, and I went head first into the juniper bushes. *Gin and tonic, anyone?* My brother, who was behind me, tried to help me to my feet, but I took him down with me. My husband slept in the spare room that night.

There it was—my final fall from grace. I quit the morning after the juniper bush incident. I felt I had no choice. I feared for my marriage and for my physical health. I had begun to notice an internal shift, from wanting a drink to needing one, waking up on days when the liquor outlets were closed and panicking if I thought there was nothing left in the house to drink, silently praying when we drove by a liquor store that my husband would turn in and not drive right past. Added to this interior drama were public humiliations like dropping the appetizer tray at a dinner party or passing out on the couch before my last guest said good night.

Alone, cloistered in a remote cottage in northwestern Ontario, I dug out my copy of *Many Roads, One Journey: Moving Beyond the 12 Steps* and reread it as I have never read before. I worked my way through Dr. Kasl's sixteen steps, feverishly making journal entries, pouring out my pain, confusion, self-pity, anger and resentment onto the blank pages, one step at a time, one day at a time. I did yoga— religiously. There's nothing like thirty minutes on a yoga mat to calm the nerves and feed the spirit. I meditated and listened to soothing music. I baked cookies and made tomato chutney. I cuddled the cat, using him as a breathing teddy bear. Slowly I began to feel better.

The memories of my WISE self-help group sustained me. I called up their faces, remembered their stories. Just knowing they were still out there, struggling, supported me. I conjured up the first meeting I attended. It was Valentine's Day. I wore a flashy red sweater with two giant hearts embroidered on my breast. I arrived first. Into the dreary church basement they came, professional women with expensive haircuts and biker mamas wearing their leathers. Welfare moms sat beside the pillars of Winnipeg society. Sarah arrived, a beautiful blonde dripping with diamonds. There were cupids on her pants! We were misfits, one and all. No matter what our income or its source, each of use was a family disgrace because we drank. These women told their stories, one by one. We laughed. I had no idea recovery could be funny. Alone in my wooded prison, I felt encouraged by the remembrances of them.

There is a conspiracy of silence around women who drink. Like the mystery woman in Morris, we are kept hidden away. People whisper about us behind our backs but don't confront us face to face. Even if they did, they would likely be met by denial or avoidance, for the sad truth about us mad heiresses trapped inside our addictions is that only we have the keys to unlock the doors of our private prison towers.

Unshackled at last, I left my sanctuary in the woods eager to share my transformation. I longed to travel back in time to the treatment centre on River Avenue, throw open the front door and invite the shadowy figures to step outside into the sunshine. I long now to reach out with my message of sobriety and hope.

To each woman imprisoned by her attraction to alcohol, I yearn to say: use the power of language to challenge the grip of addiction. Name your problem, whether it's "addiction" or "compulsion" or "dependency"; adopt a statement like "I deserve a sober self" or "I don't drink, no matter what." Say this to yourself whenever you crave a drink. Bring the problem out of hiding by telling someone else, a confidante or counsellor, about your plight. Read about the struggles of women you admire who have kicked the habit, authors like Anne Lamott (*Travelling Mercies*) or Julia Cameron (*The Artist's Way*). Start a daily journal of your experiences with sobriety. Talk about it, read about it, write about it and then do something about it. Only you can break the silence and change "she drinks" to "she drank." If I can quit, you can quit, we all can quit.

OVER THE ROCKS AND STONES

CHANTAL KREVIAZUK

I was never the popular one in school. There was always something I dreaded: failing a test I couldn't focus on enough to study for, getting nailed in a game of dodge ball, or walking into homeroom on Monday morning after not being invited to the weekend sleepover birthday party. I was the girl who cut her own hair and looked like Ringo Starr. I was the one who got picked second to last to join the team, and I was the girl who stuffed her bra and got caught by the most popular boy.

I find it fascinating now as an adult woman to look back at that time and see how my instincts kicked in, how following them led me down the path I've been on since. You see, while I was struggling to survive the cold, cruel world of growing up, there was also something fortunate about my difference, even though, back then, I hadn't learned to lean on it as my source of confidence and security. I was a singer and songwriter. I began playing melodies and performing for people when I was three years old; and in the preteen and teen years, I discovered that I felt safest when I was singing and playing piano. When I was immersed in my music I was able to shut down the out-side world completely, without realizing I was doing it. I didn't even know I wanted to—or actually needed to.

It will never be clear to me why those musical talents weren't enough. I still never felt talented, pretty or intelligent;

I always thought of myself as average. My eyes are a plain blue. I have large hips. I have small shoulders. I have thick ankles. I wear my hair in a plain, safe style, and I hate my nose. I used to try to squeeze my nose in whenever I thought of it, hoping that it might shrink.

•   •   •

The place: Shoppers Drug Mart on King Street in Toronto, where I am standing in line with toothpaste all over my pimples. The event: being asked for my autograph for the very first time. I'm in the midst of shopping for the strongest zit cream possible. My first major tour across Canada is to begin in three days, and I have the worst breakout of acne since I was a teenager. All I'm concerned about is clearing up my face. While I'm waiting to pay a girl taps me on the shoulder and asks if I am Chantal from the video. I'm humiliated, trapped, thinking only of the Colgate caking my zits. *Of course, this would happen to me.* I feel as though I'm back in private school. The odd one out again, the one who can't project the image that popularity rides on. Perfect faces on the covers of fashion magazines are staring at my blotched skin, customers are whispering, the unforgiving supermarket lighting exposes my flaws, and I honestly don't know how to answer the question; I don't know how to live up to that image of the video Chantal when I am beyond the camera lights and stage. My insecurity, the pimples, the old familiar feeling that I'm not good enough creates a force that pulls my stomach down into my toes before I answer a hesitant, "Yes."

After signing the autograph I leave the store, and before I've gone two blocks up Yonge Street I've reached the conclusion that the record company must have hired that person to pose as a fan and ask me for my autograph. Mike Roth, who signed me at Sony, continues to deny that to this day.

. . .

My first tour of Canada goes really well. I get more radio airplay as I perform in front of live audiences and with more radio airplay I sell more records. Other countries start showing an interest in me as my record starts going up on the charts. I'm asked to do promotional tours in Japan and Europe . . .

The scene: I'm on the road and experiencing what I call "burning tongue." I am constantly calling doctors in Winnipeg and Toronto, trying to figure out what is wrong with me. For all I know a huge, deadly hole is burning into my esophagus. I've put myself on a bland diet, eating nothing but white rice and pasta without sauce. I've lost weight and I'm not getting much sleep. Every day is fully scheduled, with press, radio interviews and, most often, a live performance. On my days off, I travel to the next city or country. I don't have time to heal. Stress starts to rule my body. I want desperately to do a good job. I want the record company to be happy. I want my fans to be happy. Most important, I want to protect my voice. It has always been my haven, and now it is more than that: it's one place of indisputable worth I allow myself.

Earlier on, even before I had my record deal, I discovered that steam therapy helped to open my throat. My vocal performance relies on a clear strong voice, without any snags, and I write songs that challenge my range and require a lot of stamina on the road; when I'm singing alone at the piano, I have nowhere to hide if my voice isn't *on*. One of my tricks for protecting my voice has been to immediately turn on the hot water in the shower after checking into my hotel room. I stand in the bathroom as it steams up, drinking hot tea or room temperature water and breathing the warm moisture into my airplane- or road-affected lungs and throat. The relief is always instant and the sense of calm, intoxicating.

But now things have gotten out of control—to the point that I've become addicted. Steam is like a drug. I have to have it before I can walk out on to the stage. I have my road manager call ahead to each city to find a steam room, which by the way, is not easy to find—she can always find a sauna, but I have no use for dry heat.

"God Made Me" was the first single released in America, and the record company has had me visit all the major cities to promote the song. I have been on the road for two weeks before I get to New York where Sony has organized a private performance for the radio programmers along with MTV and VH1. I have put incredible pressure on myself this night, knowing that I cannot afford to hit a snag. The stage is set in a stark, cold conference room, though candles are lit and a big vase of tropical flowers is on the piano. The table and chairs have been moved out of the room, so everyone has to stand. And they seem to be closing in on me.

While I'm singing "Surrounded" I see the guy from MTV lean over and whisper something to the head of Columbia Records. Right then I am convinced that my career is over, done, finished. In one second, one snag, one snap of the finger, I have lost my dream. I stumble through the meet-and-greet afterwards. My tongue is burning and I'm nauseous; I want desperately to go home, not home to the hotel, to my real home. But I can't—I've been gone for so long I don't know where my real home is. I barely shut the door to my hotel room before I crank the shower. It stays on all night.

My manager comes down to my room the next morning to check on me. When she walks in I can't see her, I can't see three inches in front of my face. The walls are actually sweating. I lie there in bed, with her sitting by my side, trying to convince myself that everything's normal. I am so scared that I have to cling to that possibility for dear life.

*   *   *

I am *so* far away from that hotel now, so far from all those fears and insecurities. Having recorded two subsequent albums since *Under These Rocks and Stones*, and now, while I am working on my fourth album and writing and producing for other artists and performers, I don't put so much pressure on myself at all. There is so much more to me now—with a husband and two children, my life is much fuller, and I feel defined by a range of new elements.

While the insecurities that haunted me have never gone away completely, they have lessened and a value on relationships has become strong—not only personal ones with my family and friends, but also with the global community. I attribute this sense of security to the very things that have hurt and humiliated me the most. I actually hold tight to my humility as though it's my greatest asset.

My relationship with my mother has always been bedrock for me. During the early years of my career, whenever I was teetering on the edge of some emotional precipice, she kept me from going over. I love her dearly, and not just because she's my mother. The thing about her that makes me feel continually humbled and awestruck is that she can laugh at herself. I don't just mean giggle, I mean laugh-till-you-split-your-sides laugh. She let me know that it's OK to recognize the humour in an embarrassing situation. If it weren't for my mother, I don't think I'd be able to reveal many of the things that made me anxious in the past. She has shown me that humour is potentially the very key to a stable and happy existence, that perspective is so important . . .

An image passed through my mind once when I was sitting on a plane from Los Angeles to Toronto. I could suddenly see the world from a distant perspective—off in space above me somewhere. If I had to give it a shape I'd say it resembled an undiscovered continent, a golf ball or a face without a feature. Somehow, this image of the world has also helped me to place less importance on those things that are out of my control. I don't know where the image came from, or why it chose me, but I take it with me everywhere I go— onto the stage, to a writing session, performing in front of an audience of thousands, even into the maternity ward. When I imagine the world as the size of a golf ball spinning and floating in the universe, it's hard for me to get stressed out. This image also reflects my view that each life matters. As in the story of *The Little Prince* I see each individual as being on a unique trip around the universe and having a right to chart it in a way unlike any other.

A few months ago I had the television on, blending into the other home-like sounds of a typical evening: a plane flying overhead, the heater humming, the occasional car passing by, a coyote howling in the canyon. At this point I had seen days of coverage of the tsunami disaster and endless reports of the carnage of the Iraq war. I had also been constantly checking the latest updates on the Sudanese civil war and famine, which were high on our radar, as my husband had just returned from Darfur, where there are many displaced refugees. I glanced at the television and was struck by the image of a young Middle Eastern boy lying in a hospital bed. The whole world, including the noises, all the global tragedy depicted in the media seemed to evaporate as I turned the volume up on the television.

This thirteen-year-old boy, along with twelve others, had been caught in the crossfire of the constant fighting and escalations in the Gaza Strip. Six of those boys perished. He and the other six other boys were now amputees, and suffering in the hospital. The focus of this story was on the boy's daily routine since he'd been caught in that round of artillery. His parents were at his bedside as the dressing was changed on what were then stumps just above where his knees once were. They held him down to help with the procedure as well as to comfort him as he screamed a scream that was like nothing I had ever heard in my life.

This was a new kind of horror and fear that I had not seen before on television. I don't remember what the next commercial was trying to sell me. I was crying in my bed for what seemed to be hours. Just when I would start to calm down, the pain would return. I don't know if I felt the pain of the boy being tortured in the bed, of the mother sitting at his side helpless, or of the father who, after holding and kissing the boy, changed the expression on his face and told the journalist that he simply wished his son had been killed; then he would not have to watch him die every day.

Even with all of the exposure to the hardships of the world that I have at my fingertips, the Palestinian boy that night brought home to me the clear realization that this place is also his world, his chance and his right. His story renewed and reinforced my deep conviction that every person should feel at home and safe in this world—and that I wanted to work toward that goal.

My career gives me so many opportunities to contribute. Whether I am doing a public service announcement for the Canadian Mental Health Association, or going to Iraq to work on a public-appeal documentary dealing with the effects of sanctioning civilians, I feel a distinct calling to ensure human rights. This calling sometimes seems to even overshadow my connection to music.

My career has ultimately led me to a place of rich opportunities. While I love to sing, perform, write music and be a viable part of the world of entertainment, I'm most fulfilled when I'm learning about and witnessing all of the individual stories—the suffering, the strength shown in adversity, and the hope and spirit that humanity has to offer. After all of the negotiating, business and competition I have seen in my profession, I realize that it was that feeling of giving that led me down this road in the first place. I truly believe that wanting to please others, even if it begins in a selfish place of wanting to be accepted, can lead to the most fulfilling existence possible. I have been passionate about music since I was a little girl because I saw the positive effect it had on people when I was playing or singing. The feeling of having an impact on others' lives became a core part of my being.

As I have grown older, my desire to bring peace and happiness to others has widened. I know that I am doing the right thing—that I am answering my call, because the more I give, the more the opportunities to give open up for me. A phenomenal snowball effect occurs as soon as we start doing the right thing! I was certainly not always on the right path in my life, but I now see that all the detours and bumps along the way prepared me for the road that I was meant to travel. I am now grateful for every bruise, every scar, every rock on the road I've travelled—and for every story I have to tell.

I AM A MOTHER

TRACEY ANN COVEART

This is a rare occasion. I am out for after-work cocktails and crudités with "the girls," my three best childhood friends, now adults. We are all busy, and it is hard for us to find time for ourselves, let alone one another. But we try, and once a year we actually pull it off. So here we are, sipping drinks, snacking on nachos and playing catch-up—a game I have come to dread.

Looking around the table, I am suitably impressed. We've come a long way in the twenty-five years since we first met, fresh-faced and full of ambition, in junior kindergarten. We all have university degrees under our belts. And we have all established ourselves as working women. Michelle is a lawyer with her own practice. Nora is a charge nurse in the critical care unit at Sick Kids. Susie is a senior marketing director at Pepsico. And me?

I am a mother.

Why does my job always sound like a bad act on *The Gong Show?* Motherhood is a noble, time-honoured profession, but in this you-go-girl crowd, maternal devotion flies about as well as a lead zeppelin.

I brace myself for the inevitable, excruciating moment when the conversation will get around to me; the moment when my friends will suddenly exhaust their current inventory of workplace heroics and histrionics and one will turn to me and ask, "So what have you been doing lately?"

This is the familiar version of the equally paralytic dinner party query: "And what do you do for a living?"

Both evoke the deer-in-the-headlights response. I freeze. My jaw drops open, and my mind works like a feverish terrier in a flowerbed, digging around in the dirt for something more interesting than a bone to offer up for inspection.

To my girlfriends in the bar, I make no overt apologies; a deflective "not much" is sufficient. But to complete strangers, I feel compelled to elaborate.

"I am a mother."

"Oh." (Think, Hindenburg.)

"And-I-write-books-on-the-side."

"Ahhh?"

I kick myself under the table every time I say it. Why do I need to justify my existence by being something other than a devoted mom?

There is an inherent criticism in that little disappointed word, that "Oh," like a tire going flat. People expect much more of modern, intelligent, educated women. We have our rights, and we are counted on to exercise them. It is not acceptable for a young woman with a university degree to linger barefoot and pregnant in the kitchen. Armed with the hard-won freedom to do anything she chooses, it is regarded as high treason for her to sign up for a twenty-year tour of duty on the domestic front where the work is thankless and there is no weekly paycheque, no sick leave, no holidays, no possibility for promotion and no pension.

Being an author with an income as-well-as-a-mother restores my credibility, re-establishes my value as a human being and earns me entry into the officers' mess. So I drop it like a small bomb and when it explodes, I am the only one who suffers any injury.

At times like these, when I fumble around making excuses for being what I am and doing what I do, I find myself wrestling little devils of self-doubt. Much as I try to deny it, there is a small, stubborn part of me that feels, not unfulfilled, but slightly underdeveloped—as if, in photographs I might not appear as distinctly as other women.

Was I meant to leave a more profound impression? In declining the opportunity to establish a career outside the home have I inadvertently undermined the feminist cause?

We have been conditioned to believe that our mothers and our grandmothers were trapped by their domesticity; that they were disenfranchised, oppressed; that they were prevented from exercising choice and therefore relegated to small, sad, prescriptive lives.

Today's mother is not chained to the kitchen table. On the contrary, she is expected to put bread on it. She wears a business suit, not an apron. She works in an office, not a laundry room. She carries a briefcase, not a baby. But has the pendulum swung too far? Are the expectations placed on contemporary women any less limiting than those imposed on our foremothers? Have we been emancipated, or are we simply slaves to a different, more demanding master, one who expects us to be everything to everybody?

In the current vernacular, "motherhood" appears to be a dirty word. It is fine to have children, in fact, it is presumed of a woman. But mothering is supposed to be a hobby, or at best a part-time job. We have kids on the side, like fries. The real meal, the grade A all-beef burger, is the work we do outside the home. We are not considered to be fully developed, fully fulfilled, fully contributing women unless we have established a career in the wider economic world. So where does that leave women like me?

Are we, the legions of stay-at-home moms, sending a mixed message to our daughters? Do as I say, not as I do? Will we encourage them to be homemakers, or neurosurgeons and prime ministers? Do we want them to emulate our way of life, or escape it? Are we role models or village idiots?

In our legitimate but zealous bid for liberation, have women lost sight of the real freedom—the element of choice: the right to decide for ourselves what makes us successful, satisfied, complete?

We *are* different from our mothers: we are more stressed, more anxious, more overwhelmed, more depressed. We are tortured by feelings of guilt and inadequacy. We wear a dozen different hats, and not one of them fits quite right. We are expected to manage kids and work as well as husbands, aging parents, fashion, fitness, fun and finance. We are pulled in so many opposing directions that we are drawn and quartered; dismembered, but not quite dead.

•   •   •

I began to lose my balance the day after I finished my last undergraduate class; the day I married a handsome man I barely knew. Cinderella-like, I waved goodbye to my family, friends and home, and drove off to a new life, staring into the rear-view mirror. I wept every day for two years until my son was born.

Matthew's first needy cry designed my destiny, and any career dreams that existed beyond his sphere of influence were instantly relegated to another lifetime. Patrick and Stephanie quickly followed, and with three children under the age of four, my fate was sealed tighter than a Tupperware container.

I was a mother.

Once those babies were placed in my arms there was no force in the known universe strong enough to pull us apart.

Returning to my job with a national labour organization in Ottawa wasn't fathomable. I had to stay at home to raise my children. It was a biological imperative.

Changing gears was as effortless as changing diapers. I was born to be a mother. I loved my job and I was good at it. It wasn't easy work, but it was enormously rewarding. Had I felt the need to produce an excuse for my decision, one that might placate some of my liberated sisters, those who were busy claiming their stake in the corporate echelons, I had a good one. All three of my children had been born with special needs, and my littlest angel, my baby girl, was profoundly disabled.

When my kids were small, life was rich and full and exhausting. I was too happy, too busy and too tired to think about what I might be missing. But as they grew bigger and slightly more self-sufficient, small holes appeared in my schedule that were easily filled with speculation. What if value really was equated with income? What if success really was defined by job status? I felt guilty being in the house while they were at school, as if keeping the home fires burning and-writing-books-on-the-side was somehow self-indulgent, deficient.

I considered getting a "real job" (my husband's term for full-time employment outside the home—*You have no idea what it's like to work for a living*) but there just weren't any opportunities that offered the kind of hours I could manage: weekdays 10 a.m to 3 p.m. with school holidays and summers off. I had to be—and wanted to be—at home for my children. They were my purview.

As the boys became adolescents with a healthy sense of adventure, they needed more guidance, supervision and chauffeuring than ever, and Stephanie, who had plateaued at the developmental age of five, would require around-the-clock care for the rest of her life. My services—my love, my support and most of all my presence—were still desperately needed at home. And I desperately wanted to be there to provide them. I was trapped, but I was content to live in captivity.

I was a mother, damn it.

Eventually, my husband left. More than his leaving, it was his disappointment and disapproval that deflated me. In the recesses of my soul I remained true to my own definition of accomplishment and clung to a rebellious sense of self-worth, but closer to the surface, under my thin skin, I let him get to me. I let him convince me that I was a failure. Not a good wife. Not a good mother. Not a good provider. Not a good anything. I was the "oh" at dinner parties, an underachieving embarrassment, and ultimately not worth taking along.

At thirty, I was the only one in my social circle who had the distinction of being a wife, let alone a mother. At forty, my friends were just starting their families and I had three teenagers and an ex-husband.

•   •   •

It has been two years since I reclaimed my maiden name. Slowly repossessing my sense of self, I collect small tokens of appreciation along the way and arrange them like wildflower bouquets. Good-night kisses. A ticket stub from *Mamma Mia*, a Christmas gift from Matthew, purchased with his own money. Patrick's ninth-grade essay that begins, "I don't know what I would do without my mom." A fill-in-the-blank work sheet by Stephanie that reads: "I am happy when . . . my mommy hugs me."

There are days when I feel restless, claustrophobic, a little bored, even. But I know that any professional who is worth her salt, any woman who has done the job for so many years that she could manage it blindfolded, suffers from the occasional bout of ennui.

I don't have a lot of money, and yet I feel as though I've won the lottery. In almost two decades of being a mom, I haven't missed a single thing. Not a tooth or a tear, a smile or a step; not a bath or a bedtime story, a school concert or a class trip; not a baseball practice or a basketball game, a breakfast chat or a dinner conversation. My critics might not understand the attraction or endorse my decision, but their esteem is not my concern. Achievement is a very personal yardstick. Power, prestige and personal wealth are not my benchmarks. For me, success is measured in happiness. And I am happiest being a mom.

These days, I am focusing on my epitaph. I want to be remembered as a good mother. If my tombstone reflects this great work, then I will have done what I set out to do—what I was meant to do—in this life. I may never write a best-seller-on-the-side, but I will have raised three well-loved children. And I could leave no greater mark on the world.

•   •   •

The girls—all with children of their own—are even busier now. Our get-togethers are so infrequent that they are more like reunions. Michelle moved her practice into her home. Nora took a demotion and cut back to part-time hours. Susie quit her job altogether. We still swap stories of workplace heroics and histrionics, but as the mother with the most seniority, I often lead the discussion.

Our lives are rich; meaningful; interesting; rewarding. We are not underachievers. We are not inadequate. We are not failures. We are smart, satisfied, happy women.

We are mothers.

No apologies, no excuses and no regrets.

TETHERS

BARBARA SCOTT

In 1944, at age fourteen, my mother took the train miles from her family in the tiny town of Kelvington, travelling farther than she'd ever travelled in her life, all the way to Fort San, a tuberculosis sanatorium in Fort Qu'Appelle, Saskatchewan. Too ill to be put in the children's ward, or even to have adult roommates, she was placed in a room by herself. She was laid flat on her back and stayed that way, without even a pillow, for two years. Her head was shaved because doctors were afraid a simple thing like a shampoo could give her a chill that would carry her off. Her parents were poor; there was no chance that they could visit for at least a year. Small wonder she spent the first couple of lonely months at the San crying incessantly.

The doctors and nurses explained that crying would sap her body of the strength needed to fight the disease, but she couldn't stop. Until one day two doctors discussed her sputum results while they thought she was asleep. "She won't see the New Year," one of them said. It was October. The way my mother told the story, her tears dried up in that instant. I'll show you, she thought, and bent all her will to getting better. In two months' time, her results improved 100 percent.

Even so, it was seven years before she left the San. She'd gone in at fourteen and came out at twenty-one. Her limbs were so wasted that the first time she tried to stand, she fell over. She would only ever have three-quarters of a functioning lung. The doctors gave strict parting injunctions: she must never overexert, and probably would never walk up a flight of stairs; she should not marry, as marriage led to children and she was unlikely to survive childbirth; and even with extraordinary care, she would probably not live past forty.

She took the bus back to Kelvington. All the way from Fort Qu'Appelle it rained, a heavy, cold rain that chilled her with fear—the legacy of all those years of not even having her hair washed because a wet neck might kill her. But just before she got to Kelvington, the rain stopped. As if she'd been given a special dispensation, as if even the heavens bowed to her will to live.

My mother did take good care of her health, but on her own terms. She worked on her high school diploma part-time, while doing the books for her parents' general store; she put herself on a walking regime to get her muscle strength back. At twenty-five she got married, leaving her parents to sell the store they'd bought for her security as an old maid. She bore two children, of whom I am the elder. She not only walked up a flight of stairs but also joined a bowling league, travelled and even lived overseas for several years. And she astounded everyone by outliving my father by nine years, dying at seventy-three. She was a kind of walking miracle.

But miracles can come at a price, and are not always comfortable for those who live in their immediate vicinity. I grew up in a household organized around my mother's illness, for TB remains a threat even to its survivors. One of the rules in the San was that patients must keep order in their surroundings because order creates calm, and calm means you are not overtaxing your lungs. My mother took this to mean ordering not only the physical space she inhabited, but also the people who inhabited it with her. From the time I was small, she controlled, or tried to control, every aspect of my behaviour, usually finding the results disappointing.

The standard she measured me against was that promulgated in the fifties: girls were naturally tidy, obedient and unselfish, ready always to put their desires aside to serve others. I, on the other hand, always had my nose in a book and was too apt to thoughtlessly follow my own inclinations. Frequently she would compare me with other, more tractable children. "Why can't you be more like your cousin Regan?" who was pretty and thin and practised the piano without being nagged. "Why can't you be more like Polly Pepper?" a fictional character in *The Five Little Peppers* who did housework without being asked, and didn't have any desires to put aside because her only desire was to help her mother. My first flicker of independent thought began with the mute protest, "Because you're not like Mother Pepper." Who was unfailingly sweet-tempered and encouraging, and who, I was fairly sure, if her eight-year-old daughter had asked, "Am I pretty?" wouldn't have said, "You have a long chin."

My second movement toward independence came when my father's seismic career took the family to Algeria in 1970. Because of a shortage of English- or French-speaking schools, I was sent to boarding school in England and thus spent the bulk of each year out from under my mother's direct supervision. For three years, I travelled on airplanes by myself, stood up for myself in problems with students and teachers, and sucked up the British cultural revolution that had begun in the sixties. I went to England an obedient twelve-year-old, and returned to Canada and my parents a fifteen-year-old hippy. The transformation did not make for happy relations with my mother.

The root of the problem was that, if my mother was strong-willed, so was I, and I chafed under her illness almost as much as she did. Because she frequently tried to outrun her physical limitations, her body would often fail her, landing her in hospital, or on extended bed rest at home. For the last quarter of her life she was on oxygen around the clock, tethered to a machine that delivered it through a twenty-foot length of plastic tubing. She needed to rely on others to help her live the life she wanted, and she saw me, her daughter, as an extension of herself, a kind of early prototype of the Canadarm, whose function was initially to fetch out-of-reach articles like glasses of water, pills or laundry from the basement. But when I got older I was supposed to fetch other, less tangible things: good grades, a good job, success—prizes my mother would have gotten on her own if the bacillus hadn't robbed her of the opportunities.

As a Canadarm I was pretty much a failure. For one thing, my mother had high standards that I usually fell short of: the one B plus in the line of As; the one mark shy of first class honours in my piano exam. But a deeper problem, and the source of many clashes, was my stubborn determination to grope about for my own discoveries, independent of the mother ship, especially after my taste of freedom in England. When I was young, my mother could always rein me back in with a sharp comment if she thought I'd ventured too far, or as she put it, got too big for myself. But after our return to Canada, I wasn't so easily kept in line, and our clashes got more frequent and acrimonious.

It didn't help matters that the feminist rhetoric I found so freeing in the '70s and '80s was as critical of my mother as she was of me. My mother had achieved what she had simultaneously been told was everything a woman could wish for and what she herself could never have: marriage to a good, hard-working man, two children who hadn't wrecked her figure, a suburban house and financial security. And here was her daughter turning up her nose at it all, saying "Not for me." Her daughter who quit university to go on the road as a folksinger, who changed jobs with a dizzying lack of concern for the future, who slept with men but never brought any of them home for approval. For my part, what my mother wanted for me seemed conventional and dull: not having sex until I was married because no decent man would have me otherwise; taking a degree in business or education because it would guarantee a good job; or, failing that, taking a secretarial course so I'd have "something to fall back on."

Oddly enough, though, eager as she was to direct all other aspects of my life, she was unusually reticent on the subject of motherhood. I once asked why she had had children against her doctors' advice, and she said, "Because it's what you did back then." I suppose I wanted to hear that my brother and I had been desperately longed for, were worth risking death for, that we'd only become disappointments and irritants after we got a little older. Instead, her answer implied we were simply props in the conventional life of a 1950s couple.

But distance, both temporal and physical, gives perspective. My parents retired and moved to Kelowna shortly after I married, and I saw them only a couple of times a year—circumstances that allowed my mother and me to manage an uneasy peace most of the time. Then my father died, and in watching my mother cope with his loss, I developed a new respect, even admiration, for her.

It had been a good marriage, and she was hit hard by his death, but with characteristic determination she began to rebuild her life. She joined a grief group, a bridge group and a book club. She made a killing in the stock market. I began to look at her in a new light, and to wonder if I had perhaps misinterpreted key moments in her life, by taking what she said about them at face value.

I had always assumed we moved to Algeria because my father felt stifled in his work in Calgary, and that my mother followed him because "that's what you did back then." But this decision carried serious risks to her health. Algeria had not yet reached its tenth year of independence from the French; the schools and hospitals, the infrastructure generally, were in a shambles as the country struggled to rebuild. There were frequent food shortages and political skirmishes. Resentment was mounting against the oil companies, one of which employed my father. My mother, given her fragile health, would have had every excuse to leave, even to insist that my father not take the job in the first place. She had often made her family bow to the necessities of her health, yet this time she didn't.

I think now that she was thoroughly enjoying the adventure. She loved the strangeness of the scenery and the people, the trips into the Sahara, or to Italy and Spain. She loved bartering in the markets, where she was a pit bull in negotiations; she gave dinner parties for, and made friendships with, people from all over the world. I suspect she too had been feeling stifled by her job as wife and mother and, like my father, had been only too happy to have a change. But because she spoke of the decision in terms of wifely duty, I didn't see that our overseas travel had opened up a new world for her as much as it had for me.

I realized that for many years I had been measuring her against Mrs. Pepper and those same 1950s standards of female servitude and self-sacrifice I had rejected for myself. What used to strike me most strongly in the tale of her time in the San was her extraordinary will, especially since I was bent to that will many, many times. What strikes me now is how amazing it is that a frightened, lonely, desperately ill girl had the nerve to defy the voice of authority, and to build her life on such defiance. If she had listened to the doctors, who "knew best," she'd have been, at worst, dead at fourteen, or, at best, an invalid living alone in the narrow world prescribed to her when she was twenty-one. And no matter how flatly she framed her decision to have children, even if her motivation really was the desire to follow the norm, the fact is that for her giving birth was an act of courage, even rebellion. A tractable, obedient woman wouldn't have lived the life she did.

My mother died two years ago. She left behind a number of diaries, kept in pocket-sized Daytimers, that I read in the weeks after her death. In an entry toward the end she recorded her decision to give up duplicate bridge. She had taken up this demanding version of the game after my father died, during those first, intensely lonely years of widowhood. She had always loved bridge, and was a brilliant and fierce player. Many of the diary entries kept track of her wins and, less frequently, her losses. I know what it must have cost her to accept that she no longer had the energy for the weekly competitions. But with characteristic lack of bitterness she wrote, "However, there it is—one has to accept those things one cannot change—or be miserable—and I *refuse* to be miserable. There are still many enjoyments left to me, and I *intend* to enjoy them to the full." If there is one legacy from my mother that I value most, it is that defiant determination to make all she could out of her life, even when it was shrinking to the radius of that plastic oxygen tubing.

And if I have a favourite memory, it is this: my mother was placed on twenty-four-hour oxygen just after my father retired. When she went out she took a small PortaPAC tank that held only several hours' worth of oxygen, which she filled from a big tank that was replaced weekly by a supply company. In order to travel farther than the PortaPAC would allow, my parents designed and had custom-made a stand that would enable them to take the big tank on long trips. They charted their travels throughout the United States and western Canada according to oxygen fill-up points, and my mother continued to travel this way for as long as she could after my father died. When I think of what she taught me, I see her at the wheel of what the family called the oxygen-mobile, with the green plastic tube snaking out behind her to the tank we nicknamed R2-D2, outrunning her limitations for as long as she could, and never letting anyone or anything force her to live small.

UNCHARTED WATERS

SILKEN LAUMANN

Unloading the dishwasher I pull out the Tupperware containers: small round ones for raisins and peanuts, larger ones for cheese and crackers, a square one for a sandwich. As I stack them on the counter, I look around my kitchen with a sense of wonder, noting the juice cups, the lunch bags, the enormous piles of paper from school.

This is my life. I am a mother of two small children; my existence is defined by my kitchen counter. Each day ends here—the evening unload of Tupperware, the making of lunches, the organizing to lessen tomorrow's inevitable chaos.

Motherhood can be filled with the mundane. For every moment of joy experienced in quiet bedtime conversations with my five-year-old and my seven-year-old, there are hours of asking those same children to put their toys away, to hurry and put their boots on and to close the door when they go outside.

Every day, I think about the long-term effect of my parenting, of my insistence on this boundary or that rule. I ponder how I am demonstrating my values, what my impatience is teaching my children. When I shout my frustration at muddy footprints in the hallways, at coats left strewn on the floor, I chide myself for doing so. They are so small and learning everything anew. When their pushing and teasing of each other threatens to turn me into a "monster mommy," I remember that, at first, I experienced only the marvel of them.

I will never forget the moment my son William was born. I had been in labour for hours, straining, pushing, and finally, after a violent pull from the doctor—he came into my arms. He was blue, and yellow and slimy. He was the most beautiful thing I had ever seen. His eyes were open and he seemed to be looking right through me. As I stared back in shock and wonder I knew that this was the most perfect moment of my life. That in that second of push and pull everything had changed. Everything that I was, so much of what I wanted, my needs—they had shifted.

Now, the marvel is mixed with the frustration that so much of precious mothering time seems to be spent cleaning, driving and making lunches. As well, I was unprepared for the worry and doubt. I do not make a decision without thinking of my children. Before my eyes are fully open, I feel their presence in the house, I plan our day, I gauge my emotional readiness for their energy. I know it will take a lot—that is a child's job, to take, to ask, to have needs fulfilled.

I know I can't just love them. It's not enough. It's not nearly enough. Each day I ask for the strength and compassion to be a great mother. I have not wanted anything as much as I want to be a good mother. I have never worked so hard in my life—the positive self-talk, the sheer endurance of long days, the doubt. What I want seems insignificant when measured against the importance of my children's needs. Every new skill I've learned, every wisdom I've gained, I bring to my mothering.

And yet in many ways I simply feel ill suited to it. I cannot seem to quiet that part of me that is bursting to be fully realized, that part of me that knows that there is simply so much to be done outside my little family circle. I have spent the better part of my life, so far, with my head in the clouds, dreaming of what could be, of what is possible and then making that a reality.

My Olympic journey required drive and tenacity and enormous belief; it required all my energy. To my great joy, I achieved some of my most cherished dreams. Today my professional life is a rich and delightful potpourri of speaking, writing and running a charity.

As a speaker, I am able to express who I am through my work. The lessons and insights I talk about may be universal, but they are from my own life experiences and have provided me the privilege of creating a rewarding career through sharing them with corporate audiences. As well, a year ago I started *SilkensActiveKidsMovement.com*. We are working with local champions across the country to create opportunities for kids to be active. I have watched in amazement as the idea of supervising kids in unstructured play has gained momentum and begun to unfold, with children playing actively once a week in parks and gymnasiums across this country. This professional focus can be demanding of my time and, always, of my mental energy, but it constantly challenges me to keep growing, to share what I know, and to find more effective ways of helping people be at their best.

The doubts and restlessness I feel with parenting have never been there for me in pursuing my athletic and professional goals. There, I am in familiar waters, guided by passion, ambition—and my mother's example, for she lives in this restless part of me. The intensity of my passion comes from her—of this I am certain. She was a creative, expressive woman, bursting with expectation. She was contagious; her music and energy filled every crevice of our home. Her sculptures and paintings articulated her deepest longings.

There was a part of her that the demands of motherhood could not touch: she would not be consumed, would not disappear in the role of mother.

The other night I went through my hope chest and came across one of the rare pictures of my mother—most of our family's albums seemed to have fallen through the crack of a split family. The photograph was taken on her fortieth birthday. Her blond hair cascades over her shoulder, her long and lithe body leans into the camera. What struck me most were her eyes: they look so clear, full of light and expectation. At forty she was looking at a world of possibilities. She was in art college, had a new lover and had left her marriage. There is a lightness, a clarity in her eyes I never really observed back then. Now, I notice it because I recognize that light in my own pictures.

But there was another side to my mother. She was a woman of extremes, all light and all darkness. Dark, she was self-absorbed, oblivious of her children's needs, sharp-tongued and sometimes thoughtless. In her moments of light, I still remember the feel of her soft bosom against my own thin and bony chest. She would fold me in her arms after school, ask me about my day, know immediately if I was anxious about something at school. Her ability to read my moods was truly remarkable. And perhaps that is why it was painfully confusing when she couldn't—or wouldn't—respond to me.

One moment we were learning to macramé together, the next she couldn't even look at us. We were her greatest joy but we were also the noose around her neck. We stole her time, her opportunity for greatness, her creativity. My memories of my mother have no grey.

When I turn that intensity I inherited from her inward, setting impossible standards for myself, I recognize my mother's self-talk. When I am restless or impatient with parenting because of what it drains from me, I see the potential of recreating something that I would rather avoid. I understand now that it is in mothering we grasp truths about our own mothers that otherwise might never have been unearthed.

When my sister and I were pregnant, a few months apart, we both expressed the same fear, "What if we become our mother?" Absurd, frightening and impossible, it is a thought that has brought many an expectant mom to her knees. Neither my sister nor I want to tip the other way and have self-desires override the maternal and the nurturing. Here I am in unfamiliar waters, charting a new course, unable to use my mother as a positive role model.

Perhaps I will never fully see all that is good in my mother, because I don't yet know how to. I don't yet know how to let go of the bad so completely that I can see the good in all its clarity. But having children has made me better able to understand her, to acknowledge her struggles, her inability to resolve the conflicts, her need to leave her family to pursue her own dreams, her own life. Looking at her pictures, I have flashes of insight, moments and feelings I recognize, and it is at these times I truly rejoice in her. I understand her doubt, and how that doubt can destroy many of the deepest joys in parenting.

•   •   •

My doubt is waning. I feel more confidence in my mothering as my children grow. I know I am a natural mother. Perhaps not in my ability to bake, not in my ability to stay home with my kids. But in my ability to tune in to their needs, to understand them as human beings, to love them

181

unconditionally—of this I have no doubt. (When my mother read this piece she said, "You sound like a mother who is driving herself nuts.")

And yet I am also learning to strike a balance. This Christmas, my children's father took them for several days. It was the first time since they were born that I had been alone in my own home for five consecutive days. I glimpsed another way of being. These days unfolded with a melodic ease. The days were my own, my thoughts developed to completeness without the interruption of a small voice asking for milk. I stayed up late writing, thinking, organizing, knowing that the next morning I would not be woken up at 6 a.m. by the sweet voice of my five-year-old, asking to crawl into my bed for an early-morning cuddle.

It's true, I can't seem to "pause" my dreams. I feel a deep responsibility to live up to my potential in my work and in my community, as well as with my children. I ask for complete thoughts; this is perhaps my greatest need. A need for uninterrupted thought. I wake up at five in the morning to have a few quiet hours to exercise or simply sit on the couch and experience some alone time. I would rather experience sleep deprivation than not have time alone. In my fortieth year, I created the mantra "It's all about me." I said it with glee as I traded in my fully practical but very worn Subaru for a slightly used, much swankier Range Rover. I say it every Tuesday night as I leave my children with a babysitter so I can practise yoga. The time in a handstand, my yoga instructor Elizabeth spotting me lest I crash unceremoniously to the floor, is time that I empty of all the worries, the doubt, the conflict. Some things I do are just about me, making me more capable, more aware, and able to bring more Silken to everything I do.

• • •

I hold an image before me, an image of a woman lying on the beach in her bikini, the sun falling gently across her body. Her posture is totally relaxed, her face absolutely serene. In the background her kids are playing joyfully; I can hear their shouts of glee, their ripples of laughter. This is my happy place. Somewhere I go when I am struggling to find time to write those last few e-mails or standing in the kitchen with both of my children needing my attention and the telephone ringing. Perhaps I will never have that look of serenity on my face. Full of conflict, frustration and unbelievable joy, my experience of motherhood is an intense and miraculous journey. And then, I don't really like beaches anyway.

ABOUT THE BOYS

LIANE FAULDER

It was just a casual moment, but it pricked at me, a sharp reminder of an uncomfortable sensation I'd managed to keep at bay for a long time. A friend had come by to pick up my teenager, who was heading off to the skateboard park with her son. I leaned into the car window and offered to pick the boys up after they were through.

"Oh, no, it's okay," said my friend. Her teenage daughter was in the front seat. Mother and daughter were going to have lunch together near the skateboard park and would meet the boys afterwards. No problem.

Going out for lunch together. As they all pulled out of the driveway, I waved and thought, Oh yes, that's what it's like to have a girl. With a daughter, there's an opportunity for a mother to be more than a ride. With a girl, there's a chance to be a friend.

It had been a while since I had reflected on that, though there was a time when I thought a lot about having a daughter. Growing up, I always believed that I would give birth to a girl. I couldn't have explained why I assumed this—I just did. I had been lucky enough to enjoy a tight relationship with my own mother, which continues to this day. It never occurred to me that I might not experience that same closeness with a daughter as my own life unfolded.

The birth of my first son, Dylan, didn't interfere much

with my fantasy, but by the time I was pregnant with my second and last child, I was thinking hard about what I would do if I didn't have a daughter. Partly it was because I was married to a man with four brothers. I used to feel just plain sorry for their mother, who was certainly treated with respect and occasional affection, but for the most part, entirely ignored. Sometimes I wondered what I would do with my few pieces of sentimental jewellery—a teenage promise ring, a pair of diamond studs no bigger than the head of a pin—if I didn't have a daughter. Of course, jewellery was hardly the issue. I can't even tell you where those shiny bits are now.

What I fear will be missed as time goes by is the comfort of an intimate relationship with my sons. I know what I have with my mom. I feel it every time we share a cup of tea. We sit together on the couch, discussing the small, insignificant details of our day with an ease born of blood, but also of reciprocity. It's a two-way relationship; we both want to be there.

Though I knew I would love my children ferociously every day of my life, regardless of their gender, I wondered how they might feel about me if they were both boys. No doubt they would love me back on some level—even the most acrimonious relationships between mothers and sons are rooted in that.

But would they want to spend time with me? Would they tell me when a relationship broke up? Would they phone just to talk about some little thing that happened at work? And most important, as the years went by, would they go for lunch with me, keep me in the loop of their emotional lives?

Then Daniel was born and there was no time to ruminate. Besides, when kids are little, regardless of whether they are boys or girls, much of mothering is the same. There is bathing them, and rubbing Nivea into their rough, red cheeks in the winter, and reading about Piglet, Pooh and the Heffalump. Every so often, I'd be particularly reminded they were boys and I was not. I noted in my diary when Dylan, who was maybe four, said, "Mom, wouldn't it be great if you were a boy and then we'd all be boys"—a startling statement. I thought I was the only one who noticed our differences.

There was another time in my life when I was outside, looking in. I had grown up with two brothers, both quite a bit younger, and I always felt that distance. The brother closest in age to me died when he was a young man of twenty, just as the space between us had started to close. Could it be that staying connected to a boy as he became a man would always be beyond my reach?

*   *   *

For a long and busy time, however, such issues were set aside in the rush of music lessons and soccer practice and making sure the boys' lunches were packed and their teeth brushed. Once, when Dylan was ten, I tucked him in at night, pulling the bedclothes up around his shoulders. He asked, sleepily, how it was that moms always know the right way to do things.

"Like just then, when you fluffed my blanket out and then it settled down on me. It felt so good."

That was all I needed to hear to know my place was secure. In the daily nurturing of those boys, in the spontaneous back-and-forth jumble of living together, my fears receded. There was much joy in our lives. I was a single parent when the boys were small, and so the three of us did everything together. When I went running they pedalled alongside on their two-wheelers, and the sight of their wobbly heads encased in mushroom-like helmets kept me going when I got tired. Dylan always helped me fix the vacuum cleaner, which seemed programmed to suck up valuables, and Danny always saved a place for me on the couch when we watched videos. I came to treasure the nape of a little boy's neck after a fresh haircut. I don't know exactly what the highlights would have been if the boys had been girls, but I do know this: there is nothing more gratifying than two boys competing to make their mother laugh.

Still, as they got a little older, I began to notice things. My women friends with daughters started shopping together (and not just to get school supplies). Though I get about as much pleasure from shopping as I do from eczema, I felt the pinch of absence, like being excluded from a club I yearned to join. I tried to talk the boys into doing something together to make that feeling go away. But it was hard to think of what we could all enjoy. I don't skateboard; they don't do aerobics. I wasn't up to making a bigger effort at golf. Then, one day, it didn't matter how we might spend our time together—that time had evaporated. Dylan got a girlfriend and, in a sigh, the pattern of our lives changed dramatically. She wanted to watch movies at her house, and so they did. He was hardly home.

That old saw, "A son is a son till he takes a wife, a daughter's a daughter all of her life," started roiling around my brain, a bit of a taunt, and I didn't like it. So in the last year or so, to distract myself from that hollow feeling that gets bigger as they get older, I have been trying something new. I have begun to consciously think about what it is I have gained from my relationship with the boys, what we have, and not what we don't, or won't. I look for meaning in places I didn't used to.

It's a survival technique, to be sure, but as I watch them move further into their own lives and away from mine, it is increasingly useful. Recently, I had an experience with Daniel, who just turned sixteen, and it seemed to represent the sum of my experience as the mother of boys.

It was a Saturday morning and he was sleeping in. My mother never let me sleep in when I was a teenager—there were household chores to do, after all, and the best part of the day was racing by. But I've aways thought sleeping in was a good thing for teenagers, and so I let it happen.

Around about 11:30 a.m., though, I often wander into his room with a stack of freshly folded laundry to put in his dresser drawers. I'll poke about, clearing things up, maybe humming a little just to hint that afternoon is about to spring. He ignores me, and I leave. But this time, as I was preparing to exit, he stopped me.

"Mom, Mom, Mom," he said. "Come back. Sit on my bed."

So I did. He kept his eyes closed, and said nothing. I told him a thing or two, like what I'd make him for breakfast if he would deign to rise. Maybe we should get you a haircut, I said, and, oh, Ben phoned and wants you to call him. Danny huffed some morning breath at me and murmured his assent. I stroked his head, and stopped talking. In that moment, we were together and happy with each other. I knew that, and I chose to value it.

It doesn't sound like much, does it? Compared to a cozy chat over a glass of Chardonnay and a Caesar salad on a Saturday afternoon in the restaurant at Holt Renfrew, a ritual treasured by my mom and me. And it feels like even less when I wonder how those moments will emerge in the years to come, after he leaves home. If a mother's comfort with boys is in the easy silences, the unexpected hugs, what happens when you're no longer living together?

Already, my older son has moved out. Just after he turned eighteen a few months back, he went to live with his dad, having understandably grown tired of going back and forth between two houses. I see him once a week at Sunday supper; occasionally I persuade him to let me drive him someplace, and we grab a bite. He's good about it, really, he is.

In return, I am trying hard to give him the distance he needs, to listen to him talk about his own choices, his own life, without insisting I be integral to it. I learned about letting go by watching my mother with her only surviving son, my younger brother. She has always wanted more from him than he was able, or eventually willing, to give. Through her, I have learned that what defines "enough" in a relationship is largely determined by the person on the receiving end. I may even have come to accept that if there is a hole, something missing, I will be the one to get out the shovel and look for a way to fill it.

So now, when it has been a while since I've seen or talked to my older son, and the younger one has entered a period of inscrutability, I take a deep breath. I think about what the boys have given me, and I count those blessings, one by one. They have always let me be myself, rarely criticizing me, though often poking not-so-gentle fun at my foibles. They have humoured me, and they've let me hug and kiss them on the neck, even in front of other people. The boys have given me much laughter, still do, and probably always will.

These days, when something nice happens, I virtually bronze the moment. Recently, Danny and I were driving in the car and one of his favourite tunes was blasting from the CD player.

He was singing along madly and at the end, I said to him "This song will always remind you of being a teenager, Danny. You'll hear it when you're thirty and forty and you'll

think back to when you were in high school, playing foot-
ball, hanging out with your friends." I looked over at him
and smiled.

He looked back at me, right in the eye, and replied, "And
being in the car with my mom."

You'd have to be the mother of boys to know this, but
that was enough.

part three

A LONG ECHO

WORK AND ITS DUBIOUS DELIGHTS

ARITHA van HERK

For me, the pleasure of work and a cruel sense of imperative are mixed together, shaping a force that I wrestle with every day. Having been raised within a tolerantly Calvinist family, I am motivated by guilt, by desire, and by the ineffable satisfaction of completing a difficult task. This may be the main reason that I write. The challenge of building ideas and of communicating those ideas with the sharpest and clearest of words requires an ascent to a summit that most don't want to undertake. There is immense satisfaction inherent in the journey, and of course, considerable pain. It is not at all easy to live as a writer, especially here in Canada.

And then there is the other work I cherish and toil at: teaching, talking, doing research, and chipping away at the quotidian tasks of a woman in academia. The plateau of writing breathes an air more exhilarating than academia's grubbier potion. The hallways and offices and classrooms of a university demand an unrelenting attention, compounded by theoretical wars, identity politics, a thick glass ceiling and a burgeoning concern for technology and funding.

Teaching at every level offers definite rewards, tangible as the student who develops a love for literature expressed with so much grace and gift that one can only smile and approve. Or the chronically inarticulate student who, after years, achieves some measure of eloquence. Every year I receive dozens of notes and e-mails from students who thank me for the energy that I give to my classes, and who tell me where they are in their own writing careers. Yes, my former students are themselves making a mark on this country's literature. But the precise challenge of teaching—and teaching well—is far removed from the urgent trivialities of university life, the frustrations of trying to arrive at a sensible destination in an arena attentive to so much arcane minutiae that every memo and notice becomes a virtual ankle chain.

How did I get here? I often ask myself. The students are worth the energy, and they are the primary reason for my passionate attachment to teaching. But the politics and the picayune jealousies and the jockeying for position and the backstabbing and the slow poison that leaks through the vents of decrepit buildings perform a version of cumulative discouragement. Where once there was a sunshine aura to postsecondary education's physical and psychic space, it is now obsessed with results and advancement. Students want jobs when they graduate—and what they are learning is mere conduit to that land of tech-toys and six-figure salaries, enviable cars and downtown condos. The university itself reinforces that commercial mindset: the more research dollars professors bring in, the more respect they are given. And so, imagining itself a version of a corporation, academe has allowed its halls to become the site of cloak-and-dagger competition, obsessed with arguments over space and resources, with sadly petty results.

But wait, how did I get here? In my first year as a student at the University of Alberta, I was completely and unreservedly happy. I went to my classes, I studied, I wrote papers and knew in my bones that I had found my heart's desire: to make my living reading and writing books, to make my living working with words. My notion of making my living then had to do with making a life, not making money. Money was not much discussed at institutions of higher learning in the 1970s; more important was the reading and research and the satisfaction of learning itself. And this happy state of innocence I expected to continue. But I should have taken notes, paid more attention to the worms in the apples.

I entered Honours English after an exploratory first year (as was customary at the University of Alberta) and in that very small seminar had a puzzling encounter. A young man who had been in my freshman English class was one of the half-dozen of us admitted to Honours English—and in the first Honours seminar, I was pleased to see him again. "Hi, John," I said, with friendly goodwill, and was surprised when he frowned at me.

"You've got my name wrong," he said. "It's James."

I was young and stupid enough to be quite certain that in the freshman English class we had taken together he was definitely John. "Have you changed your name, then?"

"No," he said haughtily, "I've always been James."

"But, last year . . ."

He interrupted me roughly, and with a lowered voice. "Listen, I took the course for someone else, okay? Just shut up about it."

The very notion was so puzzling to me (at the age of nineteen) that I couldn't quite figure out what he meant. He took the course for someone else? Why would one do that? At that moment the professor entered and my question was put on hold. Seeing my face, James probably thought that I was naive enough (and he was right) not to understand the ramifications of his identity switch, and when the class was over, he pulled me aside again. "I traded," he said. "He did biology for me, and I did English for him."

"But why would you do that?" I asked, incredulous.

"To get an A, stupid," he said. "He's a science student. I'm an English student. He got me an A in biology; I got him an A in English."

"But that's lying," I said.

"It's an A." He turned his back and walked away, but I had made, by the sheer accident of having been in his doppelgänger class, an enemy. And since we were Honours students together, we took many of the same courses. Where, every time I had to do a presentation or made comments in class, Mr. James (I truly cannot remember his last name), did all he could to punish me, making snide comments and challenging my critical position.

Academic misconduct of this kind was far removed from my sphere of recognition, immersed as I was in my studies, and it was less well policed than it is today. While I thought James's actions wrong, it would not have occurred to me then to report him, or even to censure him. His drive for success was so intense that he had carefully planned and orchestrated getting a good grade in an area that was not his strongest, in exchange for helping a friend in the opposite field of study. I thought he was excessively pragmatic, and that was the sum of my youthful judgment. And I did not, until years later, connect the source of his antagonism to the information that I had inadvertently acquired. Oddly, it was his early scholarly taunting that toughened me up, probably helped to sharpen my already strong feminist sense, and made me question the motivations of those who insist on humiliating others in the classroom. So perhaps I ought to be grateful.

My second shock was less accidental and more personal: deliberate harassment. Graduate students at the University of Alberta who held teaching assistantships in English were given their own freshman classes to teach. This entailed long hours of marking and preparation. As an apprenticeship in pedagogy, it was definitely a trial by fire, but I took to it with a passion and zeal predicated on my genuine love of literature and desire to persuade others to share this love. At the time, I was also writing my first novel, and my energy was happily divided between teaching and writing, all in preparation for defending my MA thesis. Because I was living in a tiny apartment, I spent long hours in my airless, windowless office. I didn't care; I was doing what I loved. I worked sometimes from nine in the morning until ten at night, eager and engaged, completely focused on literature and writing.

And then I started to get phone calls. Very strange phone calls, making utterly outrageous sexual comments. I could not understand their source at all and at first assumed that some sex phone line had a number remarkably similar to that office number. But they persisted, and a few of the male callers (they were all male) actually used my name. Finally, it was the students in my class who told me that they had seen an ad (the usual three free lines) in the campus newspaper citing my name and my number in a sexually explicit way. Only my colleagues and students knew that university phone number, but although campus security investigated, they were never able to discover who had placed the harassing advertisement—it had been done anonymously. They concluded it was students playing a bad joke, but from the perspective of time, and given my awareness that I was working far harder than most of my colleagues (and frankly, achieving greater success), I now suspect those calls may have had more to do with academic jealousy than student prankishness. Of course, the calls were so disturbing that I could no longer work in that office and had to set up a rickety desk at home. I had enjoyed having an office; I had worked well there. Now, it had been made a zone of discomfort, impossible to occupy.

These moments of shock may seem inconsequential with the passage of time, may seem to be merely about space or self-confidence, but they have a long echo, a discernibly discomfiting effect, creating stumbling blocks of doubt, distress and even, of course, danger. Older and fiercer now, I would seek to bring about some serious retribution on those responsible, but I am not sure I wouldn't encounter similar laissez-faire attitudes from administrations, student governments and even security officers. For the dominant presences within academic institutions are genuinely puzzled about women's discomfort with their scales and balances. Men like Lawrence Summers, president of Harvard University, whose remarks about women's abilities in the areas of science and engineering have brought him considerable censure, seem always surprised by the reaction they incite, despite years of information and discussion. Perhaps part of the source of unease between women and men in academe is this conflict of outcomes, the differing measurements that are imposed on goals. On the other hand, the largely male administrations of universities tend to be thuddingly and resoundingly blind to their own participation in systemic difficulty if not discrimination, so much so that they cannot imagine the changes begging to be made.

Compounding these subtle toxicities are overt collisions that can only be defined as downright thuggery, of both the silent and the spoken variety. Intellectuals are not necessarily the kindest of folks and despite the low stakes (university professors earn commensurately far less than people who work in the corporate world; writers earn virtually nothing), frustrations surface in the strangest places. I have watched men appoint themselves gatekeepers and authorities, and then bully those who are least powerful. I have seen men draft women to serve as their lackeys, their puppets in hounding other women, and I have watched those women acquiesce. The imperatives of power or friendship or debt are difficult to escape, even in a world where the higher imperative is supposed to be the transmission of knowledge.

205

As my experience as a student should have taught me, there is always a worm in the apple of knowledge. I have encountered, with frustrating predictability, actions intended to discredit and discount the work of women, as if it were inherently of questionable worth, or as if some alternative, harsher measurement were required for what women do. And yet, cowed by our own abjection or even our lack of confidence in our own value, we permit these disparagements, perhaps because there are only so many battles that can fruitfully be fought. For while universities proclaim an intellectual recognition of equality, putting that ethic into practice is another matter. The contingencies of excellence, qualification, seniority and connectedness will always trump egalitarian ideals.

In fact, the subtle hazings that go on in the academy make a high school look civilized. And a successful woman is not immune. In fact, she is likely to be the object of disgruntled or vituperative colleagues and students. I have weathered various attacks on my character and scholarly integrity; I have had to correct misinformation that was being repeated about me and I have seen other women subjected to the same subtle harassments: their publications held up to minute scrutiny, their accomplishments downplayed, their commitment to research belittled. The only armour possible is to love the work, to make the work its own reward.

So why bother staying, why continue in such a bear pit? Why not give it up and spend my time writing? The question calls for cogent answers. First, the temptations of the academy are many. A regular salary, an office (not necessarily with a view) and a version of life-schedule, along with the lure of a substantial library, are too much to resist. I am happily engaged with literature, happy to be immersed in intellectual thought. Why should I give up the work that I love because some people would like to make me miserable? Far better to refuse to be miserable. Second is my powerful sense that women must not allow the academy to function as such a punitive institution; if we flee its bruising, we leave the field open to the bruisers. On the other hand, we must also take care not to become bruisers ourselves, not to internalize the sneering, the scoffing and the quibbling. The third is the obvious delight and inspiration that students provide, coupled with the fact that students deserve good teachers, good teaching, people who give them the very best attention. If teaching in the humanities is left to those who would reduce it to its basest level, then the future of study in the humanities is short indeed. Finally but not least, I love literature and I want to instill that love in every student I encounter.

I continue to mesh teaching within a university and writing (writing across genres: fiction, history, non-fiction, journalism) because for all that an institution and its follies might seek to destroy our joy in this profession, universities exist, nevertheless, as movable feasts. At the end of Audrey Thomas's irascible novel, *Latakia*, the narrator declares to her lover, "The best revenge is writing well." Having lived through the various pitfalls and pratfalls of this profession, there is always available that comforting mergence of subject and practice. For a writer, the best revenge is writing well, but even better is to make of life material for writing. I make notes on jolly and generous and thin-skinned administrators alike, on ascetic and jealous and cheerful and eccentric academics. I talk to the cleaners and the women in the coffee shop, I try to inspire both avid and melancholic students. I cherish this work because it is material, cloth of a sort that will eventually become a story, a tale both tender and parodic. There is no stronger compensation than to make of these frictions a fascinating fiction.

FROM THE ASHES

BARBARA McLEAN

When my mother was five months pregnant with me, my sister Susan—who was five years old and the firstborn— contracted leukemia and died. I gather she was sick for a very short time. Treatment was limited in 1948, hope futile. Apparently my mother visited her hospital room every day for the paltry hour allowed, and I went with her, floating oblivious inside. I still dream of hearing her cry.

I grew up in a family that had difficulty acknowledging Susan's existence, her life, her death, her truncated potential. Perhaps their need was to carry on, to forget, to put the loss behind them; grief is personal and there is no prescriptive path. For me, having never known my sister, the need was vastly different, and for as long as I can remember I lived with a pressing sense of something missing, of a huge hole my parents stepped around that threatened to engorge and drown us all if we dared to peer into it. And yet I was continually drawn to the edge, lured not by salacious curiosity or perilous attraction, but by some intense, innate need to know.

My father refused to speak of her; I was instructed never to ask him to. My mother spoke seldom and softly, hurt, I realize now, by my questions and baffled by the insistence of my interest. "You weren't there," she said, trying to spare me pain and implication, but instead I felt excluded and denied.

When I was old enough to receive them, my mother gave me three items that belonged to Susan. A hinged locket engraved with her name, a baby mug with her initials and an elegant napkin ring. They are all empty vessels, all silver and cold to the touch. I believe my mother's need was to rid them of sad memory, whereas mine was to fill them up. My task was like trying to animate a precious shell or dress a ghost.

Information was what I wanted, and what my parents could not give me. No headstone, no birth date, no death date. In my thirties I was counselled by a wise friend to visit Susan's grave to see if that would settle the haunting and satisfy the quest. I knew she'd been cremated, so once again I prodded my mother and forced her to remember. "Where," I asked "are Susie's ashes?" Without a pause my mother replied, "We never picked them up. We left them at the funeral home." And the subject dropped like lead, like a tight-fisted ball of stiff-upper-lipped anguish sealed and compressed and forced down to sink out of sight.

It took another decade, but finally I determined to find Susie, which I realize now was really a way of finding bits of myself—my capacity to face misfortune, to handle tragedy, to approach loss, to accept imperfection.

It began on her birthday. I was driving from my farm to the city to give a paper on nineteenth-century female literary characters and medicine, a critical feminist presentation that exposed the damaging power of misogynist doctors. It suddenly struck me as I passed between fecund fields on that spring day that this was Susie's birthday. I'd somehow learned the date by then, though my parents never told me. After I gave my paper, in that moment between the last sentence and the first question, I came out of academic mode and confessed that my sister, had she lived, would have turned fifty that day.

I told my audience about her death in a hospital in that very city, about the doctors' rules which limited my mother's visits and kept her away from her dying child's side. Instead of questions I got anecdotes from many of the women there, some of whom remembered those days of maternal exclusion. They told their stories and shared in mine, infusing personal experience into literary criticism.

Having spoken in public about Susan, I was compelled to know more. I requested her death certificate and by citing my family medical history I was able to obtain a copy of the original document. When it arrived I felt an unexpected solar-plexus-punch of emotion. I walked up my lane from the mailbox, then slid the letter knife into the government envelope, withdrew the official crested legal bond and read "Full Name of Deceased" followed by all I knew of her, in elegant cursive script.

The form demanded race, and "Scotch" was written in. My father's signature verified the document in dark ink, the pen nib thick but the letters steady and sure. The saddest part was medical. The physician had attended her only on the day she died. Susie was pronounced dead by a stranger, a duty doctor. I imagined the scene, imagine it still.

To find her remains I traced the funeral home. I learned that this *does* happen, that people sometimes leave ashes, that the law allows for burial in Common Ground after a year. They had no record, however, and it took a number of inquiries to narrow down the search, but as I'd begun to look on a Friday afternoon I had to wait impatiently and impotently through the weekend until business hours on the Monday to make the final call. I hesitated, fearing failure perhaps, more loss, but when I dialled I got a recording and for the first time said her full name out loud: Susan Betsy McLean. Soon the return call came: "We have her. She's here, buried in Common Ground." Simple as that. A name on a ledger, a spot on a map. Susie's is one of perhaps a hundred urns in a crypt in an unmarked, and unmarkable grave, for it is forbidden to place a tombstone over a common plot.

Finding Susan was cathartic. All the tense excitement and bravado of my illicit quest dissolved into a surge of grief and sorrow for her, for my parents, for what could not be spoken and for my own loss of a sister I should have known. I left flowers on the spot and returned only once in a spirit of botanical sabotage to plant miniature bulbs furtively over her grave. I've not seen the result, but I imagine the snowdrops and crocus breaking through in her initials, the scylla multiplying and spreading into a blue pond.

What I learned from this experience went far beyond my own response. It incurred absolute fury from some family members and open thanks from others. I did not dare to tell my father, and when I tried to talk with my mother she stopped me, said she did not want to know. I discovered that just as there is no certain recipe for love, there is no single remedy for grief. My parents did not do the wrong thing by letting Susie go, they simply did what they were able to do, perhaps what they were counselled to do at the time.

Janice Kulyk Keefer writes: "You're born with family like a chain around your neck: metal rings, each one kissing, biting into the next. And even if you break a link, the chain doesn't dissolve. It just sinks under your skin, you wear it without knowing." Susie was the broken link in my ancestral necklace and finding her let it rise to the surface, catch the light and shine.

What I am learning not only involves my mother, my father, my sister, but also affects my relationship with my children. I am not my mother. My search for Susie disclosed my very different needs and ways. I could not respond to

Susie's absence in my mother's manner, and I see now that I cannot expect my own children to respond in mine. It has nothing to do with right or wrong; it's about difference.

As adolescents, my daughter and son had far more than their share of grief from a rash of untimely deaths at their school, from all manner of causes. They manage the pain of their losses individually, discussing it, or not. What they feel is personal and legitimate, and I must listen when they want to talk, and be still when they don't. I offer the things that help me, like poetry and music, and try to recognize and accept their personal elixirs of physical exertion, creativity and risk. I know that we react uniquely and not necessarily as we are taught.

From my sister's ashes rose not a single phoenix but a multiplicity of fledgling possibilities. Finding her fragile remains healed a painful wound, sealed a mysterious hole and exposed a missing link in my lineage. I have learned that my quest provided not what I once believed my parents wilfully withheld, but rather what I now realize they were absolutely unable to give.

It took me some effort to find Susan. Now that my parents are dead and the chance to hear their narratives is gone forever, I realize it was the actual search for my sister that settled me. The story never would have satisfied me coming from reluctant tellers. I know I had to do that work alone.

Note

Janice Kulyk Keefer, *The Green Library*. Toronto: HarperCollins, 1996.

LOVE AND FEAR

BERNICE MORGAN

I was a feckless young woman and people did not expect much of me. I knew this. I had seen surprise and immense relief in my father's eyes when he realized I was marrying the loving, steady young man I began dating at seventeen. On the faces of my kindly in-laws I recognized unvoiced incredulity: "Can our intelligent son really want to marry this callow girl?" When I became pregnant, I sensed that my doctor had similar reservations regarding my maturity. He agreed to replace a general anaesthetic with something new called a saddle block, but gently cautioned me that childbirth might not be as simple as I expected from my reading of the book *Childbirth Without Pain*.

As it happened my son's birth was very near painless. Healthy, crying and covered in white mucus he was whisked out of the delivery room before I could hold him or even really look at him. Later, back in my hospital bed, rested, washed, creamed and bedecked in a white eyelet bed jacket made for the occasion, I felt exceedingly pleased with myself. Despite what others had expected of me, despite what I myself had feared, I had succeeded in giving birth to a baby! Moreover, I had accomplished this amazing feat without making a fool of myself in some stupid, altogether childish way. If I could do that I could do anything! On that bright morning I existed inside a bubble of elation, my whole being filled with a sense of success, of power and certainty that I had never felt before—and would never feel again.

When the nurse brought my baby, rolled tightly in yellow flannel, it was clear he did not share my exuberance. He looked exhausted, his face vexed with worry. In my arms he felt weightless yet stiff and unyielding, not settling against my body as babies are supposed to. As soon as I unfolded the blanket my son began to whimper, his long-fingered hands flailing the air. Loose skin hung from the pencil-thin bones of his arms and legs, as if he had recently lost weight. I covered him and under directions from the nurse tried to get him to take my breast. While we struggled I studied his small worried face, looked into his milky unfocused eyes and touched the soft pulsing spot where his skull had not yet fused. Terrified by his fragility, I felt my euphoria vanish as if it had never been.

Despite our best efforts over the next two days, my baby and I did not seem able to get the hang of breast-feeding. He lost weight and I was frantic with worry. One of the nurses told me I was trying too hard. Later, as we were leaving, she passed me a book called *Canadian Mother and Child* and assured me everything would work out when we got home. Her voice was so kind that I knew she really did not believe what she was saying.

Back home my husband and I could not bring ourselves to put this tiny creature into the big second-hand crib I had painted pink and blue. Instead, we took a drawer from our bureau and, padding it with blankets, made a bassinet. We moved this improvised crib from room to room so that our baby would never be out of our sight. He occupied every moment of that day and most of the night. Whenever he cried I tried to feed him and when he would neither suck nor settle down one of us walked the floor with him. We began a record of how much milk he took (wild guesses), how much time he spent sleeping (accurate to the second), how many diapers we changed, the condition and colour of same. Our house became warm, and except for his crying, very quiet. The air thickened, rooms took on the smell of milk and baby powder, the antiseptic smell of the diaper pail, the fluffy smell of new flannelette. I, who had no memory of the babies I had observed taking up all this time and space, was stunned.

That winter, in 1959, was a season of blizzards and bitter cold. The baby and I hardly left the house. He took all my time, all day, every day. In a pattern that would continue for six weeks, he began crying piteously around four every afternoon, a thin mewing sound that would go on until ten or eleven at night. When his father came home he would rock our son or walk the floor with him while I took a shower. When the baby finally slept we still hovered, holding our palms to his mouth, reassured by the soft puff of his breath.

I think I am writing about the arrival of love and fear—and the terrible knowledge that both would last as long as I lived. But in that blurred, sleep-deprived winter I did not know that—could no more analyze what I was experiencing than a drowning woman might analyze the sea sweeping her under. Never had I focused so intensely on anything as I did on that tiny scrap of life. Never had I felt so responsible for, so linked to, yet so sadly, hopelessly, out of tune with another living creature.

One of my neighbours had a baby three months before I did. I remember watching her bring her son outside, marvelling at how sturdy he looked, how comfortable she seemed holding him, the assurance with which she plopped him down in a carriage while she hung clothes on the line. I told myself that if my baby lived to be three months old he would be safe and I would be like the woman across the way.

I gave up on *Canadian Mother and Child* and bought Dr. Spock's book. I gave up on breast-feeding too, and changed to formula, boiling bottles until the house filled with steam, walls dripped and one night two pictures crashed to the floor. Days passed, weeks passed, our baby gained weight, was christened, became Greg, became cheerful and beautiful.

A year after our son was born George and I had our second child, a daughter. By then I could bathe and dress two babies in twenty minutes. I could rock one baby in the carriage, feed one baby in my lap, drink tea and read a book— all at the same time. Childcare still took every minute of my day but I'd mastered the appearance of competence. Inwardly I was sick with fear, seeing danger in things I had never before given a thought to: poison plants and sharp knives, red food colouring, dangling wires, bug spray, careless drivers, ropes and broken glass and deep water.

This was in the early sixties and much of the anxiety I felt for my children was rooted in the pernicious mindset of the times: talk of our government accepting American nuclear warheads for Canadian-based missiles, school children being taught a duck-and-cover manoeuvre that was supposed to protect them in case bombs fell, talk of evil madmen (theirs and ours) pushing the button, a doomsday clock that kept ticking toward midnight—zero hour—that yellow sign with its ominous black logo and the words "Nuclear Free Zone" posted in public places. Overriding all these harbingers of doom was a male voice that spoke to me several times each day on CBC Radio—between programs designed for "easy daytime listening."

"Radiation doesn't seep. It settles," the voice said— words that still give me the shivers. After this reassuring tag line the voice would continue with tips on "how to protect your family against the potential danger of nuclear war." I must store tinned food, fresh water and first aid supplies in a windowless room. I would also need a battery-operated radio and containers for waste. The voice was male, calm, sure. A reasonable voice from which reasonable women in kitchens all across Canada were, I supposed, expected to accept direction.

I did. I made lists and without saying a word to anyone began storing things—powdered milk, candles, matches, a flashlight. I bought two large plastic garbage cans with lids—but when the alarm went off would there be time to fill them with water? And once filled how would I get them down to the windowless room in our basement? The man did not say how much time I would have to get my babies and our supplies to the room. And what about my husband at work downtown?

I read everything I could find about nuclear war, including *We of Nagasaki*, a collection of eyewitness accounts of what happened when the second atom bomb was dropped on houses and people. From that book I discovered that radiation does indeed seep—into earth and water, into human flesh, into blood and bone. Although the CBC voice was not telling me the truth about radiation I had no doubt he was speaking the truth about the possibility that nuclear bombs would fall on Canadian cities.

Nagasaki was in Japan, on an island. It would make sense to madmen to bomb an island, because the radiation was contained, the population contained. Island water and soil are separated from mainland water and soil. Newfoundland is an island—an island no one but us cares much about. Russia could scare the hell out of all of North America, could bring the president of the United States to any bargaining table just by dropping one nuclear bomb on

Newfoundland. I thought about these things before I went to sleep and when I woke up, I thought about them whenever I heard the CBC man and while I was getting meals, ironing my husband's shirts, folding diapers. I thought about these things when I spooned food into the mouths of my babies and when I watched them sleep.

In the spring of 1961, about six months before my third child was born, a group of CIA-trained exiles stormed the Bay of Pigs, a beach in Cuba—and the hands of the doomsday clock showed three minutes to midnight. Days later a yellow booklet was distributed to eleven cities in Canada deemed to be likely targets for nuclear attack. One was dropped in our mailbox: *11 Steps to Survival* was printed on the cover.

Each of the eleven steps had lists: there was a list of various sounds sirens would make to alert us, a list of ways to improvise a blast shelter in your basement, how to build a fallout shelter (Home Improvement Loans were available) places to hide if you were outdoors (culverts and cars were suggested as I recall), ways to get rid of radioactive dust and much more. Each facing page had black and red illustrations. People and houses were black, the mushroom-shaped explosion, the radioactive fallout and the firestorm that swept over the people and houses were red. There was page after page of things that must be stored in the shelter. Not just food and water, things I had never considered: shovels, an axe, road maps, a fire extinguisher, a kerosene cooker, bedding and diapers, legal papers, medicine, first aid supplies. That list went on and on for pages. There was a drawing of a family, a mother, a father, and a boy and girl, in what seemed to be their kitchen. Father was sitting at the table checking things on a list, mother was packing things into a box, sister was holding a first aid kit, brother seemed to be testing a flashlight. There was no sight of the red mushroom-shaped cloud shown on other pages, but father had a red shirt and mother a red dress with red high-heeled shoes.

I remember staring at the family for a long time. They did not seem upset or even worried. The artist had given each face a look of calm assurance, almost pleasure—they might have been packing for a picnic. I remember crying a little before I dropped the booklet into the garbage. I pushed it well down so I couldn't see it. After that I stopped storing food and used the plastic cans for garbage. Unlike the placid-faced mother in the drawing, I did not want my darlings to come up from that windowless room into a post-nuclear world. I began to think about how I could kill all of us when the time came.

I never spoke of this to anyone, not even to my husband. No one knew I was out of my mind—maybe every mother in Canada was. Maybe we should consider a class action suit against the Canadian government, for deliberately induced insanity.

That time has passed. When you love, it is hard not to hope, and little by little my hope overcame my fear.

The media image that haunted me in the sixties was that mushroom cloud; today I am haunted by long lines of dispossessed women and their starving children. What I feared, they are living through. I cannot see these women without feeling ashamed, without marvelling at their power to love and to hope—look how they keep walking through that vast desolation, holding on to their lives and the lives of their children!

Through an accident of geography I have been spared their fate—spared to see my babies grow into healthy adults, spared to become a grandmother. Yet I still have regrets, still feel guilt about any shadows my fear may have cast on the childhoods of my children. I wish now that I could have rejoiced more back then "in the beauty of the earth and the beauty of the skies, in the love that from our birth over and about us lies," as the old hymn says.

Such regret is, I suspect, the common fate of all who live into old age. Now I try to rejoice more—and try not to think too harshly of that feckless, fear-ridden young mother who didn't have the sense to turn off the radio and go out to play.

THE INOCULATION

HEATHER MALLICK

On December 9, 1980, my boyfriend and I woke to the news on the radio that John Lennon had been shot to death the night before by a deranged fan. And my first thought, unbidden, was this: Somehow, some way, by the end of the day John Lennon's death is going to be my fault.

And so it turned out to be. Despite my efforts, I can no longer recall my boyfriend's mad skein of logic: Lennon was murdered in spirit by stupid people like me who didn't appreciate his music, couldn't grasp the beauty of "the man, this great man, this fine man" (he often burbled on about males he worshipped—a bad sign) who had done so much for contemptible fools like me. Or maybe I had bought Mark Chapman the bullets. Who knows?

I was used to being belittled by my boyfriend. What was unique on this occasion was that I predicted the attack. It was my first unconscious rebellion at the abuse I'd had hurled at me for the four years since I was seventeen and fell hard for this glamorous older man with long blond hair (he was twenty-six, a drummer in a band and had read Thomas Mann). With a hideous recognition, I watched my prediction come true.

Chapters in the *Dick Tracy* adventure stories for British boys in the 1940s were apt to end with Dick trussed in a cave as the pirates ill-got their booty. The next chapter always began, "With one bound Dick was free," kind of like Jack Bauer in *24* after a commercial.

This was my chapter, on another continent and a later era, with dangers domestic and personal that Dick hadn't yet sussed out. "With one insult too many, Heather was free." Every woman glued to an abusive man has that sick-making epiphany, that moment when she realizes she must escape the monster.

I call him Fuckface because I cannot bear to say his name aloud. Okay, it was Giuliano. At least that's what he told me. His real name was Jim, but he felt he was more of a Giuliano. Here's a tip. Avoid men who rococo up their names.

I tread carefully for, sadly, he is probably still alive. I always imagine him winning a Darwin Award for boiling himself to death in a giant shrimp pot or climbing into a wood chipper on idle. No such luck. I think he lives on the West Coast now, piddling out a living on something for which he has no talent. He was entirely untalented, with one exception. He was skilled at seeking out naive, middle-class young women who had been raised to be sweet, and patiently nibbling away at their self-esteem until it resembled a flatfish. He wasn't louche so much as seedy. That's how a woman knows she's found a FF. She sees "louche" as glam; everyone else just calls it grotty.

I was a kid. I was dumb. I didn't get smart until much later, when I was about twenty-four and even then it was a near thing. When I met FF, I was in my last year of high school and Steve Tyler, Peter Frampton and the appalling Leo Sayer were my soundtrack. Underage, I met this guy in a bar, liked his long hair and the cut of his jeans, and in an act of rebellion that turned my parents into emotional auto parts—they self-dismantled—ran away to a cheap motel with a nudie bar called something like Used Tits or Strip Mall in Scarborough's scabby outer reaches, and lost my virginity to his, I now realize, tiny willy.

It was the worst sex I was ever to have, though of course I didn't know it at the time. We shall draw a veil over the details, which were unspeakable. So were his cowboy boots and his endless pretensions, but I couldn't see that, not for years. Stupid Time was still unrolling in front of me like a rubber mat. It was like getting into a taxicab and suddenly realizing you're in Scorsese's *Taxi Driver* with Travis Bickle at the wheel.

What have you done, child?

When a man tells you you're dumb, it's rude to disagree, after all. I believed him when he told me his father was a millionaire inventor. This was a lie, which my mother spotted instantly, but all her look won her was a teenage sneer and something about the bourgeoisie.

He moved into my apartment rent-free, as FFs do, gobbled my student loan, alienated my friends and neighbours— the usual. And then he proceeded to deliberately disassemble my personality. In one "Specimen Day" in my diary, I recorded that he had insulted me thirty-eight times, always for my own good. My face, my hair, my feeling that he should clean up occasionally, my taste in books, clothes, my failure to volunteer as a dogsbody, it dotted me all day like grapeshot. I washed his car and clothes, bought his food and cigarettes, co-signed his loans, paid his missed payments. Once, I may even have paid his child support. I check my diary for that time. "Today he called me a horrible little girl." But by then, ground down to a stub, I thought he had a point.

My mother had raised me to be nice. She hadn't realized there was such a thing as too nice, or that human slugs crawled the earth looking for people's daughters.

I dumped him a few weeks after Lennon's death. He was angry and patronizing. I don't think he ever quite believed that his worm had turned, so to speak. My parents took me back. They were nice. I'm not attacking niceness, believe me, just its poor aim. They repaid the money he stole from me.

Twenty years later, walking beside Lake Ontario, a body of water so huge it looks like an ocean, I apologized to my mother. Then I replaced the seal on the jar where I keep my pickled snakes, and asked her never to mention it again, which she has not.

• • •

I know what you're thinking: Why is she telling me this?

Sure, as stories go about the monstrous regiment of men, this isn't even a skirmish. FF starts out equivalent to a Ted Bundy wrapping his uninjured arm in a sling and asking pretty, young university students to help him carry library books to his car. But he didn't proceed from there to the strangulation, the sodomy, decapitation, the trading of female legs when his corpse collection built up. All he did was hijack my life in ugly interludes for five years.

But that isn't the point.

The point is the inoculation.

I could never get suckered again.

That's not the only point. The other point is that I don't want you to get suckered ever, at any stage of your life. Consider this story your inoculation. If already inoculated, make it a booster shot.

Some woman reading this might have had a FF in her life, who hit her and savaged her emotionally and maybe even fathered her children. And if she hasn't, she might well be vulnerable to one. I worry because she may not recognize her experience was an inoculation. Life isn't short. Life is long. And if she hasn't had her needle by age twenty, she might well have eighty years ahead of her to catch the superbug.

You have to bend with the blows. Hold yourself rigid and you break. At twenty, you are supple, better able to bend. At forty, fifty, sixty, without your inoculation, you are even more vulnerable to a million FFs on the prowl for you and your home, your nest egg, your self-esteem, your child. At that age, you may shatter with the blows.

Furthermore, as you age, you are less likely to have a safety net. The parental bank account, the brief move back home, the obtaining of a degree or two until you qualify for a job that pays well, all these things come from a loving family. Now, you may not have a particularly loving family, but they probably don't do to you the things that a FF will do, and that's something.

Every woman needs a pit crew. She needs solid friends (and there won't be many of them; most will melt away in a crisis, leaving a core pit crew) and she needs her family. For they offer a refuge, not just a bed and all the rice pudding she can eat in her jammies, but someone to say, "Yeah, I always knew he was one of those."

Well, why didn't you tell me? she will say.

Would you have listened? they will ask.

No.

It isn't just the pain that seals an inoculated woman in wonderful Plexiglas from brutes. It isn't even a better-developed sense of that great gift—fear. It's knowing that she is not alone.

I can spot a FF four lanes away from me on the highway now. I can smell him going down on the escalator as I go up, at the next desk, on the barstool beside me. The problem is that I fear that the young women in my life cannot. They were raised to be nice. I am of two minds about raising girls to be nice. They'll be better off if we raise them to be mean, but who wants a world staffed by two damaged genders? If men weren't violent, if they didn't have the FF gene floating among them, maybe I could feel at ease about girls being taught tedious patience and infinite kindness, especially as it relates to boys.

Girls have to know some things that I did not know, hard facts about class, that money has little to do with character and also that men without money aren't by definition good. "Poor but honest" can just as easily be "poor but psychotic." Tattoos are a bad sign, as are motorbikes and a desire to be a cop or a security guard (for a man whose dream it is to be given a gun often has an authoritarian streak in him, and it can be as domestically directed as it is publicly). Bathing is good, as is graduating. Never lend a man money.

People tell me that young women are smarter now. I don't know. They binge-drink as much as I did and they have infinitely less self-esteem, since the demand for female-body-as-skeletal-remain runs full-throttle. They refuse to call themselves feminists and like the word "girl." Even now, nobody points out the obvious to them: that sex is just awful until you either meet the right man or turn thirty—and it's their fault, not yours. The young women I know are soaked in self-blame and in hating their bodies, while the completely unjustified self-confidence of young men continues to run amok.

What this means is they may well meet men who plan to treat them like cowpats. What I'm saying to them is this. Why suffer hard and long when women like me did it for you and are offering you a FF vaccine, at no charge? If you wake up one morning and are told that you murdered John

Lennon in your sleep, apparently, and you're in trouble with your FF, you'll smile a secret smile because you have read this story and you are planning a smart exit.

I was rescued, you see. I am in debt.

And I, like other feminist stepmothers, mothers, mentors, aunts and friends who owe such a debt, will pay it off this way. We call back memories of a little girl's kisses, the sensation of the skin behind her ears at six months, her fragrance, or a young woman's smile, or the decency in a female student from a small town where she was taught the naïveté that makes her blind to her own brutalization. It doesn't even have to be memories of the young woman who needs rescuing. We are all women; we will do it in the name of a little girl we saw once, in my case a beggar in Guadalajara in 1978, to whom I gave no money, and who haunts me still. We will remember our own selves as little girls. We owe a debt to those fragile children.

And if the vaccine hasn't taken for someone—a daughter, stepdaughter, friend, sister or niece—we will stay loyal until that young woman's vision clears and she is willing to be rescued. It may take years but we can outwait FF. There's a reason FFs isolate a woman from her friends and family. He's the cult; they're the deprogrammers.

We'll always be there waiting for her return. And that is because we've had our flu shot, our misery jab, this free UNICEF-type inoculation.

Won't get fooled again.

THE BEAR WITHIN

LAURIE SARKADI

A mother black bear is visiting our house. I have awaited her return for four years. Her young ones are with her. Two. And my three sons are with me.

We watch through the big square window in our kitchen. She sniffs the air before rising onto her hind feet to walk toward me. For a moment we stand face to face, staring directly into one another's eyes. I know I have been given a powerful message, the breadth of which I will decipher later. But one thing feels certain. I am safe again.

The Pawnee believe when a bear stands on its hind legs and lifts its paws toward the sun, it is receiving its healing powers.

I live beside a small lake in the boreal forest near Yellowknife. In this sub-Arctic frontier, unburdened by the technological crush of civilization, it becomes possible to feel the ancient ways of knowing that guided the indigenous Dene peoples. This is where my odyssey of motherhood begins, alone in the woods save for the babes at my breast, the ravens outside my window and the unspoken mysteries beyond. The more I seek to unravel those mysteries, the more I see of the bear.

My husband, Francois, and I discover the bloated, fetid bodies of some three thousand whitefish, northern pike and suckers floating beside our new home in June 1991. The lake's giant ecological belch, later deemed a natural phenomenon caused by algae dying and robbing the water of oxygen, is a wonderful way to meet the new neighbours, who mind not a whiff that the place stinks. Gulls and ravens gorge on the death, yielding only to the authoritative swagger of a half-dozen bald eagles. Three black bears appear at the farthest point of our bay, eating their way closer to us each day. When they finally reach our driveway, Francois yells, "Go away, bears." And they do.

We conceive our first son in July after a spicy hot sauna and naked dip in the lake.

July is a time of estrus for female bears, and promiscuity for both sexes.

The first thing I do after confirming my pregnancy is cycle ten kilometres, rationalizing that childbirth will require the ultimate fitness and stamina. My mind brims with thoughts of the new life inside me, of how I will do everything within my power to ensure it grows safely into a healthy baby. As I near the steep hill that always defeats me, I look to my left and see a bear running beside me. We travel at exactly the same speed, glancing at each other, straight ahead, then back at each other. A surge of adrenalin wells from my abdomen, from the embryo itself as I imagine this fledgling being ripped from inside me. "Not now," I say to the bear. "Not with my new baby." The big hill fast approaches.

As I begin my ascent, so does the bear. My thighs feel detached from my upper body, now locked in a death grip with the handlebars. I reach halfway, the point where my legs and lungs normally scream in agony, without being winded. The bear veers left into the thick brush. I cycle home as if two lives depend upon it.

In time, I conclude the bear was a test. My instinctive reaction, to protect my unborn child, was correct. As for physical fitness, what further proof did I need that my body is capable of feats I cannot yet imagine? Like the bear, I am strong and protective, fit for motherhood. My prize comes the following April. A son.

Bear cubs and their mothers emerge from their womb-like dens together in April, a time of rebirth and new beginnings.

I nurse Max day and night for nearly two years. I am mesmerized by his beauty, ferociously protective and exhausted by his demands. During this period, no bears visit my house. I see bears along the highway, but always far from my home range.

Most male black bears avoid the territories of lactating females, preferring those in heat. Mother bears generally move out of another bear's territory, rather than risk a turf war.

Each day I anticipate hiking through the wilderness with Max on my back. So calming, so invigorating are these enchanted woods, compared with the nagging drudgery of housework, that I never give a thought to any possible harm. The forest casts a benevolent spell on us.

*   *   *

I am pregnant again. This baby is due in November, the same time tiny blastocysts in a pregnant black bear have to decide whether or not to attach themselves to her uterine wall.

The fertilized eggs in a sow float freely in her womb for five months until she is ready to den. If she does not have the fat reserves necessary to bear and nurse her cubs through winter, the blastocysts dissolve, sparing her the agony of starvation.

I miscarry at eleven weeks.

Sentiments of sympathy pour in, but I revel in relief. The disquieting depression that accompanied this pregnancy has been a bad hormonal trip. I drink beer and paint Zulu and

Haida designs on the kitchen and garage doors, unable to discern if I am being driven crazy—or kept sane—by my environment.

Our dog is barking maniacally at a raven taunting it from the roof. Max toddles out and conciliates the dispute by speaking to the bird *in* Raven. Then I watch all three of them walk side by side down a path, Max in the middle, the raven hopping awkwardly as it struggles to keep up, and in that moment I realize there is greatness and beauty and magic in my life, if not adult conversation and paycheques.

Come winter, I crave another baby, mating dutifully on all optimum days for conception. My pregnancy is quickly apparent. At three months, I look six months pregnant. I cup my swollen belly, musing that this cannot be just one baby. It isn't. Like a faulty gumball machine, I have double ovulated.

Copulation induces ovulation in a female black bear shortly after each encounter.

As my September due date looms larger than life, so do the pressures of toting my enormous girth. I turn forgetfully and whack it on things, nearly passing out from the pain. My stomach prevents my arms from reaching the kitchen sink, and I am grateful when my mother comes to look after me. While I insist she and Francois help me into the forest— easing me down on my side so I can pick cranberries—I am too slow and foggy to do much except wait.

As bears prepare for denning, they can spend virtually the entire day resting. This is known as "walking hibernation."

At term, I deliver my strapping twin boys naturally, without drugs. Both Calvin and Levi wriggle determinedly for sustenance at my breast, latching on hourly after that with a tenacity that leaves my nipples chafed and bleeding and fuels record-breaking weight gains within their first month.

Mother black bears nursing multiple cubs have been known to splay themselves belly down in order to stave off relentless feeding efforts.

Sleep is but a fantasy. By October, when bears crawl into their dens, I wear my fatigue like a disease. Each day becomes darker and drearier, heightening my desire to curl up and tune out. Occasionally, all three boys fall asleep with me in bed after nursing in our den of flannelette and down. The heavenly gift of sleep, the four of us enveloped in darkness. For all the times I miss the work world, this is not one of them.

By November, the mother black bear's metabolism slows to half its summer rate. She continues to slumber while her cubs are born in January or February, blind and nearly hairless. They are about eight inches long and weigh less than a pound. The mother begins an external pregnancy, or second womb-time. Even in this suspended state, she is able to respond to her cubs' cries and needs, maintaining a level of subconscious caregiving.

The bears are out in force the next summer, all around our house. Our first encounter is a mother with two tiny cubs and a much larger third, shambling across the road. She manages only a glazed stare of forced interest in our direction. Her ribs show through her dull and matted fur. "They're sucking the life right out of you, aren't they," I commiserate.

The twins are in baby swings on the deck watching Max tour in his push-pedal car. I am doing dishes. Two cubs play in a tree at the back of our house while their mother grazes below. When Francois spots them, he tells them all to go home. The mother gathers her young and walks away.

On August 19, 2002, a healthy black bear in the resort town of Fallsburg, New York, knocks five-month-old Esther Schwimmer out of her stroller and carries her into nearby woods, where she dies of head and neck injuries. A wildlife pathologist says the bear may have been attracted to Esther's milky odour.

Daily hikes are still integral to my happiness, but when the twins get too big to carry in my *amautik*, an Inuit coat, I push them along the highway in a double stroller. One day in September, a cold, snowy rain pelts down on the back of an icy wind. I put off the walk until I can no longer stand the anxieties that accumulate after a day cooped inside. The twins howl in protest as I strap them into the stroller, while a raven stares down at our spectacle from a tree. "I hope I get an especially good reward for this," I say to the bird.

We've managed the equivalent of a city block when the dog bolts across the road and begins chasing a bear, toward us. I turn the stroller around and order Max to head home. "Don't run!"

Fleeing-prey behaviour can trigger a bear's predatory pursuit instincts. In July 2000, Canadian Olympic biathlete Mary Beth Miller of Yellowknife is killed by a black bear while jogging outside of Quebec City.

When the galloping bear is right beside us, it glances at me then veers in the opposite direction.

•   •   •

Max is five. We take him on a fishing trip to a pristine lake accessible only by a gruelling trek through five kilometres of swampy, mosquito-infested portages. The night before the trip I dream I am standing with the children on a concrete platform of stairs surrounded by lake and woods. Francois is canoeing toward us when a male bear, snarling and frothing at the mouth, appears in the water behind him. When Francois tries to climb onto the concrete the bear claws and eats his arm and back. I clang on a pot with a wooden spoon.

The bear rears on its hind legs, twists its head toward the sound . . .

I awake so tired and distracted, I forget to tell Francois the dream.

Five minutes after launching the canoe, we see a bear on a flat outcrop of rock ahead of us. It paces back and forth then sits complacently on its haunches, content to watch us drift silently past.

The ensuing summer is fraught with forest fires, ambitious house renovations and long spells of single parenting while Francois joins firefighting efforts along our road. I worry more about keeping my three energetic boys from slipping unnoticed into the blackness of the lake, or dismembering themselves with the workers' power tools. A cousin arrives in the midst of this mayhem with her three-month-old son, whose tiny lungs cannot handle the black smoke outdoors, or the choking drywall dust inside. I feel trapped and personally responsible for everyone. Daily, I consider fleeing my home range.

Mature mother bears may spend 75 percent of their time in the company of their offspring, compared to males, who remain solitary except when breeding or when congregated at plentiful food sources.

I am driving in our truck with Levi to pick up bookshelves. When we return, the other two boys and my neighbour are playing on the driveway. Levi is asleep in his car seat, so I open both truck doors wide to keep him cool and load myself up with wooden shelving. A few strides past the truck I hear the *crack* of a branch snapping under enormous weight. I turn to stare directly into the black-rimmed eyes of an adolescent bear. An unsavoury list of options flashes before me. I choose to run, lumber in hand, up to the house, yelling at the others to get inside. I grab a pot and spoon from the kitchen, race back outside, then freeze.

I do not want to confront this bear.

I do not want it to maul *me*.

I *have* to rescue Levi—I know I *will*—but I do not *want* to.

These fleeting, unmotherly thoughts make me feel selfish and ashamed.

Clanging the pot and bleating strange noises, I leap up and down to make myself appear large and foreign as I head blindly toward the bear, unaware my neighbour has already scared it away by rattling gravel in a metal dog dish. She is standing near Levi as he awakes. I walk over, draw him close and breathe him in deeply.

My relationship with the bear changes that day. I am afraid to go camping, afraid to pick berries, afraid to fish. Bears disappear entirely from my natural landscape, and I struggle to understand why. Have I offended the mother bear's protective spirit? Am I being punished for having put my own safety before that of my son's?

Three years later, still without a sighting, still with fear, I am painting the deck when I hear on the radio that a black bear has killed a camper about two kilometres from my house. Helicopters swoop overhead with infrared scanners and SWAT teams and wildlife crews assemble to hunt the marauding killer. June 2, 2001, eighteen-year-old Kyle Harry becomes the first recorded person fatally attacked by an American black bear in the Northwest Territories, suffering more than two hundred severe puncture wounds from teeth and claws over most of his body. His left arm and lower back are eaten. The bear is shot, but only wounded, by an RCMP officer. Search crews scour the region. Parks close. Roadblocks and traps go up. I am oddly calm. My anxieties having born fruit, Kyle's tragic death feels sadly conclusive.

Wildlife officers shoot and kill the wrong bear before eventually gunning down a second, which has matching bullet

fragments in his body. This emaciated animal has other puncture wounds, including a large hole through his sinus that
probably blinded his right eye. Experts say he was likely
attacked by another bear, perhaps a week before Kyle's death.
I am relieved to learn the killer may have been going mad.

It is still another year before the bears make their reassuring return to my kitchen window.

Perhaps I was not being punished. Perhaps the mother
bear's spirit was guiding me all along, instilling fear to protect the children and me. For all I know, the young bear
I encountered that fateful day with Levi was the same adult
male that later killed Kyle Harry. A medicine woman I con-
sult tells me punishment is never part of an animal's psyche,
or part of our own higher self or the divine. It only creates
fear. And you either live in love, or you live in fear, with all
its manifestations. She suggests I created the fear because
I felt I needed to punish myself.

For what though?

For harbouring ideas of abandoning my relentless
responsibilities? From the entropy of housework, the daily
hand-to-hand combat with human excrement, the unsexi-
ness of fatigue, the stress of keeping everyone alive, the
longing to resume my career? All true. But ultimately love,
beauty and magic have a greater hold than any of this.

When the bears come back to me, it feels counterintuitive
to shoo them away. I can't hide my true feelings from one I
see on the escarpment behind our house.

"Oh, all right, I do love you," I confess in exasperation.
"But twenty-seven people will be camping here tomorrow for
a family reunion. It's best if you stay away." It listens, then
lumbers up the hill.

Two days later, at 4:45 a.m., the dogs are barking.
Francois eventually spots a bear heading away from the

house. My sister-in-law later notices the clock has stopped at 4:50. She changes the batteries, but it never works again. Jung calls these "meaningful coincidences" synchronicity. The Dene call it medicine.

For me, it is subtle communication with the otherwise intangible forces of nature. Magic.

Notes

Jeff Fair and Lynn Rogers, *The Great American Bear*. Minoqua, Wis.: NorthWord Press, Inc., 1994.

David Rockwell, *Giving Voice to Bear: North American Indian Myths, Rituals, and Images of the Bear*. Key Porter Books, 1991.

Tony DeBruyn, *Walking with Bears, One Man's Relationship with Three Generations of Wild Bear*. New York: Lyons Press, 1999.

Dean Cluff, "First Fatal Bear Attack, Northwest Territories, Canada." *International Bear News* 10, no. 3 (August 2001).

THE ONLY WAY PAST

MAGGIE DE VRIES

My sister Sarah disappeared from Vancouver's Downtown
Eastside in April 1998. Four and a half years later, her DNA
was found on the Pickton property in Port Coquitlam. In May
2005, a murder charge was laid against Robert Pickton for her
death. Sarah was eight years younger than I. She lived downtown
for fourteen years, most of the second half of her life, supporting
herself as a sex worker and struggling with addiction. When
Sarah's life ended, I was ushered onto a journey of discovery—a
profound and pain-filled one—that continues to this day.

Seven years have passed since my sister vanished, but her loss is as fresh and painful as it was the first day I realized she was gone. While Sarah was alive, I struggled to maintain a meaningful relationship with her, riddled with guilt at my inability to help her and desperately uncomfortable with everything about the world in which she lived. Ever since Sarah disappeared, I've focused on her life, on celebrating it in a way that I wish I'd been able to when she was alive. I helped plan a memorial in which we remembered living women— Sarah and the others who had disappeared from Vancouver's Downtown Eastside. I wrote letters to Sarah as I remembered her. I wrote a book about her life and in the process, she became a whole person for me in ways she wasn't when she was alive. I learned that she was a creative and loving person in a supportive community where she helped others and they helped her. From her diaries, I learned the extent of her suffering and the nature of her deepest longings.

What I learned about my sister I had a profound need to share. For years now, I've spoken about Sarah at book clubs and conferences, at high schools and women's clubs. I've talked about Sarah's life and how we can change our thinking, our behaviour and our laws to allow women like my sister to live with dignity. When I talk about her, I try to keep Sarah's spirit close—I wear the earrings she gave me fifteen years ago, gold-plated hearts with a pearl dangling from each one. I read her poems, her letters and her journal entries aloud to audiences; it is almost as if she speaks through my mouth. I bring a large photo, my favourite, in which she grins broadly, glowing with beauty and love of life, and ask people to look at her instead of me while I read her writing. Some do. Others close their eyes.

When I give these talks, I'm able to inhabit my relationship with Sarah fully, to honour her with each word I speak. Each time I'm drained, but I receive something precious all the same. And only now, as I write this, am I able to define what that something is: I receive Sarah back again, Sarah at her strongest and most loving.

•   •   •

Until recently, even though I talked about Sarah extensively and embraced every opportunity to meet someone who knew her or to hear another anecdote about her life, I kept myself as far away as I could from the circumstances of her death. I can see now that, right from the beginning, I was trying instinctively to protect myself. When Victim Services first contacted me several years ago, I was mortified. I didn't want to hear from them. I was not a victim, I thought, Sarah was the victim. I still feel a twist in my stomach if someone uses the word "victim" with reference to me.

When I speak to an audience, someone often asks me about my anger. Where is it? they want to know. Over and over again, I have told groups, calmly, that I cannot feel it, it's too big to feel, I would not be able to bear it. I've also said that I do not plan to attend Robert Pickton's trial, read the reports in the newspapers or watch the clips on TV that will describe what was discovered on the Port Coquitlam property. "I don't want those images in my head," I say. And I move on, calm and cool and in control.

Or I try to.

At one event recently, I was calm enough, but an elderly woman with a long braid wrapped around her head was not. She was seething with her own rage when she asked me about mine. When I said I didn't want to know the horrors of my sister's death, she cried out, "The truth will set you free!" and glared at me. She went on to say that we need to face up to the fact that the world is a sewer. I didn't take her seriously, not at the time. I'd seen her before at another event, witnessed her anger, her seeming irrationality. She was a person to be "dealt with," not listened to—just like the others who wanted to talk about the details of my sister's murder.

No matter how outraged people seemed to be when they said such things as, "How could someone do that?" or "So, what's up with the trial?" or "I heard that . . ." I felt that their words trivialized my sister's death and my insides recoiled. My response actually had more to do with me than with them.

I understand now that each of those people speaking about Sarah's death had been unwittingly pushing me closer and closer to the truth held out by the braided lady. Each of those times, I recoiled because I didn't want to look, because I was afraid to know who killed Sarah, how they killed her or how they disposed of her body after she was dead.

In the weeks that followed my encounter with the braided lady, her words rang inside my head and whispered in my ears. The trial is coming, I thought to myself, and suddenly the idea of keeping at bay all the gruesome details that would be revealed in that courtroom made me tired. I wasn't going to be able to do it, I realized. I remembered that in the Bernardo case I tried not to take in what was being reported, but I didn't succeed. I didn't succeed then, and I wasn't going to succeed now.

I decided I couldn't bear the prospect of waiting for the trial to learn, along with the rest of the world, how my sister died. Such deliberate ignorance was exacting a cost. I was using enormous energy trying to keep at bay knowledge related to her death, but really I did know. Instead of keeping it at bay, I was actually keeping it buried. I had taken the bits of news that had been reported over the years and packed it in a deep dark place within me. Along with that information were all the thoughts and feelings it evoked— my anger at Sarah's murderer, any anger I might feel toward Sarah herself, and all my grief about the manner of her death, all the horror of not having her body, of not knowing for more than four years what had happened to her.

•   •   •

Recently, with the help of my therapist, Patrice, and my husband, Roland, I have been easing up the protective lid of denial and peeking at the pain inside of me. I now know I must feel my anger and my grief. Patrice told me that the only way to the other side of all this pain is through it. There is no other way past. I can either live my whole life on this side, using much of my energy to keep pain locked in and locked out, contorting myself to avoid feelings and thoughts that I don't want to have, or I can let myself learn and feel in a supported way.

That is the key—the support, the talk.

Support can come from unexpected places. Recently, I read an interview between Oprah and Bishop Tutu. She asked him how he could hear all the testimony that was shared after apartheid ended and then go home and eat dinner with his family. "We were told not to be like vacuum cleaners," he said, "taking in dirt and keeping it in a bag, but like dishwashers, taking in dirt, then passing it out. Otherwise we would have been traumatized." That image has stayed with me.

Patrice, who is trained in helping people deal with vicarious trauma, is leading me to an understanding of how to approach what I kept buried for so long. She told me I needed to speak the terrible thoughts in my head, to speak them to someone who could reflect back to me what I was saying, someone who would not try to take away my pain, to diminish what I was saying, but who would be able to stay with me as I go through this in the coming months and years. That someone is Roland, my husband.

I must face not only the hard, cold fact of Sarah's death, but also the details of the findings at the Pickton property. During Robert Pickton's preliminary hearing in 2003, many of those details were revealed in the courtroom in Port Coquitlam, with the accused sitting behind glass and family members of many of the victims in attendance, along with two or three dozen journalists. I stayed only for the first three hours of the first day and then left, not prepared to hear what was going to be revealed in that room. A publication ban kept the words that were spoken there from reaching the public. But the people who were present heard them, and the journalists recorded them.

At first, I thought I'd ask one of the journalists to pass on to me the written material from the preliminary hearing, but Patrice warned against that. The learning needed to be shared, she cautioned, spoken and heard in the same moment, talked about. So I arranged to meet with one of the journalists, a man who agreed to do that sharing. We were both afraid: He didn't want to hurt me, and I didn't know what he would say, how it would feel. But I had to trust him and trust the process that Patrice and I had discussed. Piece by piece he told me what he knew. Piece by piece I repeated it back to him and recorded it in my journal. The details were gruesome, explicit, and the implications were monstrous, but the two of us kept on going together until we were done.

After our meeting, I took a break, as Patrice had suggested, and then wrote about what had happened. I also wrote a letter to my sister—not recognizing that, once again, I was skirting something by bringing her to life for myself. I felt relief, a sense of completion. I had done what I feared for so long, and had survived. And really, hadn't I known most of what the journalist told me all along? Hadn't I, at some level, been working on assimilating this information for seven years? Now I had taken the last step—I thought.

I told Roland all that had happened, told him of my sense of relief, of completion. And really, I said, whatever happened to Sarah's body after she was dead has more to do with her murderer than with her or with us. I went to bed and slept soundly that night, no nightmares lurking anywhere near.

The next day I went to see Patrice. I still felt jubilant. I opened my journal and told her everything, explaining why

I felt it would not be that difficult for me to move on. It took her all of three minutes to return me to reality, to have me sobbing in my chair. And I realized that I had been trying to do, once again, what I had been doing for seven years—pack away the horror of Sarah's death, keep from facing it fully by focusing on her life.

(257)

That night Roland rented the movie *Troy*. It was not the best movie I'd ever seen, but we both found the story compelling. Toward the end, Achilles, in an act of grand vengeance, comes to the gates of Troy to engage Hector in single combat. Achilles triumphs, killing Hector. He then ties a rope around Hector's ankles and drags the body behind his chariot back to the Greek camp. Under cover of darkness, the Trojan king slips into the Greek camp and into Achilles' tent. "Please," he begs, "return my son's body to me." At that moment I began to weep. By the time the movie was over, half an hour later, I was sobbing openly.

When I saw the Trojan king beg for his son's body, I recognized the extent of my own loss for the first time. I understood that when Sarah's murderer killed her, he committed a heinous act against us, against everyone who loved her. And when he disposed of her body in such a way that we would never see it, never be able to confirm her death through her body, never be able to bury her or scatter her ashes or place an urn containing her ashes in our family plot, he not only dishonoured her, he took something infinitely precious from us.

For seven years, I had tried to convince myself that what happens to a body after a person is dead does not matter. Now I know that it does. Now I can no longer separate Sarah's murder or her murderer from myself.

So, this is what I know: It's better to feel our feelings, no matter how painful, than to lock them away. Now my mind and heart can turn to Sarah's death, but I don't need to force that. I may regret the seven years, but seven years is how long it has taken. I now know that our minds and bodies and hearts can guide us, but we need outside help as well. We must never try to face the horrors in our lives alone.

* * *

I am trying desperately to make meaning out of all that I have learned from the last numbing seven years. Someone killed my sister. That same person may have killed many other women and disposed of their bodies in such a way that even their bones are gone from us. Now, that murderer is my litmus test. When I hear generalities about human nature, about spirituality, my mind flies to him first. Yet I believe that the world is essentially a good place. When I was ten or eleven, I wept at Anne Frank's words: "In spite of everything, I still believe that people are really good at heart." I want to believe her words even now.

I don't know if the game Mastermind is still available. I played it a lot as a kid. It involves trying to match a row of four or five coloured pegs to a hidden row of pegs with the help of clues from the opponent. It requires rigorous logical consistency. That's a metaphor for how I try to live my life. I want rigorous, logical consistency. But sometimes life refuses to reveal its logic or to abide by logical principles. People are capable of the most terrible acts against one another, and people are capable of transformative acts of love. No explanation of the world that does not accommodate both of those truths is adequate. Sometimes, we try to make meanings that trivialize or ignore the range of human experience. I must reach some understanding of what someone did to my sister and of what she may have suffered, and in that understanding, I must not diminish or shirk the possible truths, nor must I lose sight of love.

I've turned the dishwasher on, but it could be a long cycle, and I may have to stop it now and again to load in another item or two.

NO BEATLES REUNION

J. C. SZASZ

In Memory of
Rick Wallensteen

For seven years I typed Informations—criminal charges—on multicoloured carbon paper. The yellow and pink copies were for our office, the white for the Court Registry.

Sixteen years later, I can still recite the section numbers for a variety of Criminal Code offences as if I were saying the alphabet: Section 267(1)(a), assault causing bodily harm; Section 348(1)(b), break and enter to commit theft, and Section 235, murder.

I began my stint at the Nanaimo Crown Counsel Office over a handshake and a promise that my part-time hours would grow into full-time. They did. Crime was on the rise. Back then, if I told anyone that I worked for the Crown Counsel they'd think I worked for a crown corporation—not the prosecutor's office. We were invisible to law-abiding citizens; most weren't aware that we existed. But the inmates at Wilkinson Road jail knew us well—our telephone number was written on the wall above the public telephone. Our small office included prosecutors and secretaries, and our clientele was the common criminal—mother, daughter, father, son—predator and prey.

The most eligible of the lawyers, Jack, had arrived from Dauphin, known as the perogy capital of Manitoba. There was also Gordon, a big man with a big heart, who introduced me to the margarita. I swear he carried a blender and frozen limeade in his briefcase. Then Rick, who worked evenings and weekends and always wore a grey tweed jacket and a red knitted vest over his white shirt. And Clive, the oldest, who had been an RCMP officer before he hung up his red serge and donned a black robe. A tough old bear, he thought my thirteen-year-old daughter had beautiful blue eyes and once sang to her Bobby Vinton's *Blue Velvet* in an aisle of our local grocery store.

The secretaries or "support staff" (this politically correct term from Headquarters always made me think of hosiery) included Jessica, who could rattle off the Young Offenders Act while running in steel-tipped stilettos to a ringing telephone. Sandra, who had fire-engine-red hair and pumped out subpoenas when she wasn't trying to pump water from the well at her rustic home. And then at the front desk there was Jana. It didn't matter if you were a first-time offender or a career criminal with a record as tall as I am, Jana took no crap from anyone. Granted, she made an extra effort for those who said "please" and "thank you," but she did not tolerate raised voices or swearing.

The office expanded and we grew to include a Victim Services Branch. Three great women came on board, who, for a number of years, made the scary adversarial court system more bearable for five-year-old victims or seventy-year-old witnesses. Those women, Pam, Lois and Susan, gave hope not only to our victims but also to the rest of us. When we felt frustrated, unable to stop the repeated violence, they reminded us that we were cogs in the wheel of justice and we all needed to do our part. They were our cream-puff-baking, spiritual angels. Then the government laid them off.

When our prosecutors needed a document in court, one of us would run it up the street to them—snow, rain or sleet. If they needed a rush release order sworn, we'd swear. Or, if they needed help lugging three large briefcases from our office to the courthouse, one of us would lug one while they struggled with two.

The prosecutors in their black robes gave us all a sense of pride in our role in the fundamental struggle between good and evil—we worked for the good guys, fought the good fight. There were no heroes, only victims, and every day we uncovered another tragedy. With the Charter of Rights and Freedoms, we often felt our hands were tied, and the fight then became downright nasty—sometimes unfair.

The obtaining of physical evidence was fundamental to a strong case. But *how* that evidence was obtained was critical—sometimes even more critical than the allegation. "You are not obliged to say anything, but anything you do say may be given in evidence"—this was true only if the arresting officer had given the Official Warning before the accused started confessing to the crime committed. The last thing we needed was a judge ruling a confession inadmissible. Try explaining that to a victim.

Some horrors detailed in the police reports that passed over our desks were simply filed away because there was "no substantial likelihood of a conviction." That was the test; the policy directive practised throughout the ministry. We could not charge what we could not prove. Again, try explaining that to a victim. Weak or strong, a case could swing sideways if a police officer didn't show up or a witness changed his or her story. Either way, the prosecutor took the responsibility and the blame.

The Crown tried to shield us from the brutalities of our work. Most of the time binders of autopsy photos were labelled and secured with elastic bands. Yet sometimes, usually five minutes before court, an unsuspecting secretary frantically searching for a file would find herself looking at photographs of an old man stabbed twenty-five times in his own living room, or of children: babies beaten and bruised, some murdered. Those were the pictures that kept me awake at night, wishing that just once we could have saved instead of prosecuted.

Before each trial we gave our prosecutors a Superman's send-off. I remember telling Gordon, "Go fight for truth, justice and the Canadian way!" Sometimes Gordon returned from court victorious, other times slaughtered, his shoulders sagging in defeat.

One time, near the end of the day, Gordon had returned triumphant after slogging it out in a ten-week murder trial. With a slight smile on his face, he hummed as he strolled past my desk and casually asked, "Margarita, Jo?"

But within a few months the Court of Appeal had over-turned that murder conviction. A new trial was ordered. Gordon won a second time but again the Court of Appeal overruled him. The third time, he won; by then he could have done that trial in his sleep.

We numbed our losses with shots of tequila, but we couldn't chase away the nightmares. Then there were the media to contend with, and the *suits* from Criminal Justice Headquarters, who demanded to know what went wrong.

Our victories were bittersweet and congratulations to the prosecutor awkward. Although a son had been found guilty of killing his father, a murder conviction would not bring his father back. After the thirty-day appeal period, I would close my file and put another life on the shelf. Tomorrow, next week or next month, I would come across yet another grue-some police report, open a file, categorize another horren-dous act. And once again the Crown would prepare for a trial.

Despite the violence we waded through, we found time to laugh and tell jokes. At one point three women in our office had become pregnant at the same time. The joke was that they had all ridden the elevator with bachelor Jack and later returned with child. None of us would ride in the elevator with Jack after that! We also developed lasting friendships. We shared stories about our children. We knew each other's spouses by their first names. We partied at each other's homes. Our camaraderie and fun attracted attention: lawyers and secretaries from bigger cities tried to break into our circle. Shamefully, I'll admit, we weren't too inviting. We wanted to keep what we had.

Then, gradually, things started to change for me. I regarded every person on the street as a potential criminal. In one week I warned my daughter three times about sexual predators. My tolerance was wearing thin. I trusted no one. I had to escape.

There had to be life without crime.

My husband had also outgrown Nanaimo. He wanted to expand his career in the grocery retail business. On my advice, he threw his resume out there and got an interview for an assistant produce manager's position in Victoria. He landed the job. Our lives were about to change.

By the time I left, Rick had been lured into private practice, defending criminals instead of prosecuting them. Gordon—well, he stayed in Nanaimo and became a Headquarters man. Bachelor Jack moved to Victoria. The only one still around was Clive. He retired three months after I moved on. Nothing was left of our original crew but scribbles on Post-it notes attached to dead files that would eventually be shredded or archived.

The final change came three years later when Rick was killed in a car accident. He was one of the good guys—one of us. E-mail messages about his death blurred from our tears. Bound by our grief, we reached out to each other.

Some of us car-pooled to his service while others stole away on their lunch hours to light candles and say goodbye in a local church.

No more red knitted vest or tweed jacket. Rick's robe is draped on a hanger now and not on his shoulders. Things will never be the same. There will be no Beatles reunion.

For years I had earned a good paycheque. I hadn't stayed at that Crown office because of the money though; I stayed because of the people. I was a female in the traditional female job—secretary. Growing up after the women's liberation movement, I was conditioned by our society to believe that my chosen profession was not an important one. Little girls do not skip down the street singing they're going to be secretaries when they grow up. But to the men and women prosecutors of the Nanaimo Crown Office, I was important. I was regarded as an equal. A Crown loss was our loss, a Crown victory our victory. Our respect for each other transcended gender, job titles and job descriptions.

No one was better than anyone else.

We were a motley crew but one hell of a team. We did our jobs to the best of our abilities. Lives were at stake—the police had passed the baton and the courtroom was our finish line. To say the work didn't get to us would be a lie, although we'd never openly admit it. I've finally stopped triple-checking the locks on my doors at home. Twice is enough now.

Our office did not land the biggest contracts; we never achieved record sales. With what we were given, we tried to prove a case beyond a reasonable doubt to a judge and a jury of twelve—and what a pain if it was a hung jury.

Trials are expensive, and when it comes to the administering of justice there are no bargain days at Sears. When we were successful the celebration was short-lived; another trial loomed around the corner. We didn't want accolades because we knew they came at a price—a human life. Our rewards were sporadic and came in the form of a wood-carving or a child's drawing. For the men, women and children whose lives had been robbed of innocence and trust, we couldn't remove the scar, but we could help it heal.

Our crew has moved on but we still stay in touch. We're coping with new jobs—all except Clive, who's enjoying retirement on his boat. We all cling to one common thread—our time at the Crown Counsel Office.

At one of my recent jobs, I tried to replicate that experience. It didn't work. Different time; different place; different people. Our Nanaimo Crown experience was unique and we knew it. We also knew that it was too good to last. That's what made it special.

FÚ:
THE TURNING POINT

JANICE WILLIAMSON

earth   thunder

After my neighbour lost her beautiful newborn, who was missing half his heart, I knew I wanted a child. I had almost witnessed the child's birth. It mattered not that as birth attendant, I missed the actual event when a trip to the hospital concluded a long labour. Five days later, in an afternoon crushed by grief, the infant corpse, yellowed by jaundice and too little time, lay in a small cradle at the foot of the family bed. As part of the memorial service, I called out "Finlay" once, and then "Finlay" and "Finlay" again, sounding out his small being in a sombre naming ceremony.

This cry, suspended in the hollow listening of mourning, was the moment of conception when my plot to become a mother was hatched. I knew I wanted to adopt. Even as I write this I hear thin brittle walls of fear crack open after decades of resignation to my infertility. That the Alberta provincial child welfare authorities deemed me too single and too old (at forty-eight) for domestic adoption would prove only a minor setback.

In one child's going, mine would be born in south China, oceans away.

AUGUST 6, 1997

Dear Daughter,

Who dressed you in a special red quilt coat, swaddled tight in spite of August heat? Kissed you for the last time? Laid you wet with tears in another's arms—grandmother, father, aunt, husband, lover?

Who bicycled before first light to cradle you on the ground under the shade of bridge or palm, near enough to the road so the one who crouched behind the still green leaves could watch?

Who waited in the shadows until you were found?

Did passersby notice your cry?

Who found you?

Who knew?

THE BLANK PAGE

I want to write in detail about that room in a city, town or village where my daughter was born, but her origins are mysterious, shrouded in secrecy and hidden in bureaucracy. A wide river flows beneath the bridge where my daughter was found not far from the orphanage. A woman writhed in an apartment or house nearby or in a far-off place, under a clay-tiled roof or beside a concrete wall, on a farm, in a hospital or clinic. Her story exists somewhere in a place that won't be known. The map can't lie flat enough on this table to tell me how I might navigate to a place that only exists as an adoptive mother's dream.

JANUARY 1999, GUANGDONG PROVINCE, PEOPLE'S
REPUBLIC OF CHINA

On this first journey to Maoming, by plane, train, bus, taxi and van, my mind was overwhelmed with anticipation of a child as I talked excitedly to my travelling companion, my mother, who calmly prepared to meet her new granddaughter. Occasionally, I turned on the rented camera, but the video looped and bumped with every turn in the road making the recorded image as nauseating as any arcade's Drop of Doom. I remember the paved highway, fast-moving cars beside our bus, tense individual murmurs of eleven families anticipating their new child's arrival, a blur of square whitewashed farmhouses, walled courtyards, a water buffalo's lumbering gait, chemical belch of smokestack, cluttered metal of factory yard, the still pools of roadside water, green-spiked rice paddies neatly squared, ingenious farm plots snaking through ditch or road allowance, the scented shape of longan fresh from the tree.

Details of my daughter's orphanage lodge in my memory like night lights in a home. We visit the courtyard only. No foreigners allowed inside. Vines and pink-trimmed balconies edge every floor of the main wing where my infant daughter grew, one of many sleeping two by two in blue metal cribs. The courtyard is deserted except for a few older children dressed against the winter chill. On seeing us, the nanny hurriedly rushes them inside. A line of dark laundry for tiny invisible children hangs from the balconies of an adjacent grey cement structure. Ribs of bamboo scaffolding hide a new wing under construction, funded by foreigners' donations.

Mrs. Zhang, the orphanage director, asks whether I want to visit the place where my daughter was abandoned and without hesitation I say no.

How much does an adoptive mother's life begin with dissimulation, a first refusal that makes the story begin again? Did I not want this memory for my daughter to keep? Much as I told myself to remember every second, to document, for my daughter's sake, every location, every encounter, I wondered, did I want to erase this part of her history? What part of me liked to imagine my first meeting with my daughter as a new birth for the two of us, an erasure of long months of care by others?

ADOPTION, LIKE TRAVEL, EXPANDS THE WORLD YOU INHABIT

What is strange becomes familiar as the small being in your arms becomes as much of you as a child can be. And you become hers. At the end of five years you notice your behaviour has changed—sometimes for the better. While you never imagined your adoption to be a matter of altruism, you have become more generous with strangers. You seek nourishing communities and caring neighbours where you cultivate aunties and uncles for your daughter. Still an atheist, you join a compatible Unitarian congregation to surround yourself with others who care about what it means to live in a just world. Less mobile now that you clothe and feed and house a child, you contribute more to the well-being of those with less, especially motherless children. You are not able or willing to rush through life. You know more about your daughter's birth world, a smattering of language. You acquire new music and a library of books.

JUNE 2004, MAOMING, GUANGDONG PROVINCE

Your daughter's world opens you to the unexpected. Her questions become your own. When she is six, you return to her birthplace to seek a backdrop for the absent centre that is her first family. You want to people a landscape, find a substitute for the sudden erasure of genealogical connection.

In a small provincial Chinese city, you discover a rootless traveller's ease. At home in a strange land, you reinvent your desire. You once loved McIntosh apples; here dragon fruit turns you on. You thought the big sky of prairie or taiga lipped by Rocky Mountains thrilled your heart, but here you love the spare horizon, the beat-up lineage of a seaside resort, the South China Sea. In settled Western Canada you followed the clean order of gridded urban routes, but here your mind bends through looped rings of narrow streets. You liked the comfort of barely peopled spaces, but now catch your breath, sigh in the crush of bodies, the swirl of crowded squares. You found comfort in shades of grey monochrome, but now your eye is nuzzled by gold-threaded cobalt and red silk. You preferred the plain speech of a secular life, but weep in the incense fog under this blackened Buddhist temple roof.

Your centre of gravity shifts.

MY DAUGHTER STANDS AT THE ENTRANCE TO HER ORPHANAGE

She asks where she lived as a baby and I point to the building on the left, each floor lidded with balconies and hanging vines. The director, well dressed and cautious, ushers us into the reception room, acres of table ringed by chairs. My daughter wants to explore in the playground sheltered on the first floor. She likes monkey bars and shinnying up poles at home. Here she wraps her suntanned hands around the chipped paint of the swing's upper bar and looks into my camera's lens; her slim body hangs suspended, pink skirt, pink T-shirt, pink cheeks flushed by the heat of the tropical sun. Imagine the photograph: a glance, sadness deep in her eyes, the tentative upturn of her lips.

Afterwards I sit alone in the orphanage courtyard dwarfed by a giant white stone statue of "the one who loved China," Madame Ching-ling Soong, who had established the first Chinese Welfare Institute, a safe haven for surviving orphans after World War II. Just above us in my daughter's immaculate, illustrious orphanage, sixteen infants bounce in one room's shining new stainless steel cribs. Stuffed animals hang suspended just beyond their reach. My child's dark brown eyes are rimmed with a watery look. Madame Soong is obscured behind the pillar.

As we are about to leave, my daughter refuses to pose with me for a family portrait. Instead she stands on the other side of the lens and snaps my picture.

ALL ALONG THE RIVER, WE FOLLOW YANGJIANG ROAD

We photograph places where babies have been left. Here is one site, a stone's throw from the Hedong or Guandou police stations several blocks from the orphanage; or here in the bustling marketplace by Guandou Bridge; or here in front of the Yangjiang Restaurant renowned for its culinary treasures, *dim sum*, translated literally as "little hearts." Right here beside the spot where another child was found not long ago, I begin to imagine a crowd of shadows, invisible women and men crowding the streets, hiding behind the trees, waiting in doorways, casually dilly-dallying at a market stall to mull over fish or greens or a pile of shining key chains, all watching, all waiting for someone to look down, then look again; startled this time, they listen for the cry. Maybe they retrace their steps, stoop down and hurry away again. Maybe they say out loud, "Look, here's a baby." Or maybe they say nothing, pick the infant up, and show her to someone. Or they carry her into the restaurant and call the police. Or maybe they themselves take her to the station. One police station meets and conveys to the orphanage about ten children each year; nearby, another encounters even more.

When we arrive at the station where my daughter was first taken at three days old, her umbilical cord still attached, the chief of police can't stop patting her slender shoulder. Smiling, he bends down on one knee beside her to pose for the photograph. What must it be like to be the intermediary of so many children, bearing them from their mysterious past into an institutional future?

Standing at the market, hiding in the grove of palms or squinting into the sun on the Guandou bridge, my daughter frowns but doesn't say a word. Later she proudly tells a stranger, "I live in Canada, but I'm Chinese," explaining that Maoming is her favourite place in all of China, because "that's where my orphanage is."

On our visit to a Maoming elementary boarding school, where rural children are sent for a better education, the youngest dress as sunflowers to sing and perform for us. Only forty of the three hundred students in the school are girls. "Girls have more patience for farm work and stay in the countryside," a teacher explains. They might attend a rural school, but boarding school funds are reserved mainly for boys who will care for their elders and maintain the family name.

ADOPTION INEVITABLY SPEAKS THE "LANGUAGE OF CELEBRATION AND LAMENT"

You imagine her as Mother Moon, always present even when we can't see her. Over time, a particular woman's face comes into view. At first she looks like every other Chinese woman—the way some Caucasians say "all Chinese look alike" when they don't look carefully enough to appreciate the differences. You notice how this particular woman's eyes—beautiful, deep brown-black, almond-shaped—are tired around the edges. You imagine her up early to look after her children, only one of them official unless she lives on a farm and can justify more for the field labour they perform.

Today you watch as she takes her bicycle to the market before dawn to find her way almost by touch in the dark to the small shop where she sells soup pots and small wicker kitchen implements. Or you pick out her silhouette among dozens and dozens of women as she sits on the factory floor and in a flash sews the Disney T-shirt front to back, front to back, for eleven to sixteen hours, six or seven days a week. She maintains her quota in spite of her back, her fingers and the deterioration of her sight. Or follow her to where her walk ends in a rice paddy and see her hat dip to the rhythm of arms and torso as she curves into and over the green spiked water. Or watch her stretch a weary arm for the branch of lychee fruit, another migrant worker in the civil servants' ancestral farm. The surrounding hills are rounded with groves of trees or squared off in concrete-block solutions to overcrowded cities.

This woman birthed a most beautiful baby daughter in the early morning of an August day in 1997, somewhere near Maoming in the southern Chinese province of Guangdong. She knew that this child would disappear, never to be spoken of again. She knows this now and weeps.

FÚ

To become mother and daughter, we've both crossed great distances. Any woman who adopts at forty-eight knows that a midseason turning point can be a revolution.

Tattered pages of the *I Ching*, the ancient Chinese book of divination that I consulted as a hippie in 1971 become my transcultural adoptive mothering manual thirty years later. "The time of darkness is past," says the *I Ching's* six-lined hexagram *fú*. This image of earth over thunder means "return" or "turning point" when the December winter solstice marks the seasonal shift that stimulates good fortune. Here at latitude 53 where winter's night endures almost forever, signs of changing seasons are delayed. Chinese New Year fell in February this year. That's when millions of red paper squares, embossed with golden brushstrokes of the Chinese good luck symbol, clung to doorways from Beijing to central Alberta.

The ancients advise, "Position the golden strokes of *fú* upside down to ward off evil and bring great good fortune." This tradition began in the Qing dynasty (1661–1911) when one of the servants accidentally displayed the symbol for *fú*, or luck, upside down on the palace and storeroom doors. Justifying the error, the housemaster noted the word *dào* or "upside down" is the same character as "arrived."

Soon after I adopted Bao, our friend Rose from Shandong taped the red Chinese New Year sign to the oval glass in our purple Edmonton front door. For Rose, who knows the difficult trails of Chinese migration, my daughter and I have truly arrived—only luck, the one-child policy and uneven economic development could have brought us together to share this small house.

Luck is also often the topic of conversation when we visit the Garden Bakery for our tasty Chinese coconut buns: the friendly woman proprietor tells me my daughter is "lucky." In Noodle Noodle, our favourite restaurant across the street, uniformed waitresses echo these words. These brilliant Chinese women travel to Canada in search of a better life only to trade in their PhD in engineering or forestry for a *dim sum* cart, shift work in a water bottle factory, or an extra job cleaning houses for penny candy tips.

LOVE'S FORTUNATE PIVOT

"I'm so lucky, Mommy," says Bao as we nibble on the *har gau* shrimp dumplings, *dim sum* culinary treasures.

"Why, Bao?" I ask, knowing that when others describe our luck, the comment erases my own good fortune and the tragedy of her early life.

"I'm lucky because everyone loves me," she says.

At night my daughter looks up to make her wish. That faraway Chinese god of luck, *fú xing*, twinkles her starry eye at us.

Note

The phrase "language of celebration and lament" is from Jacqueline Rose's discussion of feminism in *On Not Being Able to Sleep: Psychoanalysis and the Modern World*. Princeton: Princeton Univ. Press, 2003.

DIVORCING
YOUR MOTHER

JODI STONE

STEP 1: RISE

Up until now your life has been a wrestling match, with obligation and guilt in one corner, free choice and self-preservation in the other. You have always known which corner wins the small battles—after all, you have been conditioned to revere your parents, respect your elders and "Honour thy mother." But now your bulging belly has added a potent element to the fight: a protective maternal instinct. Lean in close to the mirror. Closer. Examine those dark hollows above your cheeks. Raise your gaze a little and stare into those frightened eyes. See how they belong in a smaller frame, that of a young girl no older than eight? Now inhale deeply, right down into your extended belly. Breathe for both of you. Think of him and feel that tingle of clean tranquility. At the dawning of your son's life, it is time to reclaim your own.

STEP 2: REINFORCE

After your son is born, your mother will burst into your hospital room. You made a valiant effort to break ties with her during your pregnancy, for the sake of your son's health. That first phone call flagged it, when she moaned about her husband's inadequacies and ignored your good news. You tried to hold in your disappointment and shame for having thought she would be happy for you, but your husband watched you sob. It was when he asked Why put yourself through it? that you fully understood you had a choice. For the eight months that followed you did not call her and you felt free and clear. But now your term is up and tradition is stepping in. Know this: your husband will call her after your son is born and she will cause a commotion. She will ignore visiting hours, argue with doctors, and pull your fresh stitches as she strains to grab your son.

You will notice, not for the first time, that her eyes do not meet yours. At that moment, you know you cannot wish a mother-daughter bond into being; it doesn't exist and never did. This realization is painful, and in your weakened state it may be too much to handle. Secure some time with your son and lick your wounds. Then, when you are alone and ready, close your eyes and begin remembering.

STEP 3: REMEMBER MR. SMITH

Drift back to when you were seven years old. It is a Snow Day and you awake excited that school is cancelled. You hear your mother swear and slam the kitchen cupboard. You do not know why and your father is not home to translate. Your mother throws a jacket on you, neglecting hat and mittens because she is late. You are cold as you walk to Mr. Smith's house but are afraid to say anything because nothing can soothe her anger that erupts at everything lately. Recall the basement with the dim lighting and the stand-up piano in the corner where she left you. Hear her voice blend with Mr. Smith's behind the door. Feel the wooden stairs you climb up and away from spiders and strange sounds. See her face a horrid mixture of shock and ecstasy as you open the door and watch Mr. Smith climb off her. Watch her slap you, but do not feel it. You are no longer that seven-year-old girl.

STEP 4: REMEMBER BROKEN BLOOD VESSELS

Now you are thirteen. You are washing dinner dishes in the aftermath of an argument your mother has had with her new husband. She sits at the table, head down, with a butcher knife in one hand aimed at her bare wrist. She is crying and talking to a dead relative. You have seen this before and wish now that she had completed her treatment at the *nuthouse*—as she called it—instead of kidnapping you from your father four years earlier. At the time you missed her motherly comforts—her Sears perfume, her pickled beets, the special way she tied your hair in braids—and even prayed for her to come home. So when you saw her climbing through the kitchen window when your father was at work, you happily went with her and did not ask questions. Not even when Mr. Smith moved in. But now even he is gone and you are alone with her. Left to wipe her eyes and hold her and tell her that everything will be all right. But tonight you just don't feel like it. Tonight you want to be a child for once. You ignore her cries and head toward your room. But she is suddenly behind you with the knife at your back and it starts to dig in. She drops it and gasps. You turn to see her face cloud and distort again just before she starts hitting you, open handed, and yelling that you are ungrateful and useless and now your insolence has caused her to break blood vessels in her hands. She walks into the night without a coat, leaving you alone and clinging to a broken banister.

STEP 5: REMEMBER THE LEGION

This last recollection is of fresh memories. Approach them slowly. There, see that day in the Legion up north where she lives. You drove three hours to visit her on that weekend your husband was at a seminar. Of course you

287

called her, double-checked that your visit suited her well in advance of your departure. She was already drunk when you got there and out of a strange sense of obligation you drove her and her husband from their cottage on the lake to the Legion in town. There, she flirted shamelessly with a man. Her husband buried his face in a glass of beer across from her and you felt a sad kinship with him as you both tried to ignore her. Only when she stood up, pointed at you, and commanded all legionaries to look at your funny hair did you start paying attention. As you stood to leave, she pulled at your pants, slid them down mid-thigh and pointed out the difference between your build and hers. Later, as you drove her home, her head out the window like a dog, you tried to explain how hurtful her actions were. Then, by the side of the road, while you held her hair and wiped the vomit from her shoe, you were fairly certain she hadn't heard you.

STEP 6: REMOVE

This step may seem very simple at first. And, in truth, it is. You begin by not answering her phone calls. You strike her birthday off the calendar. You hide all the photos you have of her. Then you sit down, inhale deeply, and draft your letter to her. It should cover a few essential points:

a) State that you are writing to her neither hastily nor in anger. You have thought this over for the better part of thirty-five years and are ready to begin living your life in peace.

b) State that she is not a bad person but you are done with the horrible drama. You are done jumping every time the phone rings and crying for hours after. Life is precious and short and you want to start enjoying it.

c) Explain this new, overwhelming instinct that
instructs you to protect your son and finally yourself.
This means severing ties with her. You hope she
will understand one day.

Reread the letter before mailing. It is not advisable to call
her as her dry sobs will invariably sway your decision—you
will only kick yourself later. Prepare for her response: com-
mending you, thanking you for the honesty, explaining that
she is undergoing new therapy and is better now. You have
heard this all before. A phone call from her most recent ex-
husband will make you more comfortable in this difficult
time. He will tell you that she is getting married to a new
man, a man she adamantly denied any involvement with.
Smile at having learned the fine art of recognizing her lies.
You can practically feel her web slip from your shoulders.

STEP 7: RENEW

The first morning you wake after a complete month of
freedom from her you will be a little frightened. This is only
natural. It is the little girl inside of you who wants approval
and now has no mother to pat her on the head and tell her
she has made the right decision. This is when you realize
that you never really had an attentive mother in the first
place. Dry your eyes, dispense with self-pity, and vow to be
as good a mother as conceivably possible without smother-
ing your son. Walk to the nursery with your head high. You
are free. But now fresh worries will plague you: how will you
explain the missing grandmother, and will he accept your
choice? This is when you sit down by the cartoon lamp
beside his crib and begin writing another letter. This time it
is for him. Within it you will explain your perception of free
choice and condone it when laced with a healthy dose of

soul-searching and responsibility. After all, it is your responsibility to protect him. You need not offer intricate details but be prepared to tell the truth if he asks, because you will no longer lie for her. You notice that the filth on your conscience is beginning to wash away, and you like the feeling of lightness.

STEP 8: REVERE AND REMIT

You have undergone intense deliberation and countless sleepless nights and now it is time to enjoy the fruits of your labours. Take time to revere the child who gave you the strength to sever that bad relationship like a gangrenous limb. Sit in the room with him, enjoy his innocence—for you have done a lot to protect it—but *do* stay away from it. Don't touch it: it is his and his alone. When he is sleeping, get acquainted with yourself; admire this new confident woman capable of caring for her family. And in those moments of fading euphoria, when guilt starts jabbing at your shoulder with worn boxing gloves, learn to forgive yourself. It was never your intention to hurt her. In moments of doubt, when you wonder if your son will understand or if you are teaching him that relationships are disposable, rub that little scar on your back and repeat the word *protection* until it is no longer a word but a part of your breath.

STEP 9: RESUME

Now that the vacant space inside you has begun filling in with a liberating lust for life, know that she will often creep into your thoughts. Beware of times when you would usually think of her: holidays are hazardous. When you recall with awe the heaps of chocolate macaroons she prepared for Christmas mornings, take your hand off the phone and go back over steps 3 to 5 if necessary. Should you choose to tell friends and colleagues of your actions, on those days you will learn to dub *weak days*, be prepared for their shocked looks. They may never understand your situation. Divorcing a mother is not for everyone. A long history of tradition and societal expectation goes against your actions. At such moments breathe deeply, find your reflection, and note the distinct absence of that frightened girl behind your eyes.

STEP 10: RESTRAIN

As you raise your son, know the difference between involvement and interference. He is entitled to make his own decisions, as you were. Be forewarned that freedom may have a price. One day, when his independence blooms and his monthly visits trickle down to a thin, infrequent stream, take this book off your shelf, read over the section on free choice repeatedly until you fall asleep, spine straight, on your bare wooden floor. When you awaken with wide, clear eyes, revisit your reflection and look for similarities between yourself and your mother. The arms may appear different: hers were loose, yours may be worn and red. After you carefully consider the term *overprotection*, allow air to fill your lungs, wrap your arms around your body, and then smile in gratitude for having lived a self-guided life, unclouded, clean, and your own.

part four

GIFTS BEYOND RECKONING

CONSPICUOUS
VOICES

FRANCES ITANI

The afternoon my aunt's house burned down, she was upstairs, wearing an old pair of shorts and a worn blouse with the sleeves cut off. She was barefoot and had been cleaning house when she suddenly noticed large, quick flames about to encompass the room. She did not know, at the time, that the fire had started outside. She grabbed her toddler by the wrist and dragged him downstairs and out the front door. Fire trucks and police cars arrived; sirens were heard throughout the town, and people ran toward the scene. My aunt was distraught, but refused to leave. She stood in the middle of the road, in shock, and stared at murderous flames that raced within and from room to room, devouring everything she owned—every sheet and pillow and chair, her Sunday hat, her two good skirts, the rest of her wardrobe, the silverware she kept "for best," even her jars of pickled beets. One of her sisters was phoned by a neighbour to come and collect the child. A rumour about no insurance was whispered, with some authority, through the crowd. My aunt was put in the back seat of a police car to keep her away from the heat and devastation, but as soon as the car door was shut she wriggled across the seat and out the other side. Her pots and pans continued to melt. Her other four sisters arrived and dragged her away. The roof fell in with an astonishing crash.

297

I heard this story over and over during my childhood but, gradually, a second part was added on and this became the real story, the one that could make us laugh. It was the part about my aunt being driven to her parents' farm, the home of my grandparents, several miles outside of town. My deaf grandmother, shocked at her daughter's misfortune as well as her appearance, sat her down at the kitchen table, put the kettle on to make tea, and then disappeared upstairs. She came back down with a pair of pearl earrings and handed them to my aunt. It was all she could think of at the time. My aunt had nothing. No furniture, no food, not even a pair of shoes. But now she had a pair of pearl earrings. When this part of the story is told, along with the fire story, my mother and my aunts laugh until tears overflow from their eyes. I try to picture my grandmother, her concern and her instinct to help. I hear her voice, her oh so familiar, dulcet voice (a voice I managed to capture unwittingly on tape when my own children were toddlers). But everything else is drowned in the laughter of her five daughters. Even the aunt who lost everything she owned in the fire laughs until she cries.

I am not sure how and when I began to understand that these voices, the caring voices of the women who were in the foreground of my childhood, are the important voices inside me today. As a writer, I can only say that I am thankful. Each voice can be called up individually across the shared experience of birth and life and now death, for one of my aunts has recently died. I drove my mother several hundred miles so that we could say goodbye. When it was time for us to return home, I turned back to look from the hospital doorway. My aunt was propped up in bed, frail but vibrant, her sisters and sisters-in-law grouped around her. They were telling stories. There was a good deal of laughter while, outside in the hall, there were also tears.

The voice of my late deaf grandmother, no less influential, was absorbed by me in a different way. Deaf from the age of eighteen months, my grandmother married a hearing man. Together they raised eleven hearing children, five daughters and six sons, my mother being the eldest. Because my grandmother was an expert lip-reader, my language memories of her are largely visual. Her eyebrows are slightly raised; her steady brown eyes watch for the message on my lips. After a slight pause—for the moment of understanding—her quick and inimitable laugh is heard, and her kindness seen. If my grandmother happened to be worried or upset, she moved deeper into the silence of her internal world. At those times, she moved her lips as if talking to herself, but she turned aside so that no one could lip-read *her.* She twisted her wedding band around and around on her finger, a sure sign of distress. Or sat on a chair with one knee crossed over the other, her foot bobbing steadily.

•   •   •

I was a lurker, a watcher, a listener, beguiled by storytelling, enticed by the circle of laughter. And yet, after I began to attend school, all of this must have taken place during holidays—Easter or summer—because when I was four years old our family moved to a small village in rural Quebec, three hours by train from our much larger extended family in Ontario. My father and my uncles were present on many of these occasions, but it was the women who were my role models and they were the ones to whom I paid most attention. Still, I did not want to become these women—what young woman, after all, wants to turn into her mother? But at some level there was an awareness of being shaped by the collective of female voices. Voice and story. One story rolling into another. Teasing and laughter all around.

In my grandmother's kitchen, ongoing language was visible. Words were shapes—written into the air, or spilled from a pair of lips, or outlined by the speaker's hands. Because of my grandmother's deafness, even the youngest grandchild took part in the "acting out of language." When I recollect what seem to be the crowded scenes of my childhood, the aunts always have something in their hands: a spatula, a tea towel, a dishcloth, a rag. They are wiping—small children's faces, sticky fingers, the countertop, the heavy oilcloth on the table after a meal. There are children between their knees, iodine is being painted on scraped shins, burrs are brushed from someone's hair, buttons are being buttoned. But my aunts were equally at home with a wrench in their hands, or a screwdriver, a hammer. They could take apart a house and put it back together—and one of them did. They knew how to farm, how to pitch hay, how to saw steaks off a frozen side of beef, or raise turkeys. It seemed to me that my aunts could do anything they set their minds to. What I could not have articulated at the time was that I was watching and learning strength.

My mother and my aunts did not seem to take themselves seriously. At least, not publicly. One of five children, I had already learned that you had to laugh if you wanted to survive. Survival was more complicated as the family group became larger. If you could not laugh at yourself, you could be hooted out of a room. Every one of us, girls and boys, knew that. I also knew that life was not easy for the adults in my life—my parents, my aunts, my uncles. As children they had lived through difficult years during the Depression. After they married and began to raise children, they had crises and responsibilities to deal with. Still, it was impossible to be dreary in that family. As we spread out, stories criss-crossed the widening space and connected us back. Stories were ravelled and unravelled just as surely as porridge was made, dresses were sewed, shirts were ironed and children patched up and comforted, skills that every one of the women could carry out with expertise.

How else, except by being with my mother, my grand-mother and my aunts, would I have learned that the best way to measure a bolt of cloth is from nose-tip to fingertip, stretching your arm horizontally to one side? "It's a yard," my mother said. "A yardstick measure. As long as you don't turn your head." (It didn't matter that I had questions about the length of a person's arm, or that I would never learn to sew; I was more interested in the stories.) How else would I have heard of the jilted boyfriend who loved one of my aunts and never recovered after she married another man. Fifty years later, when he met her in the street, his lips shaped the silent words "I love you," because he remembered that she could lip-read. His wife was beside him and none the wiser, as the two walked past. How else would I have heard the expression that someone was wandering aimlessly, "like a buck in a rainstorm." *Buck?* I thought—or did she say duck? I didn't ask. Or the story of WeeWee the fish who died in his goldfish bowl and was floating belly-up, only to be revived because my aunt raced to the rescue and gave him a few drops of brandy with an eyedropper. And how WeeWee died again and again, surviving for another twenty-five years because he was sure to be revived by an eyedropper dose of brandy dripped into his bowl.

How else would I have learned about the hobos of the thirties when my mother was a child, men who made their way up the long and dusty lane from the rail yards and were never denied a meal at my grandparents' farm. My grandfather was absent during the week, because his work allowed him to be home only on weekends, but food was passed by his daughters through the doorway to the hungry men who sat outside in the shade while they ate. Or the story of my grandmother, trying to think up a special dessert for her children and serving peach halves in pink Depression-glass nappies that had been purchased at Woolworth's, five cents apiece. In the hollow of each peach half she added a half teaspoon of my grandfather's rum (while he was away) and a dollop of whipped cream. Money was scarce but milk and cream were in abundance on the farm, Depression or no.

Throughout my own childhood, if a visitor (or an entire family) arrived unexpectedly around mealtime—at my parents' home, or the homes of my grandparents or my aunts—an extra plate was laid, whether or not there was enough food. If there was not, the main course was shared and, to compensate, extra slices of bread and butter were heaped onto the platter in the centre of the table.

The generosity of spirit that surrounded me in childhood helped to shape my optimism and endowed me with hope. The adults of my world—especially my aunts and uncles—bestowed love and laughter, gifts beyond reckoning. The intimate and loving voices of the women helped me to find my own voice—as a woman, a parent, a writer. And though our large family is now widely scattered while generations continue to be added, and though my grandparents, four of my uncles and one of my aunts have died, the early voices still demand to be considered and heard. They are as surely inside me as an arrow is inside a compass. I could no more remove them than I could remove my own genetic code.

IN THE PRESENCE
OF GRACE

CATHY STONEHOUSE

JANUARY 7, 2003. VANCOUVER WOMEN'S HOSPITAL

It's 2 a.m. and I'm finally in labour. My husband, Wayne, lies on a foldout cot beside me while I toss and turn, nauseous and feverish from the prostaglandin suppositories placed in my vagina every four hours since ten o'clock yesterday morning. The contractions started rapidly, but for the last few hours there haven't been any. My body seems to have shut down. The night nurse fusses about, attempting to find a vein for an IV. Maybe I'll be the first woman ever for whom the hormones won't work. Perhaps they will have to cut the baby out of me.

DECEMBER 13, 2002

The first time we see our baby, she or he appears on the grainy screen of the ultrasound monitor in profile, one hand raised as if in welcome or dismissal. I want to peer closer, but am afraid to. The results of a routine test of my blood showed an abnormally high level of certain hormones associated with genetic disorders. Although they assure me that the test is renowned for yielding many false alarms, all I can think about is that this serene-seeming creature may be fatally damaged.

Later that day, while a long silver needle plunges into my uterus to sample my amniotic fluid, Wayne holds my feet and I try not to jerk as the pierced muscles go into spasm.

305

The doctor performing the procedure is holding an ultra-sound wand steady against my belly, enabling us to see the baby's echo once again. Our child is curled up like a hibernating mole in a corner of my womb.

CHRISTMAS 2002

The two-week waiting period for the amniocentesis results coincides with the Christmas holiday. After some debate, we decide to spend it with Wayne's family in the Okanagan. It seems like a better bet than sitting at home.

Yet there is no escape.

On Christmas Day we sit in Wayne's parents' sunny living room listening to an old recording of seasonal favourites, opening bag after bag of tiny sleepers, pastel crib linens and hand-knitted booties so small my thumb can barely fit in them. Everyone knows there might be a problem with the pregnancy, but once in motion the gift-giving train is hard to halt. Behind my cheerful exterior a sudden thought sears me: What will I do with all this if the baby dies?

DECEMBER 28, 2002

We're back home and the phone is ringing. My husband hovers, helpless, in the doorway while I grip the receiver so hard it squeaks. To disguise my pregnant state I'm wearing jeans zipped up tight, the straining top button lengthened with a rubber band.

"Hello?"

"It's trisomy-18," the midwife says matter-of-factly, and then, "It's a girl."

I bend over, cradling my belly, as if I've been kicked in the stomach.

The following day, the medical genetics counsellor at the hospital shows us pictures of trisomy-18 babies and lists our daughter's likely abnormalities: severe mental retardation, heart problems, liver problems, intestinal problems . . . most fetuses with this abnormality are lost to miscarriage. The odds are against even those that survive to birth: 90 percent die in the first month of life.

"But aren't there some babies who survive to adulthood?" I ask, hoping my child might somehow be the exception.

"No," the counsellor answers. "There aren't."

Our child's fate hangs over us like a heavy, metallic cloud. We know what we must do but not how to say it, the word "terminate" unspoken between us, with its kinship to the term "exterminate."

"If you decide not to continue with the pregnancy you have two choices," our doctor tells us. "A late-term abortion under general anaesthetic, or induced labour."

We opt for plan A. It seems the most painless: I'll be asleep and won't have to go through pointless pain. And although we've been told that seeing, even naming, our child will help us to grieve her loss, neither of us can imagine doing that. Rather than providing solace, the pastel pink hospital pamphlets with their reverential tone provoke in me an irrational rage: to hell with hospital bracelets and miniature nightgowns! If this is the end, let it be quick and clinical. I refuse to obscure this loss with sentiment, with angel wings and teddy bear smiles.

JANUARY 6, 2003

I've changed my mind. Lying in bed last night, I recalled the day, two months ago, when my daughter seemed to speak to me. Walking on the beach in the rain, I heard a little voice from inside say clearly *I'm a girl and I'm okay.* These words now seem like a cruel joke, but then again, perhaps they aren't—perhaps she *is* okay with her condition. And if she is, then I must be. I am, after all, this child's mother. Having made the unthinkable decision to end her life, the least I can do is to allow death to happen in the most natural, dignified way possible. Perhaps, in fact, this is what mother-hood requires of me—not to deny her, but to stay present with her through this dark passage.

My husband and I switch to plan B.

Now, the house feels strangely expectant, the congratulations cards I received when I spread my good news still displayed on the living-room bookshelf. Wayne and I get out our daughter's ultrasound snapshot, light a tiny beeswax candle in front of it, and attempt to say goodbye. But how to say goodbye to someone who hasn't arrived?

JANUARY 7, 2003

At 5 a.m. the grief of my loss twists me up in it like a tor-nado, carrying me away for a while. After crying for over an hour, I feel the contractions start up again, and now, at 8 a.m., the baby is ready to be pushed out.

"Try sitting on the toilet," suggests the day nurse, a sturdy Irishwoman who has seen many women through this procedure. She helps me up from my bed, places a plastic bowl inside the toilet seat, and I sit down. I feel something weighty pressing against the lips of my vagina, then in one slippery motion my baby comes out.

"It's happened," I yell, unable to actually name *it*. The nurse hastens back into the bathroom, bends down between my legs and cuts the umbilical cord. I get up hurriedly, aware of something red floating in the bowl.

I just gave birth! Back in bed, I deliver a tiny placenta. For an instant I feel like a real mother. Then the nurse passes my tiny daughter to me, laid out on a folded sheet. Dead.

Wayne nestles up close. "She's beautiful," he says.

Together we examine her minute body, marvelling over every inch. At 20 weeks, her skin is so thin you can see the veins and arteries beneath it. A bloodless umbilical cord bejewels her tummy. Her eyes are sealed shut. She looks strangely peaceful. And although her tiny ears and elfin features—the classic characteristics of trisomy-18 babies—confirm what the test results predicted, to us she is perfect, a wonder of vulnerability, blessed with the long, lean legs of my husband, her whole length a cooling presence barely bigger than my outstretched hand.

When the nurse asks if she can take her away for a few minutes, it's hard to let go. In one brief moment our daughter has charmed us completely: a being tender with newness, reminiscent of an exposed human heart.

When she comes back, the nurse has dressed her in a tiny woollen cap and pink nightgown. Although intended to acknowledge our baby's realness, this dressing up does not bring comfort; the minuscule clothes seem only to diminish her. Her body, fragile to begin with, without firm skin or fat, is not the body of a living full-term child but something more mysterious, something as soft as a chamois glove.

Oh, Grace, I say, stroking her torso tenderly. This is the name we have chosen for her—or rather she has chosen for herself. It arrived in me unexpectedly one afternoon this past week, while I was sitting, crying, at the kitchen table. *You chose well*, I say to her.

Eventually we're asked if we're ready to leave. Time is advancing, and there are questions to answer. Would we like an autopsy? Should the hospital mortuary arrange cremation, or will we? Throughout the process of letting go—the showering and dressing, the signing of papers, the choosing of a box, painted by volunteers, in which to store our baby's keepsakes—it's her name, Grace, that holds me together:

hopeful, respectable and slightly old-fashioned, like a cameo brooch or a pearl pin.

JANUARY 23, 2003

When we arrive at the crematorium it's raining. Nervously, we step into the empty chapel, where our daughter's casket, plain white and only a foot long, has been placed before the altar. In the absence of an audience it's hard to know what to do. Weep? Pray? I feel slightly embarrassed, as if my husband and I are overreacting by cremating and mourning a child who never actually was. Wayne and I caress the textured surface of the casket, while I suppress the desire to rip it open and look once again at the body that emerged from me.

Eventually a young man in a crisp white button-down shirt appears. He carries Gracie's casket down some steps and into a room we can see only through a pane of glass. Wordless, we watch him place her casket in the mouth of the oven, and close the door.

FEBRUARY 3, 2003

Gracie's ashes have arrived. What's left of our daughter is now just a plastic bag of grey-brown ash, no more than a couple of tablespoons, held together with a wire twist-tie and labelled with a circular metal tag.

We don't feel ready to scatter them. Instead we decide to put them in a cedar box I bought last November, intending to give it as a Christmas present. It's good to have a container, something firm to hold on to now that I feel skinless, without edges.

I'm still bleeding from the delivery, and my breasts have been leaking milk. These are not the only changes. It's as if, since my world shifted on its axis, a new law of gravity has set in, pulling some people toward me, pushing others away. Some friends will examine photos of Gracie, while others meticulously avoid using her name. I've realized that, although my daughter definitely existed, to some she will never be a person. Compared to living, breathing children, she is merely a lacuna, an absence, an unfortunate mistake.

I've also unearthed secrets. One of my friends has had several miscarriages, both my aunts had babies who died shortly after delivery, and my sister-in-law had a twin who died in utero. It seems these ghost babies are everywhere.

And I can't stop seeing live ones—giggling, snoozing, babbling, wailing—casually parked in strollers or backpacks. How can their parents ignore these precious live beings, even for a second? I have to restrain myself from rushing up to them shouting, *Wake up and look at your babies!* Desperate, demented, I walk on by with my mouth clamped shut and arms tightly folded.

Wayne and I line the cedar box with eagle down collected from Jericho Park and a handful of sheep's wool from England. Then we wrap up the bag of ashes in a fresh green Tibetan prayer flag. It feels good to swaddle Gracie.

We hold hands and gaze at our daughter, silently. We've become closer because of her, and I'm glad of this. Whatever anyone else thinks, we're Gracie's parents. And as her mother, there's an emptiness in me I want to savour. It's all I have left that holds her shape.

THE WRITERS' CIRCLE

ANDREA CURTIS

There's something feral about this street. Rambling, once-grand homes now carved up into cheap boarding houses jostle for sidewalk space with immaculately restored Victorians, boasting topiaries and fierce wrought-iron gates. The tension makes the spring air snappish, and I tug at my old coat, trying to close it over my newly swollen belly. The crackheads huddled in the slushy laneway north of Dundas turn to watch me as I pass. I pick up the pace, looking straight ahead and walking briskly in what I imagine is a purposeful way. I have to work harder at this than usual since I have taken on the unmistakable sway of pregnancy; it makes me feel unbalanced, vulnerable.

I turn in at a large three-storey brick house dripping with ornate blue gingerbread trim. There are two women dressed in puffy black jackets talking at the front gate. They watch me as I buzz the door. I can hear shuffling inside, then a pause while someone looks through the peephole.

"I'm here for the writing group," I say to the door, with as much conviction as I can muster. A staff member lets me in. She looks me up and down as if I'm a stranger, though I've been coming to this women's shelter to lead the Writers' Circle nearly every Thursday for three years. When I began volunteering here, I imagined I could share my passion for writing fiction and its therapeutic sidekick, journalling, with women who, perhaps more than most, need the release it can offer. I've stayed because their stories have stuck in my head.

I turn to my left and lean into a large room filled with people sprawled on mismatched couches and chairs, a television blaring the latest news about Michael Jackson. A few women look up and nod languidly at me.

Though the house has been stripped of most of its former grandeur, you can see its past carved in the ornate ceiling, intricate rosettes where crystal chandeliers must once have hung, deeply embossed crown moulding marking the perimeter of the room. There's a laminate bookshelf stacked with donated detective novels, and some plastic garden chairs. Two girls in low-rise jeans and hoodies are sitting at a coffee table playing cards beside a woman with matted hair who's rifling loudly through her collection of plastic bags.

I follow the staffer down the narrow hallway, past the pay phone, past a room misty with cigarette smoke, past the showers and staff room to the dining area where the writing group meets. There's a lingering aroma from the shepherd's pie that's just been cleared away and some people drinking coffee and Red Rose tea at the round tables. Behind them on the bulletin board promoting AA meetings and support groups for incest survivors and for women with AIDS, there's the faded poster I made last year to try to get more people out to the Writers' Circle. It's hard to know if it worked because the group, like the population of the shelter and this neighbourhood, changes nearly every week. Sometimes two women will show up, other times there will be two tables full. I take comfort in the handful of regulars who try to make it each week though they are no longer living at the shelter: There's the earnest young woman from Boston who lost her high-paying job at a big corporation and moved to

Canada because she was convinced the government was poisoning the water; the voluptuous forty-year-old with metallic green eye shadow and ruby lips who tells me she's a movie star, friend to Barbra Streisand; and the domineering girl with a wicked temper and a gaggle of followers who lost her baby to the Children's Aid. I've been rehearsing in my mind how to tell them tonight is the last time I'll be here.

Each week we write for a little more than half an hour, then we read our work out loud. I come armed with pencils and paper and a general topic intended to spark their creativity (the person who has influenced you most in your life, summer memories and so on). I act as a facilitator, answer spelling questions (despite my protests that it doesn't matter here), encourage the hesitant and generally try to make sure no one offends anyone else. Mostly the women ignore my topic and write about themselves. They all have stories.

Tonight, an unusually large group has gathered, and we have to pull together three tables to accommodate them all. Passing out the paper and pens I suggest that they write about how they felt today and whether their mood affected their relationship to others. It's often loud during this post-dinner hour, but tonight the only sound is the hum of the fridge and someone clanking dishes in the giant stainless steel sink in the nearby kitchen. As the women settle into their writing, one girl, her eyes like narrow slashes in a grey, drawn face, tells me about the stillborn baby she had two days ago and how tired she is from walking around and crying all day; another, staring vacantly out the window, says she'll write about how it felt when her husband beat her up.

I write, too. I have always loved the freedom of this hour, my anonymity in this group and their easy acceptance of each other and me. Tonight, maybe because I know it is my last, I find myself writing about things I can barely admit to my closest friends. How I'm terrified to be having my first child. How the first thing I did when I found out I was pregnant was burst into frightened tears, the weight of responsibility pinning me to the bed. About the way anxiety no longer seems so easy to shake off and how some weeks, I cry about nothing every day. I haven't told anyone this because I don't want to acknowledge my ambivalence by releasing it into the world. I worry, too, that my friends and family will think I'm a bad mother if I confess these uncomfortable feelings. Anyway, no one wants to hear about my worries. People steer me away, telling me how happy I must be, how I can't wait until the baby is born. To admit that the little fish thumping and swooshing inside scares me half to death is to transgress some unwritten social stricture. But here, with these women whose lives are complicated by drugs and deadbeat boyfriends, depression and poverty, my fears seem unremarkable. The words pour out sticky and messy like syrup.

It's seven-thirty by the time everyone has finished. The young woman with the tired eyes has slept through the last half hour, her cheek pressed against the plastic tabletop. Another girl left to have a smoke and didn't return. But the rest want to read out loud and a native woman volunteers to be first. She calls her piece "Anxiety." She's anxious, she reads from her hesitant script, because she's just been diagnosed with diabetes and she's worried about who will care for her and how she'll cope if it gets bad. She doesn't know much about the disease except that lots of people from her reserve have it. She's a former alcoholic and is thinking about quitting smoking, but even the thought of that makes her more anxious.

The others thank her for her story, and then one woman launches into a tale about her sister who has diabetes and is going blind and might have to have both legs amputated. I wonder momentarily if I should put an end to this story before the anxious woman is in tears, but the storyteller finishes before I can decide. Anyway, the diabetic isn't fazed. She asks questions and nods as the grim details of her future are catalogued in enthusiastic detail.

A small, neat, grey-haired woman from Finland goes next. In short, abrupt sentences, which she reads as if they were questions, she tells us that she's happy after a nice day spent wandering the Eaton Centre. I'm sure the other women are also wondering what she left out. They know better than anyone that no one comes here if they're really that happy. As she finishes I can see the woman beside her breathing deeply with her eyes closed, bracing herself. A striking Trinidadian with a smooth high forehead, she reads of betrayal and violence in a gentle island lilt that makes her story sound like a song. Her husband beat her, she reads. She doesn't know why because she loves him. She's been running it over and over in her mind and doesn't think she can forgive him this time. She's crying now, though you wouldn't know it if she hadn't stopped to swallow the lump in her throat and dab her shining eyes. Now there are tears on cheeks all around the table, nods of recognition. When she finishes everyone claps.

I read next, hoping to slip in while the others are still reeling from this last outpouring. The women listen quietly and nod at my story. I tell them I'm not going to be here for a while because of the baby. And they tell me that they also felt scared when they were pregnant, that I'm right to think that my life will change when I have children. That kids make you see everything differently. The woman who thinks she's a movie star tells me that what I really need is a good nanny. I laugh. It's a relief.

We listen to an addict talk about how frightened she is about trying to quit crack, and the movie star rambles incomprehensibly in beautiful, carefully chosen language. Then, over the PA, someone announces it's time for drop-ins to leave. We clear away the saltine crumbs and wet tea bags and most of the women scatter without saying goodbye or even collecting their work. Often I feel deflated at the end of our writing session, rattled by the litany of misery I've just heard, but today I'm oddly buoyant as I gather the pens and papers together. Liberated, perhaps, by my confession, thankful for the good-natured embrace of these women. The loud one, the woman who had her baby taken away by the CAS, helps me return the supplies to the staff room. As I'm gathering my coat and bag together to go home, she waits by the door and stops me before I leave. She puts out her arms and pulls me in toward her substantial bosom, squeezing gently. "Good luck," she whispers in my ear.

I walk home feeling light, even graceful, despite my lumbering gait. For the first time, I can see myself as I've always seen other pregnant women—strong, vibrant, beautiful. I talk under my breath to my baby. I want him to know about this unlikely community I've found, about the women who shared their struggles with me and made all of us feel stronger. As if in response, the baby jabs me in the ribs with a tiny, powerful foot. I rub the spot he kicked with the heel of my hand, and smile.

LARRY'S
LAST RESORT

SUSAN RILEY

My thoughts are a mother's thoughts as Jo strides toward our little family group in the parking lot in front of the grey institutional building, the sunlight on the mountains behind her. A faint breeze lifts a few strands of dark hair across her cheek. I'm glad she made it around that construction on the highway. She's too thin, I note, and her cheek is swollen from the dentist this morning. But here she is, bending to hug her great-aunt Lois, at eighty-four the sole survivor of the three siblings who grew up in Winnipeg during the Depression. The oldest was my mother, Jo's grandmother, Sheila.

Lois was always the shy one, haunted by secret fears, outshone by older sister Sheila, the beautiful and talented one. Lois was there with us fifteen years ago to bury my mother, struck down by Alzheimer's at a young age. Now Larry, the adored, fun-loving and risk-taking baby of the family, is dead too. And Lois, the last of the three, is here to bury him.

Jo reaches up to embrace Lois's husband, Tom, who will give the eulogy at this afternoon's service. My daughter Jo is twenty-nine and gorgeous (a mother's opinion), muscles toned by Pilates and marathons in Vancouver. She has worn simple black pants and a light sweater today, no jacket. We agree that her cell phone should be locked in the trunk and then remember we should leave our bags there too, for we know they would be searched at the door.

The last time Jo and I were in this parking lot, Uncle Larry came out to meet her. That was back in the spring, just before Larry's eighty-first birthday. He told us he really wasn't supposed to go as far as the parking lot but he wanted to say hello to his grandniece and her new husband. No one stopped him.

Uncle Larry collapsed in his cell in the Ferndale Institute in Mission, British Columbia, after surviving seven years in a federal penitentiary. He died in an Abbotsford hospital on Thanksgiving weekend. He would have been eligible for parole in another year and a half. Our family dream was that we would take him back to the Lake of the Woods in Ontario where he had built his own cabin retreat he called Larry's Last Resort when he was in his twenties. He was my favourite uncle back then, blond with soft blue eyes and a smile that promised an adult world full of fun. He had been a bomber pilot in the war and, when I was growing up, he had glamorous girlfriends who had jobs and drank beer on weekends, a red Alfa Romeo Giulietta Sprint sportscar and a 25-horsepower outboard motorboat that pulled water skiers bouncing over the waves. To us kids, his life was full of everything we dreamed about.

Aunt Lois had not wanted a service of any kind. This wasn't the way her brother's story was supposed to end. But the prison chaplain had persuaded her to attend a simple service in the Ferndale chapel. He said it would be "important to the men." The family agreed to come. I found an eight-by-ten portrait of Uncle Larry in his RCAF uniform, taken when he enlisted at eighteen in 1942, and brought it with me from Winnipeg. Lois and Tom worked on a simple message from the family for the service. We joked that Tom, a retired university professor, would finally have his dream: a captive audience.

Jo's arrival from Vancouver completes the group of about a dozen family members and friends and we file in together.

While we wait to sign in, we read the names of other inmates on a chart on the wall. We recognize one: Colin Thatcher, son of the former Saskatchewan premier, convicted of killing his wife in her garage, in a celebrated criminal case many years back.

The Anglican chaplain who will be leading the service is wearing long black-and-white robes that flap in the breeze as he leads our tiny family group to the chapel. I feel Jo beside me. Although she is looking around with curiosity, she is quiet. We hear the sound of inmates lazily batting tennis balls back and forth on the nearby courts as we move between prison buildings. At the chapel door, an inmate has been posted to greet everyone, to thank us for coming and shake our hands. The simple gesture is calming, a welcome human touch. The usher guides us into the dimly lit chapel with its rows of folding chairs, a red hymnbook on each, and a whiff of fresh flowers and candles in the air. The familiarity of this church-like place steadies me. Jo picks up a hymnbook and begins to leaf through it. Candles and flower arrangements adorn the altar at the front and the picture of teenaged Larry in his airforce hat, smiling with youthful enthusiasm as if the world were not at war, reminds everyone why we are here.

Jo and I sit together, Lois and Tom in the row behind us. The room holds about fifty and gradually the chairs fill up, leaving some of the men, dressed mostly in jeans and sweatshirts, lounging against the back wall and in the aisles. One man directly across from us has tied his shoulder-length hair loosely with a bandana; beside him another with a shaved head crosses tattooed, muscular arms over his chest. The men stare silently straight ahead at the altar, some clutching their hymnbooks, while the organist plays solemn church music.

Jo and I tense as the last family member slides into the row behind us. Larry's son, who lives in a group home nearby, has arrived. Today, he is accompanied by a guard and his social worker.

We all know the story. When the police arrived at the West Vancouver apartment in May 1992 in response to Larry's frantic 911 call, they found him covered with blood cradling the body of his wife of thirty-five years, blowing air into her lungs. It was a violent murder; she had been struck repeatedly with a knife sharpener and tinsnips. In the five years of trial after trial, Larry never allowed his defence to focus on the evidence that their son lived around the corner, suffered from paranoid schizophrenia and had a history of difficulty with his mother. Larry never let his lawyers tell the jury that like many parents he and his wife had never got around to telling their son he was adopted. It also went unmentioned that, the week before the murder, their son was deeply upset when his birth mother showed up after somehow managing to find him. Larry's calm insistence that "it must have been an intruder" could not be backed by evidence, and he was convicted in the third trial and sentenced to life—ten years without parole. He arranged through friends to make sure his son was well cared for and could come and visit him regularly. He always maintained in discussions with me that the justice system did not show an understanding of mental illness and, consequently, the mentally ill were not protected or given proper treatment inside. When I tried to disagree, he would remind me that he was side by side with the mentally ill in prison. I had no response for that.

Sitting in the chapel, our family is feeling all the sadness and seeming futility of Larry's sacrifice; comfort doesn't seem possible. But we have agreed to come, so we sit through the first reading and dutifully rise to sing "The Lord Is My Shepherd." The inmate in charge of transparencies switches on the projector light to reveal that the words to the hymn are upside down on the screen. The chaplain pauses, glowering through bifocals down at the offender, and waits, tapping the lectern with his forefinger. The inmate fumbles with the pile of transparencies but they are slippery and escape his hands, landing scattered on the floor. He scrambles to pick them up and throws another on the projector plate. Now it's backwards, still unreadable. He tries once more and, finally, we are able to read the words right side up. We begin to sing, our voices hesitant and flat. "Yea, though I walk through death's dark vale yet will I fear no ill . . ."

Tom is invited to the front to give his eulogy. The men chuckle when he says Larry wrote a story called "How to Escape." It turns out the story is about escaping in the mind, transcending physical barriers with imagined journeys. We assume this family message will mark the end of the service. Then the chaplain says, "If anyone else wishes to speak about Larry, please do so." He looks pointedly at the men across the aisle from us and nods to an anxious-looking, short, stocky man with a day-old beard. "Yes, Robert."

Robert shuffles to the front. He doesn't use the lectern but stands unprotected in front of us with a paper in his hands, which are visibly shaking. "I was illiterate when I met Larry," he begins. "I started in his creative writing class and now I'm a poet." He shares a poem with us that he and Larry worked on together. Each of the seven stanzas begins with "to my brother of words." Robert ends with the line "the spikes that come out of my mouth will be sharp as arrows and cutting like a hot knife through butter" then returns to his seat, his face flushed with pride and relief.

Next is Deltonia, a muscular, handsome man with a big grin and a wide white headband around his forehead. "I had a prepared speech I wanted to give the family," he says. However, it seems he couldn't get the printer to work, so at the last minute he decided to "speak from the heart." Until Thanksgiving weekend, he had shared a house with Larry and two other inmates. He tells us how, just last week, he was troubled and depressed. Larry noticed and asked what was wrong. Deltonia explained that his one-year-old daughter had been having seizures and he was worried about not being with her, about how his wife would cope. "Larry taught me to meditate and relax. He said to start from the top of my head and slowly work down to my toes, concentrating on relaxing each body part. And, you know, it worked. I started to feel better."

The next speaker, an older man with a soft voice and calm expression, talks about Larry as a father. "He was a devoted father. He was determined to find out every medical fact about schizophrenia. He was sure he could cure his son."

They come to the front one by one, six of them, to speak about Uncle Larry and what he meant in their lives. Because visiting was difficult and always under surveillance and because Larry didn't write about these men in his letters, our family, before this moment, knew almost nothing about Larry's life over the past seven years. As the men tell their stories, we slowly begin to understand the profound effect Larry had on their lives in that world hidden from our view. We sit in rapt attention as this touching picture emerges, and gradually the cloud of sadness and futility hanging over us begins to lift.

We are invited to stay for coffee and dainties after the service. The inmates have been baking and a table at the back is piled high with Nanaimo bars, iced cupcakes, chocolate chip cookies, banana loaf and lemon squares—like the ladies' auxiliary table at any church bake sale on the Prairies.

As we chat and help ourselves to cookies, I watch my daughter. A young man in baggy black pants, with metal studs in his lip, nose and ears and Walkman earphones draped around his neck, is earnestly talking to her in one corner, his face leaning close to hers. My first thought is that he might be bothering her. I quickly join them only to hear her suggesting movies he might like. An East Indian inmate tells us Larry was great because "he had been in the war and he knew things—like how to make bombs." Everyone laughs and we suggest perhaps he shouldn't be saying that in here. He adds, seriously, that he couldn't speak a word of English when he was sent here and that Larry taught him ESL.

Deltonia, a former U.S. Marine, now standing near us, says some of the older inmates have a rough time on the inside, but not Larry. "We felt respect from him and so he got our respect right away. No one would dare touch Larry with us around—we took care of him." Another gift for the family.

Our initial trepidation gone, Jo and I are now eagerly sharing stories with the men. We tell them about the time Larry got in trouble in university when he flew his rented plane dangerously close to the ground trying to drop pamphlets for the campus election. They tell us Larry was given a motor scooter when his legs got weak and he drove it like he flew a plane, with speed and precision. As chapel was about to start on Sunday mornings they would hear the scooter roar up and stop within inches of the wall and, moments later, Larry would limp in grinning. When the time comes to leave the reception, we wish everyone good luck.

But we know we're the lucky ones. By whatever combination of fate and circumstance, we are able to walk out into the sunshine and go home.

As Jo drives me back to Vancouver, we talk the whole hour and a half about family, our lives and whether we're making the most of them, about success and how it's measured. We remind ourselves that taking risks by entering uncomfortable places can open up new ways of seeing. We're both lawyers. In law school we learned about the concepts "beyond reasonable doubt" and "innocent until proven guilty." We wrote exams in criminal law, applied legal reasoning to cases and learned that people with mental illness could be found "not criminally responsible." But today we discovered how all this can play out in the real world, where someone like Larry could be found guilty "beyond a reasonable doubt." Today we are humbled by the complexities of "justice."

Even though I didn't always agree with Larry, I know he did the only thing he could as a parent and lived the consequences with dignity and meaning, not self-pity. And to add to the richness of this day for me, my daughter and I shared Larry's unexpected lesson together.

MY FATHER'S
LAST GIFT

NORMA DePLEDGE

Like many men of his generation, my father saw his main role starting and ending outside our home. He was a man's man, beyond the world of women and children my mother and I lived in. When friends, neighbours, or even his own father died, he handled arrangements purposefully, appearing not bereaved but simply strong. He seemed to stand above—or at least outside—the stresses that shook my mother and me, taking my mother's chronic sadness in stride and not apparently affected by it. My mother and I reaped the rewards of his stability: through his work, he kept a roof over our heads; through his public life in many service organizations, he guaranteed our place in the community.

As a child, I felt great pride in him. I remember a July 1, Dominion Day, when I was ten. My father had parked our car at the best spot on the parade route. I was sitting on the hood, wearing my cowboy hat. I could smell the horses, hear the high-strung clatter of their feet on the pavement. There were rodeo clowns throwing saltwater toffees to the crowd and kids like me swarming into the street, then darting back to our mothers' skirts, pockets full of candy. I remember the soft slump of toffee on my tongue, the bicycles with crepe paper threaded through their spokes and frames outlined in Kleenex flowers, the John Philip Sousa band, the floats drifting past like tall ships, the stampede queens in swimsuits.

Then, at the end of the parade, came the part that only the men stayed to watch: the balers, tractors, swathing machines, and last of all, the combines. And my father, standing on the rung of the ladder that ran up the outside of the cab of a combine, hanging on with his right arm, riding along above the crowd on the outside of the roaring machinery, talking with a man who was driving, his head thrown back in laughter. He was grand—tall, straight, and seemingly set apart—not like the men watching from the sidelines or hurrying back to a car or truck, carrying a kid in one arm and dragging a bicycle along with the other. I was proud of my dad, proud that he couldn't be made soft by people like my mother and me.

The combine passed so close I could have called to him, but I didn't. He was separated from me by a gulf I would never have presumed to shout across. But I do remember a kind of longing—longing to know what he and the driver could possibly be saying to each other, what it must be like to have him climb up the side of a cab just to be with you.

I grew up, unwittingly following in his footsteps, focusing on security and doing everything I could to appear self-sufficient. Turning away from things that might make me soft, I poured myself into my education and later into my job. I took control and I worked unstintingly to maintain it. No one needed to worry about me. I was fine.

At times, I carried a heavy weight of sorrow over the disappointments in my own life, and I knew, in those rare moments when I was honest, that I would have given anything for my father to hold me like a child and make everything better. But I also knew it was never going to happen, so I convinced myself that I didn't need him; after all, he didn't appear to need me. Over the years, to protect myself from the hurt of his indifference, I developed an armour of disdain and dislike. And so the decades passed.

•   •   •

After my mother's death, when my father was eighty-two, he and I were thrown together because I didn't have the backbone to abandon him altogether. His response to grief was rage. He stormed through the days, ordering me to do one job after another. I felt mean-spirited when I refused, yet I often did. I also felt unnerved watching him blunder ahead, wrecking everything he touched.

He painted the inside of the house, but his eyesight was so poor he couldn't differentiate between the strips he'd already covered and those he had not. He had chosen an untinted white. I could imagine him going to the hardware store, picking up a can, taking it to the counter. "Now that's an exterior paint, Jack," they would have said. "Are you sure that's what you're looking for?"—knowing him, knowing that he was too unstable on his feet to paint, knowing, as everyone in the town knew, that he'd just lost his wife, that a man who'd vested his life in being in control was disintegrating.

"What the hell do you know!" he would have barked at them. "I was painting before you were even born."

When I saw what he'd done, I felt childishly frightened, grief-stricken and trapped. The once-green walls of what had been my mother's music room were a crosshatch of roller marks—a diary, a record. He'd reached up and swiped at ceiling tiles, covering no more than two-thirds of the space, catching the metal frames on some of his passes, missing them on others. Slops of white paint had splattered the carpet and run down the walls like slow rain.

I was desperate to turn away and run. I wanted to yell at him to stop making such a terrible mess, and I was ashamed that a daughter could be so mean. When he wasn't looking, I broke down in tears.

Before long, he couldn't stay in the house by himself. After a fall, he ended up in hospital and then in a seniors' lodge—an independent living facility. Single room; single bed. A cell with a television. His rage grew and he took it out on everyone, including me. He demanded that I find him something to do before he went crazy. Then he ranted at the stupidity of what I suggested. He ordered me to get him out of there at least for an afternoon, take him to the bank. Then he shouted at the tellers. I did laundry; I cleaned up urine on the floor of his bathroom. He bellowed, "For Christ's sake, leave things alone."

On my visits, I began to notice how many people were watching him, waiting for him to screw up: the lodge administration, the homecare people, staff—alert to any evidence that he could no longer muster the level of independence demanded by independent living facilities. My father seemed to go out of his way not to disappoint them, either unaware or not caring that each time someone other than he carried his meal tray, each time he refused to take a pill, each time he wet the bed, lashed out at a staff member, or caught his foot on the edge of a carpet and fell, each time he cried— all these deteriorations were tallied up. I was anxiously aware that when he'd made one mistake too many, he would be forced out. At last, my father and I had something in common: we both hated the lodge.

Sure enough, the day came. Dementia and Parkinson's had gone too far. He was having more and more trouble walking. He couldn't control his bladder, and he was refusing to come to meals. I fought the administration because, like my father, I had grown angry at everything. But the decision was out of my hands. They moved him to an auxiliary hospital.

Once he was there, there was nothing left for me to do for him. His laundry was whisked away daily, his meals were delivered, a catheter took care of the incontinence. Even the bed was automated. Every few minutes, the motor kicked in, dropping the mattress away from his heels where blisters the diameter of baseballs formed under his translucent skin. The bed also shifted his feathery weight away from the bedsore that grew ever larger on his left hip. At first, he thought the motor in the computerized bed was an electric current. He would fight the sleeve of his hospital gown, his agitated fingers struggling to uncover the skin to show me that he was being electrocuted. "For God's sake, shut it off," he would order me, partly in anger, partly in fear. I wanted to do it for him and end his distress, but I knew it would only make things worse. He couldn't understand why nobody would help him, especially me.

Then, thankfully, for no reason I could fathom, he seemed to lose track of the distress. The fight went out of him. But when I sat beside him as he slept, his body relentlessly on the move, raised, lowered, rolled, shifted, the perfect solution for his fragile skin, I wanted to tell him I was sorry he'd been robbed even of the power to be still.

Although he slept much of the time, the two of us also spent many hours sitting in his room, waiting. Circumstances had thrown us into the same small box and left us there. Out of desperation one afternoon, I suggested that we sing. "How would you feel about a little tune, Dad?" I asked, and he said, "Why not?"

They'd gotten him up that day. He was sitting in his wheelchair between the bed and the cupboard. I remember it so clearly. I pulled my chair up in front of his and we sat, knee to knee. I can still see the thin concave of his chest over which his loose sweater drooped. I remember his hands folded together in his lap, his voice thin and reedy. I remember him reaching for the notes, the catch in my throat when he missed them. We sang the oldies with only the hum of a computerized bed for accompaniment.

The second time, or maybe the third or fourth—it became our routine—I brought a little handheld tape recorder and we made a recording, so I've got one of his chuckles on tape and a little conversation that I treasure: "How about 'I'll Be With You?' I asked. "Oh, you decide," he said. "You're drivin'."

In time, we branched out from singing and started looking at old photograph albums to fill the hours. We tried to remember names and places. We talked about memories, and I wrote them down as if he were dictating a diary to me sixty years after the event. We talked about his dying and what I wanted him to know before he left me. We even talked about my mother, whom he hadn't mentioned since her death. I'd seen him rage against impotence and fallibility. Now I saw him cry in grief.

•   •   •

One afternoon toward the end, bedridden and in pain, my father gave me all that he had left to give. It happened when a nurse came to get him up. The only way he could be lifted out of bed was with a hoist. The staff used it to transfer him to a wheelchair so they could take him down to the bath or lift him into a wheelchair bed so he could escape his room for a few hours. It was after lunch. Dad and I were reading the local newspaper when the nurse came in.

"I better go now," he said to me when he saw her, as if he were ending a phone conversation. "There's someone here."

She leaned across him, slipping her arm behind his back, rolling his body over as if he were inert. She pushed the sling under him, rolled him back, and hooked the metal rings over the stork-like bill of the hoist. Then she flipped the switch and winched him slowly skyward, the slack going out of the straps first, his arms following the ascending chrome bar, drawn up over his head. The sleeves of his gown dropped back, baring loose flesh. The nurse told him, "Hang on, Jack" as he gripped the chrome trapeze bar, just as he had gripped the bar of a combine forty years before, only now his arms were trembling with effort. His softness resisted the drag, and the downward pull of gravity made his body droop like dough while his arms, raised above him, looked as if they would pull off in ropey strands. Then he was clear of the bed and, shockingly, he swung forward, suspended in space, his white knuckles clenched around the bar, his swollen knees naked, his hospital gown flapping open behind him. The thing I remember most, which brings me both gratitude and pain, is his mouth twisted into a determined grin, a reassurance, as if irony could erase the helplessness and ignominy of it all, as if he were letting me know—as I think he had always tried to do—that I didn't need to worry about him, he had everything under control.

Many times during those two terrible years, I prayed for it to be over. No one could have convinced me that having his life end this way was anything but a travesty. But I came to believe that without my father's catastrophic disintegration, I would never have come to know the person he had been at pains to hide all his life. And without my own despair, which left me so vulnerable and open, we could never have discovered how deeply we loved each other. We learned it only because we reached a point that we had nothing but our presence left to give. It was the one thing we hadn't thought of before. It turned out that it was all either of us had ever wanted.

MOSS CAMPION

C. B. MACKINTOSH

High on the ridge of Cascade Mountain, far from the swarm of tourists on Banff Avenue a thousand metres below, lives one of my perennial heroes. She makes her home in open, alpine spaces. She thrives, small and determined and hopeful, in a windswept, barren landscape of talus and scree. Where grey-weathered slabs of limestone pierce the sky with their jagged teeth, she flaunts her softness and her colour. Her name is *Silene acaulis* and she is a member of the pink family.

I first met Silene in 1994, when I came to Banff to work for the summer and fell in with some local kids, a group of fun-loving, competitive cross-country skiers who went for three-hour bike rides after work and climbed mountains every weekend. They asked me along and, naively, I went, which was how I often found myself, weak-kneed and light-headed, on Silene's terrain.

They called her moss campion, her common name, and they warned me early on to watch for her. Though she is one of the faster-growing alpine plants, her existence is delicate: her first flower won't bloom for ten years, and a single misplaced human step could destroy her. As my new friends led me into the backcountry, stepping from rock to rock to avoid landing on living things, I could see that they cared for Silene; they respected her tenuous hold on the ground they walked on, and they taught me to do the same.

Most young people come to Banff to leave their cares behind. I suppose the truth is I came to Banff that summer to get away from my mother. Some part of me believed that, with only a sleeping bag, my hiking boots and a plane ticket, I could save myself from drowning in her quicksand moods; I could sever her hold on me and rise to the surface, three thousand kilometres from home, buoyant and happily sputtering.

There were other things too, other reasons to flee: poor job prospects, a failed relationship. But my mother's depression was a dark shadow, a wall of snow moving up the valley toward me, threatening to obliterate the landscape and turn the rocks beneath my feet all slick and untrustworthy.

I stayed in Banff. I learned to dress for extreme weather. Following the heels of the person in front of me up the eight steep kilometres to Cascade's natural amphitheatre, I ignored my body's objections, my face burning, my arms heavy, my heart pounding in my ears, drowning out the sound of my friends' easy banter. As their voices drifted farther up the trail away from me, my head swam with slogans and clichés: *One step at a time. Just do it!* I kept my head down so I couldn't see how steep the path was ahead of me, and measured each breath to keep from hyperventilating.

If I kept moving, I had a purpose. At the end of an eight-hour hike, life's big questions were diverted to the comforting dilemma over which to do first: sleep, shower or eat.

Altitude became my therapy. When I stood on a mountaintop, there was so much *space*; it absorbed me, carried me out into the dizzying gulf between Mount Rundle and Cascade, and wove me into the sky-strewn landscape. I was so small, and yet I felt so *mighty* to be part of all that lives and grows at the tops of those lofty peaks.

In Banff, people were always leaving. I could try on a whole new version of myself each time the ski season ended, each time the air turned sharp, the days shortened and the summer staff returned to school in the East. Even the mountains, my steadfast sentinels, bathed in sunset or clutched by clouds, never looked the same.

I moved a lot. I changed jobs a lot. Boyfriends, co-workers, roommates, even my cat, came and went. I went back to Ontario, but only to visit. My mother was in and out of the hospital, taking too many, or not enough, pills. Everything there was the same. Suffocating.

I lived alone in an apartment above the bookstore: one small windowless room, surrounded by slamming doors and an alley that erupted with garbage-truck noise every morning at 7:00 a.m. This was not home to me. Home was the river's edge, where I would break from my run to watch the water pucker and swirl, its mirrored surface mountain-deep. Home was the beating of ravens' wings, and moonlight casting a tangle of tree shadows on the forest floor; the swish-scuttle of stone on ice, and the other-worldly call of elk rutting. Home was that moment outside time when the sound of rocks falling meant the rocks had already fallen.

Relationships were steep, sliding slopes of scree. After a string of boyfriends who either wanted too much or too little of me, I began a year-long, self-imposed moratorium on dating. I bought myself Bernard Callebaut chocolate. I lit candles and drank wine with dinner. I carried my notebook and pen to the sun-drenched tip of Mount Fairview, in Lake Louise. I travelled alone, overseas. I went to work. At night, if I needed company, I wrote, or read, or watched TV. Ten months later I met Lach.

We met in January. In February, we lay in each other's arms, huddled beneath a nylon sleeping bag in his shivery basement suite, naming our children. Being with him was like being in the backcountry, beyond the trappings of civilization, outside the constructs of time and productivity. He was my hard-earned destination, a place of rest and beauty where I could allow myself to just *be*.

Love happened like a windstorm, a sudden gust felling trees, thinning the forest to reveal a path of limitless possibility. We moved in together. We hiked, played tennis, went to concerts, went to Paris, got married, bought a house, moved to Canmore. Making a life together, and making a child together: that was our dream.

•   •   •

Jerked upright in bed, like a marionette. *By what?* Silence. Drenched in sweat. My T-shirt clinging to my body. My ears straining for the sound of her while the house holds its breath. I wait. *Nothing.* The clock glows 3:00 a.m.

Two hours since the last feed, she'll be waking soon, God. Should try to get more sleep. Need to shower. Change my clothes. Dark wet circles dilate across my chest; my breasts are full, throbbing. I get up, shivering in the nighttime coolness of the house and cross the hall to where she sleeps in her bassinet. She's on her back. Her arms are bent up by the sides of her head in a body builder's pose, her little hands forming fists. *So strong, so beautiful.* Her face turned sideways is peaceful, her features delicate. I want to pick her up and hold her to me, smell her baby smell, nose pressed to the top of her head. Then: *What if I pick her up and throw her out the window? . . . That's crazy. It's just . . . I don't know . . . I'm so tired, my incision hurts, everything hurts . . .*

My mind plays these tricks, creeps up on me when my guard is down. Like yesterday, on my way downstairs to the laundry room, past the side door, a thought, a cat-like pouncing in my head: *I could just walk out* . . .

I leave the baby's room, turn into the bathroom and strip off my clothes, stare at the body in the mirror, at the long scar across the pubis and the bulging flesh above and below, at the staple marks. The breasts are twice their normal size, pale and luminous and marbled with veins. The face is pallid, the eyes abandoned, like vacant windows. *Who is this woman?*

I hear the shower door close, feel hot water pouring down my face, neck, breasts. Cold air shocks the parts of me the water can't cover. Afterwards the towel is sandpaper on my nipples. I peer down to examine them and cringe at the angry red slashes I will soon be offering her hungry mouth. *Will life ever feel normal again?*

My mother has come. While I weather this storm of postpartum depression, she beams with a love for my baby that I cannot feel. She is strong now, thriving on the hope that sprouts from new life, new beginnings. As I cling to her lifeline of clean counters and folded laundry, I reach for her hard-earned understanding of what it means to survive.

It is April 2004. I am alone, now. While my husband goes off to work each day, I crouch in the corner of the living-room sofa, my baby balanced in my arms, the sun beaming like an alien spaceship behind the closed blinds. I have survived the first six weeks.

Mostly I stay indoors, topless, my nipples smeared with lanoline, or air-drying in breast milk. A soundtrack of screaming Oprah fans accompanies my scenery of failures and foreign objects—dirty dishes, stuffed animals, scattered laundry, an electric breast pump, a vibrating bouncy chair.

Venturing into the world outside my living room is an exhausting feat of logistics squeezed in between sleeps and feeds. Against a backdrop of world-class-tourist-destination peaks, I push our all-terrain stroller slowly around the neighbourhood, wary of bumps, fending off the slightest breeze with binder clips and a receiving blanket.

Back inside I cling to the couch, my mind held hostage by the weeds growing in our yard; the dust-streaked windows; the empty flower boxes. I sit motionless, watching the neighbours industriously cutting and watering their lawns, planting their gardens, paving their driveways.

I have forgotten what wilderness is. I have forgotten Silene, who among the arid, ancient-seabed shards, with no soil or water within a human arm's reach, sprouts her cushion of tiny, bright green leaves.

Ten years ago, as the wind whipped my hair into my face and I looked for a safe place to plant my feet, Silene showed me the strength and beauty of her vulnerability. Like grass growing up through a crack in the concrete, she showed me how, one tender green shoot at a time, Nature reclaimed the old mining town of Bankhead, at the foot of Cascade. And as I climbed higher up the ridge, my lungs aching, my heart beating its way out of my chest, it occurred to me that *I* might belong to the same glorious, vital, and yes, obstinate life force.

It has been ten years since I first saw myself in Silene, and in my stillness—immobilized on the couch, my baby latched to my breast—I can't see that I am blooming. I can't see that in this new wilderness of motherhood, my roots are growing deep; that my roots will sustain me.

•   •   •

When Amanda is three months old, I order a backpack carrier from Mountain Equipment Co-op. After inspecting and adjusting all the straps and clasps, I snap her in, hoist her onto my back, and check us out in the bathroom mirror. We look happy.

I decide to take her for a test run up Cougar Creek. It's June. All spring, the sun's rays have been gathering strength, and a steady trickle of water winds its way down the creekbed toward the highway. I hear the sound of it, like laughter rippling through a crowd, gently dissipating. Summer is coming.

Pavement turns to gravel, and gravel gives way to a worn path through rocks and boulders, where Silene waits. Hoodoo sentinels guard the cliffside on my left, while across the creek, on my right, the bright red roof of a modern ranch house gleams against its backdrop of evergreens. I pause and crane my neck around, trying to catch sight of Amanda in the carrier behind me. All I want is to watch her, my tiny, triumphant pink flower, seeing everything for the first time.

ANIMAL LESSONS

LORNA CROZIER

Mark Twain claimed that if a cat were crossed with a human it
would be to the cat's disadvantage. But oh, what we would know
of night, leaf stutter, mouse quiver, the sinful taste of birdsong on
our tongues!

On both sides of my family there is a penchant for drink
and horses. My maternal Welsh grandfather brought the
two together. His father was a wagoner, working on an estate
just north of the border, near the town of Shrewsbury where,
my grandmother said, the church was round so the devil
couldn't corner you. From the time he walked straight-
backed out of school in grade four because the teacher
wrongly accused him of cheating, he worked every day
beside his father, taking care of the horses and driving wag-
ons back and forth from the fields to town. He was allowed
to ride one of the draft horses if he wanted to go off on his
own after the farm work was done. The gelding he chose was
a Shire named Billy, seventeen hands high and an uncommon grey with white feathered fetlocks above hooves that
spread wide as platters on the plowed fields.

When Grandpa reached drinking age, he and Billy
made nightly trips to the local pub. Luckily for him, my
grandfather was a singer like many of his Welsh country-
men, and inside, at a table near the window, he bartered a

song for his first pint. Perhaps he wasn't melodious enough to get a second or a third sent his way. Those were provided by Billy. It worked like this: my grandfather didn't allow himself to down his first beer. He had to have faith like the thirsty man who primes the pump by pouring a ready bucket of water down the top, believing the sacrifice will pay off in a fresh stream gushing from the spout. When Grandpa raised his pint, Billy, tied up outside, poked his head through the open window and guzzled the beer down, his master feigning surprise and outrage. The patrons were so delighted they kept the drinks coming for the man and the insatiable horse until closing time when the two would stumble home in the dark. Grandpa said he didn't know who was the shakier on his legs. Some nights he thought he'd have to carry Billy on his back.

*   *   *

Unlike the dog, its opposite, a cat shuns anecdote and goes for the lyric. Know that a cat is music given bone and muscle and the grace notes of paws.

*   *   *

The story of the drunken horse sits side by side with my mother's tales of my grandfather's strictness and pride, his meanness to her and her six siblings on their Saskatchewan farm. As a kid, if she hadn't done the chores exactly as he'd wanted or if she'd come home late from a dance in the schoolhouse three miles down the road, he went after her with a willow switch, slashing at her bare legs as she squirmed on her belly into the farthest corner under the bed. Though he'd mellowed in old age, his daughters, wary of his temper, tried to keep me and my cousins from getting in his way.

Often when the family gathered at the farm for holidays and celebrations, he'd retreat to the barn to curry the wide backs and haunches in the stalls or haul hay to the feed troughs, the tall animals swinging their massive heads to watch him lift forkfuls of dry grass. The qualities the Shire draft horse was bred for—endurance and willingness to work—were also his, and almost all I got to know of him.

355

*   *   *

A cat sleeps sixteen hours a day because owning so much wears him out. "In a cat's eyes, all things belong to cats," so the English proverb goes.

*   *   *

Bitterness intact, my grandfather pounded home his hatred for teachers and school, told me to pinch a dog's ear to make it listen and to down a healthy dose of castor oil to clean a body out in spring. His and Billy's shenanigan is the only complete story I can remember him telling. It shows a warmth I never saw in him, a sweet affection for a creature that was more to him than just a beast that pulled a plow or wagon and lessened his own heavy labours on the farm. I tell it to myself over and over because it gives me something I need to know: Nothing and no one are wholly what they seem, especially those difficult to love.

Sometimes I think we're allotted a predetermined amount of pleasure that we can take from life. The measure the blessèd receive is enough to fill a water tower, a bounty that would provide for all the houses in a town. In my grandfather's case, his limit was a dipperful. He used his pleasure up when he was young except for what he kept alive in Billy and their story. Thinking of my grandfather and that horse, the two alone weaving their way down the narrow country road under stars unwashed by city lights, both having to rise at dawn to work in the fields, I feel a tenderness for what gets lost in living. Now when I give my horse her head she leads me to the country of my grandfather's birth and the years of his young manhood. Thin child from the future, in the barn's close scent of hay and horses, I wait for him and Billy to come safely to their rest before the sunrise, a rest companiable, bone-deep, and brief.

*   *   *

Swallow two whiskers from the cat you've loved since she was a kitten. Now without a torch, you can navigate the neighbourhood at night and walk without bruising through any stooped and narrow doorway.

*   *   *

When I was four, into the kitchen of our house my dad carried a toy Pomeranian tucked in his coat pocket. He had traded, unbeknown to his boss, a half tank of oil from the green Co-op delivery truck for one of Mrs. Rittinger's pure-bred pups. Furry and red as a fox, the pup was smaller than my father's hand. Lying on my belly on linoleum warmed by the fire in the wood stove, I watched her small pink tongue lapping milk. The thread of white stretching from the surface to her mouth didn't break until she'd licked the bowl clean. Never had I gazed at anything so long and hard, sensing for the first time that beauty, when you open up to it completely, brings both a wonder and a wound.

My mother named her Tiny, and she became my brother's dog. Seven years older than I, he'd sometimes let me tag along when he and his friends played kick the can or built a soldiers' fort out of the log ends waiting to be chopped for the stove. As soon as he grabbed his jacket from the hook, I was at his heels like a second dog, dumber in canine ways but just as loyal and underfoot. Some days he'd order me to stay in our yard. Other times, by the caragana hedge, he'd tell me to hide and he'd count to ten, and then he'd never find me. Tiny wasn't sent away unless the games spread too far afield. "Go home, Tiny," he'd say, and she'd wend slowly down the block, head and tail lowered. I knew exactly what she felt. She made an image of my sadness.

   •   •   •

Cats are confounded by mirrors and the surfaces of pools. Strangers to Narcissus, they don't need the compliment of their reflection. There's so much in the world: sunslick and dapple, moth blunder, black spider skating on the porcelain of the bathroom sink.

   •   •   •

On winter mornings from the picture window, I'd watch Tiny and my brother head off on his paper route, her trotting ahead, running up the steps to the houses that took the news and passing those that didn't. Our neighbours thought this was the smartest, cutest thing and tipped my brother with change left over from the milkman. Once I went off with them because Mom was curling in a bonspiel out of town and left the house early to make the first game. All down the block every house or so, Tiny leapt straight up as if springs had been buckled to the bottom of her paws so she could see above the snow piled on both sides of the shovelled walk. When my brother's bag was almost empty, he lifted me and set me inside on top of the papers he had left, Tiny bounding ahead on her short legs and doubling back. I was so happy then. If he'd told her any time, "Go home," she'd have known exactly where to go, but she didn't have to. The three of us had work to do, lights coming on one by one in the windows down our small town's winter streets, blue as they were back then, before the dawn.

Because my brother tossed too much in bed, Tiny slept with me. A cranky little dog, she'd nip if I moved my feet. I learned to lie like a courtly lady's effigy on a tomb, dog on a carnelian cushion at my feet. I can still sleep like that, the blankets and sheets flat and smooth when I wake in the morning as if no one lay all night in that neat bed. What else did I learn from her? No matter what I did, she remained my brother's dog. No matter how much I loved her, the same love didn't come back. My brother reaffirmed this lesson when he left home. He was eighteen, I was eleven, and though I don't blame him any more, he rarely wrote and never visited. I missed him, but he didn't miss me. Two years ago, a friend stopped seeing me because of some terrible thing I'd done, she said, but she couldn't explain it. Next to my husband and mother, she was the most important person in my life. My saying that out loud meant nothing to her. Again, my love for her was more than what she felt for me, and there was nothing I could do to make things right.

·   ·   ·

A cat can walk on snow without breaking through; it can walk on clouds. If you follow one for a day in the garden, your feet will grow lighter. By night, you'll be walking on your dreams. This is the first lesson in flying without wings.

•   •   •

A few Januarys ago, a freak snowstorm hit the West Coast, where I now live. Before the worst of it when we couldn't make it through the backyard, the snow thigh-high, my husband and I walked to the pond to check on the gold-fish. Two of them lay still, embedded in a skin of ice. He broke through to scoop them out and set them on the snow at the edge of the circle of stones while we peered in the pond to see the others. Alive, they drifted in the cold viscous water as if suspended between two elements like someone waiting to be born.

I stared at the two dead fish. Their presence seemed mag-nified, weighted with significance. Part of their power was the startling beauty of paradox—against the snow, two gleaming fish the size and colour of candle flames broken from their wicks. No matter how long I looked, I couldn't figure out what they meant. They remained unreadable, like glyphs from a language not my own. Looking at the fish, a still life on white canvas, was like looking at the sky where some believe a paradise is waiting. If it does exist, there are few signs of it more powerful than the small miracles you find right here.

•   •   •

The inventor of the camera's shutter and light-filter mechanisms had been studying the pupils of his cat. Every photograph has a parallel a cat has taken—without a touch of sentiment, a perfect composition of the never-seen and shadow.

•   •   •

The black-and-white cat on my lap under the apple tree stares at the fir against the fence. When I follow the translucent arrow of her gaze, look over and up, I see the raccoon I didn't know was there, peering down at us. The blue-eyed cat on the deck fixates on the ivy that climbs the chimney, his ears swerving left then right. I sit beside him and hear a woodrat's feet scuttling along the stems of the vines under the sticky leaves. Instead of multiplying cat years by seven to figure out how old they are in human terms, I divide my age when I'm around them. I grow younger, alert to what a cat attends to. This morning I am eight and full of wonder. Over a hundred years ago, Charles Baudelaire wrote, "The Chinese read the time in the eyes of cats." The time, he said, was eternity. When I spend my hours with cats, make my eyes their eyes, note the twitching of their ears and their nostrils' flare, this is the eternity I sense: the smell of rust in the air before rain; all things the wind startles into beauty; the winter hare in the belly of the moon, its heartbeat soft and sure as the fall of paws.

A THOUGHT,
OR MAYBE TWO

JUNE CALLWOOD

I'm not sure anyone can explain how wisdom is attained; yet many people are wise. Unhappily, human development is an exceedingly private matter, so secret and individual that it leaves no footprints for someone else to follow. The nature of inner growth is mostly snail-paced and evolutionary, rather than the clap of a revolutionary resolve that calls attention to itself.

For instance, my work habits are of the nose-to-the-grindstone, obsessive-compulsive variety, but I don't know why. My parents were hard-working people; maybe that accounts for my somewhat driven behaviour.

Also, I find that adversarial situations depress me, my strong preference being for the bliss of amiable collaboration, but the anguish I feel when tempers rise can't be attributed to early influences because there wasn't much open conflict in my childhood. If my family members didn't like one another, they kept it to themselves. Unless you count as a contributing factor to my horror of conflict the fact that my mother hated it too. It would drive her out of the house, and her mother was the same. A clue there.

The literature on the subject of early childhood maintains that good (or bad) behaviour is shaped early in life according to a seamless twining of the infant's innate character and the environment in which the small person is raised.

Conditioning often results in a degree of permanent patterning, but it is also true that most adults retain a capacity to be impressionable. Profound change can happen in a click because of someone's example, or a casual comment that sinks in because it holds a truth. The power of random events to alter behaviour is grist for fiction and the real stuff of human lives.

It takes practice, I'm told, to upgrade a personality. Aristotle said that humans are what they repeatedly do. It's hard and lonely toil, without end, as people stumble from peaks of sweet harmony to the caustic depths of regret. I'm a work in progress myself and I'm in my eighties.

Jean Piaget, a Swiss child psychologist of note, decided that humans acquire knowledge and their distinctive dispositions by a process of accretion and substitution. Accretion is the layering of information (how to tie a shoe, the names of clouds) and substitution is the factor of *Oops, that was wrong, better not do that again.*

In my experience good people can't explain why they are good. I once asked an outstandingly fine woman who lives a selfless life why she is such a good person. She said, "My parents were good people." That's a reasonable answer, since people are shaped more by parental example than anything adults may pass on in the way of instruction. But in her case it doesn't really explain much. Her brother is in jail.

If people are a mystery to themselves, which is what I think I am getting at here, I don't know what any of us can offer the young beyond loving them and setting as decent an example as possible. The rest is rules, such as to be punctual (it is inconsiderate to keep people waiting); to strive for economic self-sufficiency (you're safer); and don't step on ants (they have a life too). The objective is to shape a conscience that neither produces crushing guilt nor forgives bad behaviour easily.

• • •

I can't think of any life-enhancing counsel I have ever passed on successfully to our children, except that they all know not to interrupt writers when they are thinking—only when they are typing. One of my grandchildren, indeed, was asked this very question on television. Said the interviewer, "What life lessons has your grandmother given you?" She responded, "How to butter bread." Oh well, good table manners always come in handy.

Similarly, on a television show I was hosting, the producer scheduled an item which featured my mother and older daughter. The point was that we were to discuss the continuity that flows from mothers to daughters, and back. I addressed the pivotal question to my mother. I asked, "What do you think we three have in common?" She answered thoughtfully, "We all wash dishes the same way."

My answer would have been, "We all have a sense of humor," but it amounts to the same thing. She wasn't prepared to offer an analysis, which, at best, would capture only a thread or two of the thick fabric that binds our three generations. "Washing dishes the same way" was the short form of the very complicated stuff of family relationships. In our gang we are affectionate and loyal, we have similar views on matters of social responsibility, and we laugh a lot, but we are very, very different people. Even love, which Freud poetically called the "oceanic feeling," can't dissolve the secrets a heart holds.

Behavioural scientists say that people discover when they are only two years old that adults can't read their thoughts. That realization carries with it a shocking message that, essentially, every individual is alone and unknowable. The universal search for the meaning of existence owes much to the uneasiness felt by those who sense, to their horror, that they are hunkered down alone on the high seas of perpetual angst, and where is land?

This gives rise to dread, which in turn accounts for the popularity of how-to books and advice columns. The field is a splendid one for the improvement of a writer's income, however clueless the author may be. I myself used to be quite good at giving advice until I noticed one day that no one was paying the slightest attention—unless what I had to suggest coincided with what they planned to do anyway.

In any case, dramatic and helpful insight often comes unsolicited and out of the blue, and from unexpected sources. When I was about twelve I was a member of a swimming team in Kitchener, Ontario. My best event was highboard diving, and I was taking first place in every competition until Dorothy Schaeffer came along with her forward layout flip. I couldn't bring myself even to try it, so she moved into the winner's circle. One evening during a meet, she over-rotated and went into the water with a huge splash. I was delighted. "Oh good!" I cried. A boy next to me, also twelve years old, said in a low voice, "That wasn't very nice." Drenched in shame, I discovered in that instant that I wanted to be a nice person a whole lot more than I wanted to win a ribbon. On reflection, I count him among the most influential mentors I have ever known, and I can't remember his name.

Ever since the night of the swimming meet I have been working on a theology which looks pretty simple: it is that kindness is as close to godliness as humans can ever get. There is a law of physics that states that the only thing absolutely true in the universe is the speed of light. But light bends, I believe, so maybe that isn't exactly true either. I am unalterably convinced, however, of the truth that kindness is holiness in action. I am not speaking of the one-way kindness of acts of charity, that humiliate the recipient, but of the kindness that leaves both parties feeling better.

If I hold a door for strangers following behind me, the strangers are no longer exactly the people they were before that happened, and neither am I. They have been brushed by a very small act of consideration, which cost me nothing, and the world seems to them minutely more friendly, and safer. And I feel better too. On the other hand, people who let doors shut in someone's face lower the human pool of goodwill.

I doubt anyone becomes kinder by being ordered to, but everyone can learn civility, which actually amounts to the same thing. Rules of good conduct are quite precise. "Please" and "thank you" are signals of respect. In most cultures, people greet one another by saying some version of, "How are you?" That show of concern has become ritualized, but it still carries a message that the well-being of others is an important matter. Similarly, the prohibitions on lying are not because the liar might be caught and suffer censure, but because the lying breaks the code of trust that is the glue of relationships. Good manners, fundamentally, are exercises in empathy. If we were not helpful to one another, our communities would turn into jungles full of angry animals, and every inmate would be lunch.

"We are all in this together," sighed Kurt Vonnegut, "whatever this is."

Thoughtfulness for others generally is learned in childhood when the principal adults in a child's life show consideration to all comers. Rules of behaviour can be learned by rote, of course, without the support of genuine thoughtfulness, but they don't do the essential job of warming a room. People have an unnerving capacity to reflect what comes at them. If there is a primary assumption that another person is reasonable and good, that individual is quite likely to react by being both. On the other hand, the expectation that the other person is of a lower order of intelligence and worth deeply discourages co-operation. The best people can give one another is respect; actually, that's a lot.

The rudder of conscience that steers me is homemade. Since I don't know what built it, I am not in a position to pass on a training manual and, in any case, I cannot presume that it would serve another person. Mine is customized to fit me, just as others put together individualized rudders out of the stuff of their own lives.

It is, therefore, not particularly useful for me to pass along something that gives me calm, but I'll end with it anyway. I find peace in my sense of insignificance; if I ever thought otherwise, I would be immobilized. I learned this about myself when I was a teenager racked by confusion. One hot July night when I dragged my mattress out to an upstairs balcony to be cooler, I discovered stars. I was enchanted. Such glory, such constancy, such mystery. By day I studied astronomy and at night I picked out the galaxies. At some point I was awed to realize my irrelevance in the vastness of space. Perspective set in and I felt my adolescent angst evaporate.

Since I live in a city now and the stars are opaque, I restore equilibrium these days by watching endless waves break on a shore. They rise and fall, rise and fall, one after another, after another, after another; forever. Long after I pick up my beach towel and depart, long, long after I am gone from the planet, the waves will still be coming in, as indifferent to my absence as they were to my presence. That is a comforting thought.

CONTRIBUTORS

MARJORIE ANDERSON

My life was first made rich by being part of a story-telling family living on the edge of Lake Winnipeg, where we were surrounded by the wonders of its mists and lore. After years of teaching various combinations of writing, literature and communication at the University of Manitoba, I've shifted my professional focus to editing and being immersed in literary projects such as this one. My personal joys are still being with family and spending time at the edge of water, now with the mists and moonlight at our lake cottage.

MARGARET ATWOOD

I am the author of more than twenty-six books of poetry, fiction and non-fiction, and my work has been translated into more than thirty languages. My most recent novel is *Oryx and Crake*. I live in Toronto.

JUNE CALLWOOD

I've been a journalist for a very long time, and I don't know any other profession that gives such a window on the world. In my era journalists rarely were college graduates and I never heard of a journalism school, so we all learned from patient colleagues—and developed a newsroom camaraderie that isn't common any more. For a nervous teenager, far from home, newspaper city rooms were my introduction to the kindness of strangers.

TRACEY ANN COVEART

Growing up, I was described (not always kindly) as a mother looking for a place to happen. Eventually, I happened. I blossomed with my three children—now teenagers, two on the verge of fledging, one a perpetual nestling—and they are my opus. A full-time mom and part-time writer and editor, I live on a hill in Port Perry, Ontario, within spitting distance of the world's most devoted parents. Over the last twenty years I have managed to wedge a number of works—both published and unpublished—into the nooks and crannies of the time-space continuum.

LORNA CROZIER

Precious moments have come when I'm able to erase the outlines that separate me from another species and enter their sensory world, even briefly. I try to do that while being Chair of the Department of Writing at the University of Victoria, where I teach poetry. I've recently become more interested in the personal essay, partly thanks to Marjorie Anderson and Carol Shields, who first invited me to explore the form. I live and write in an old house on Vancouver Island with a big garden tended by Patrick Lane and appreciated by our two fine cats.

ANDREA CURTIS

I grew up in the shadow of Georgian Bay with my nose in a book, went to school in Montreal, tree-planted in Northern Ontario and wound up as a magazine editor in Toronto. My first book, *Into the Blue*, is a creative non-fiction work about a 1906 Great Lakes shipwreck that devastated my family.

I live in Toronto with a houseful of boys. "The Writers' Circle" recalls a time when I yearned to write more, imagining that committing words to paper would not only free me, but might also offer solace to the profoundly marginalized at a Toronto women's shelter.

NORMA DePLEDGE

"My Father's Last Gift" is part of a larger work in progress, the working title of which is *How Slight the Shadow*. Other pieces of my short fiction have been published in literary magazines—including the *Malahat Review, Room of One's Own, Grain*, and *Atlantis*—aired on CBC Radio, and anthologized in *Love and Pomegranates* (Sono Nis). In collaboration with my friend and colleague Claire McKenzie, I published a writing textbook with Prentice Hall. My novel, *A Better Plan*, was published in 2004 in broadsheet format by the *Victoria Literary Times*. I live and work in Victoria.

MAGGIE de VRIES

After five years as children's book editor at Orca Book Publishers in Victoria, I am in the middle of a transformation, from commuting editor to at-home writer who edits. All of a sudden "at home" means more to me than it ever has before: husband, cats, garden, friends, family. I wrote "The Only Way Past" because I wanted to tell about learning to face life squarely, no matter how hard that might be, and now I find that the life I am facing delights me.

M. A. C. FARRANT

I was born in Australia to a wandering mother and a Canadian seafaring father but, luckily, at age five, was settled on Vancouver Island to be raised by my father's sister. These events are the subject of my memoir, *My Turquoise*

Years (Greystone/Douglas & McIntyre, 2004), and of the piece included in this book—my early training about men and Amazon housewives. I have also published seven books of humorous and satirical short fiction. Writing full-time and occasionally teaching at the University of Victoria, I live near Sidney, B.C.

LIANE FAULDER

I've lived most of my life in Edmonton, though I came to love Toronto while a journalism student at Ryerson. As a feature writer with the *Edmonton Journal*, I've learned to work with the material that comes my way, and that's been helpful in my life too. My contribution to this anthology was inspired by my two sons, Dylan and Daniel. Being the mother of boys came as a shock to me, and I've been figuring out why ever since.

NATALIE FINGERHUT

After eight post-secondary institutions, five cities and four careers, I have finally found a happy place for myself as an editor in Toronto with the love of my life, Rob Winters, and our beloved Raphael. Though the misfit's journey to personal acceptance is long, the rewards are many, namely being able to pass time at bar mitzvahs by talking wrestling with the guys and debating diapers with the gals.

MARIE-LYNN HAMMOND

I'm an air force brat; got my love of storytelling from my Franco-Ontarian *maman;* became a singer-songwriter, with detours through playwriting and broadcasting; now work mostly as a writer and editor. My remaining sister and my niece make life worthwhile, along with all critters great and small and my dream of someday doing flying changes on a little black horse. Why this essay? Because I want humans to remember we're animals too and ought to stop fouling our nest. Because maybe you don't need a guru, a therapist or a million bucks; maybe all you need is a cat.

HARRIET HART

I'm migratory, a snowbird who winters by the shores of Lake Chapala, Mexico, and summers on Kagaki Lake, northwestern Ontario. Born on a prairie farm, I've been cast in many supporting roles on my life's journey from Manitoba to Mexico: daughter, sister, wife, mother, divorcée, other woman, friend, employee, landlady and stepmother. In retirement, I play the leading lady in my personal drama. I wrote "She Drinks" to share how I quit drinking and did it my way.

FRANCES ITANI

I grew up in a Quebec village and began to travel and study at age fifteen, when I finished high school. I've been writing for more than thirty years, and my books include *Deafening* and *Poached Egg on Toast*. I was born with energy and optimism of spirit, and am thankful for both. I love children and have two of my own, now adults. Voice and language have always been of interest to me in my work. I wrote "Conspicuous Voices" as a tribute to the extended family that surrounded me in childhood, one more thing to be thankful about.

MELANIE D. JANZEN

Three years ago, I decided to leave my rewarding teaching career to return to university to pursue an interdisciplinary master's degree in Womens' Studies and Education. It was through my coursework, my amazing advisers and my research in Uganda that I have come to truly appreciate the extraordinary circles of women in my life. My life in Winnipeg is further enriched by the unwavering support of my husband, Keith, our foster daughter Cayla's teenaged antics and the love of my family and friends.

GILLIAN KERR

I live in Toronto where I have a career in food marketing and retailing. My profession has taught me the shortcuts available in supermarkets that make it possible to serve food with pride and love without having to sacrifice the best part of a Saturday afternoon. I have been writing creatively for five years. Many people have asked me how I learned to cook. "Tiny Tomatoes" is an answer to that question as well as a reflection on the ways creativity is taught. It asks: what do our talents owe to the passion of our teachers?

CHANTAL KREVIAZUK

I lived in Winnipeg, Manitoba, for my first twenty years, then moved to Toronto when I released my first album. Now I commute between Los Angeles and Toronto, where I live with my husband and our sons, Rowan and Lucca. Our life together is fulfilling, juggling the demands and joys of parenthood, the rich careers as artists and writers/producers, and the work we do for organizations such as Warchild Canada and the Canadian Mental Health Association. My career has taught me there is so much more to living in this world than self-perpetuation and consumerism. Therein lies my greatest discovery.

SILKEN LAUMANN

My life is a medley of parenting, inspirational speaking and writing, friends and family and time for my own growth and reflection. It is wonderful when a writing project can touch upon all of these. Writing this piece was cathartic in that it provided an opportunity to reflect on all that is contradictory as well as all that is beautiful in mothering; I find myself more peaceful in the experience now. I live an alternately harried and peaceful life in Victoria, B.C., when not travelling for speaking engagements all across North America.

JODI LUNDGREN

Words and movement have impassioned me since childhood. Victoria-raised, I earned a doctorate in English at the University of Washington while training and performing as a modern dancer. I published a novel, *Touched*, and have recently written another for young adults from the perspective of a teenage dancer. After spending two years as writer-in-residence at Thompson Rivers University, I now live in Nanaimo, B.C. In "Pitch: A Dancer's Journal," I explore the place where discipline and exhilaration coincide.

ANN-MARIE MacDONALD

I am a novelist, a playwright and an actor. I have performed in theatres across Canada and in numerous television series and feature films, including *Better Than Chocolate*. My plays include *Goodnight Desdemona (Good Morning Juliet)* and *Belle Moral: A Natural History*. I am also the author of two novels, *Fall on Your Knees* and *The Way the Crow Flies*.

C. B. MACKINTOSH

I was born and raised in Walkerton, Ontario, but my heart found its home in Banff, where I work among artists and walk up mountains on my lunch hours. I wrote this piece because my husband saw the call for proposals, and my mentor, Marni Jackson, suggested, "Write something about the mountains." Writing is, and has always been, my trail through the wilderness. I am currently navigating my first book.

BARBARA McLEAN

Permanently a farmer, temporarily a teacher of English and Women's Studies, I combined my passions in my book, *Lambsquarters: Scenes From a Handmade Life*. As a shepherd I am acquainted with grief and interment, for keeping live-stock inevitably results in deadstock: stillborn lambs lie buried in the bush and extinct ewes sprout alfalfa in the fields. The death of my parents makes it possible to print the story of what I discovered through finding my sister's ashes.

HEATHER MALLICK

I am a constant reader, a feminist, a socialist, a francophile, a columnist and a number of other things. My first book, published by Penguin Canada, was a diary entitled *Pearls in Vinegar*, and I am now working on two new works of non-fiction. My essay, "The Inoculation," written with much wincing and disinfection of typing fingers, is intended as a donation to women and girls, in the hope that it might direct them away from similar disasters.

BARBARA MITCHELL

I am a writer and a university lecturer living in Peter-borough, Ontario. I was raised in High River, Alberta, where, at the age of fifteen, I met my husband on a piano bench. For the past fifteen years we have been involved in a writerly duet—two volumes of a biography on his father, W.O. Mitchell. "Finding My Way," about family connec-tions and disconnections, was sparked by my musings about the time spent buried in Mitchell history and the recent discovery of my own repressed family history.

BERNICE MORGAN

I was born in Newfoundland and have lived all my life here— a place that fills my imagination, exhilarates me and drives me to despair. My parents, Sadie Vincent of Cape Island, Bonavista Bay, and William Vardy of Random Island, Trinity Bay, came into St. John's during the Depression. Stories about the outposts they left behind provided the background for my novels, *Random Passages* and *Waiting for Time*. Wartime St. John's is the setting for most of the stories in my third book, *Topography of Love*, and I hope the novel I am now working on will lead me eventually into St. John's of 2005.

LORRI NEILSEN GLENN

I was raised in railway towns on the prairies and moved to Nova Scotia over twenty years ago. After years as an ethnographer, a professor and an author of books on research and feminist issues, I began to write poetry and essays, and now wonder what took me so long. The ocean, the prairie horizon and stories of dauntless women inspire me equally. I was appointed Poet Laureate of Halifax for 2005–2009.

PATRICIA PEARSON

I was born in Mexico City into a Foreign Service family and spent my childhood trotting after my parents from country to country, occupying myself by writing stories and telling fibs. One of which was that I was born in Mexico City "during an earthquake." This love of embellishment was tempered by a career in journalism, but has recently been given free rein again in my novels *Playing House* and *Believe Me*.

BETH POWNING

I spent my childhood in a creaky, mouse-ridden farmhouse in northeast Connecticut. I studied creative writing at Sarah Lawrence College and in 1972, at the age of twenty-three, moved to New Brunswick with my husband, Peter. I've written about our remote maritime farm in the memoirs *Seeds of Another Summer, Shadow Child* and *Edge Seasons*. My first novel, *The Hatbox Letters*, drew upon my memories of my grandparents. I'm one now myself. Maeve and Bridget live just down the road.

JUDY REBICK

I have been an activist on various issues since my late twenties. I've just turned sixty and am still at it. Young people always ask me how I have stayed active for so long without getting discouraged, so I thought I would contribute a piece on how my life as an activist was born in personal rebellion and moved on from there.

SUSAN RILEY

After twenty-five years writing for newspapers and producing for the CBC, I studied law at the same time both my children were in university. I am now working as a lawyer, living between Winnipeg and an island in Lake of the Woods and writing about things that matter to me. I wrote about Larry because his story inspired my daughter and me, to our surprise, one sad fall weekend.

LAURIE SARKADI

I moved to the Northwest Territories as a young woman and travelled the Arctic as the *Edmonton Journal*'s northern correspondent. I'm still here, raising a globe-tripping family in the wilderness, grateful for the natural grandeur and insightful people in my life. ("Hi Mom!") Sometimes I work at the CBC, sometimes I write songs . . . and once, I had the luxury of spending months at home in silence to write "The Bear Within."

BARBARA SCOTT

I work as a freelance writer, editor and creative writing instructor in Calgary. My first book, a collection of short stories entitled *The Quick*, won the City of Calgary W.O. Mitchell Book Prize and the Howard O'Hagan Award for Short Fiction. I recently co-edited an anthology of essays on the experience of publishing a first book, entitled *First Writes*, and am currently at work on a novel. In writing "Tethers" I realized that while my relationship with my mother was difficult, it led me to the writing life I treasure—her greatest gift to me, even if unintentionally given.

JODI STONE

I like to spin yarns. I spun them in Edinburgh for a few years, then in Liverpool. I returned to Ontario to spin some more and wove a family instead. While writing, editing and publishing provide me with immense satisfaction, my husband and son are my greatest joys.

CATHY STONEHOUSE

I grew up in the UK and emigrated to Canada in 1988, receiving my MFA in Creative Writing from UBC in 1990. I've published poetry, fiction and non-fiction in a wide range of Canadian magazines and anthologies, edited the literary journal *Event* for three years, and currently spend my time chasing after my not-quite-toddling daughter and making notes for future writing projects on the backs of envelopes.

This essay pushed its way out of me during the first raw months after my (living) daughter's birth. Writing it has felt like a partial completion of the unfinished journey that was Gracie's life.

J. C. SZASZ

As a child I hated reading, but the *Bobbsey Twins* series inspired me to write my own stories. In 2006 Napoleon Publishing/RendezVous Crime will publish my short mystery "Egyptian Queen" in their *Dead in the Water* anthology. My novel, *The Change Agent*, is currently seeking a publisher while I write its sequel. My family and I enjoy skiing and kayaking on Vancouver Island. I am honoured to write about the humble heroes of the Nanaimo Crown Counsel office.

ARITHA van HERK

I've been asked if I am a writer who teaches or a teacher who writes, but I consider this a false division. I teach and write, sometimes simultaneously, sometimes in a wonderfully challenging juggling act of words and ideas. I have been teaching Creative Writing and Canadian Literature at the University of Calgary for twenty-two years, and what is best is being able to make my living reading books and being able to hide in the biggest library in the city.

JANICE WILLIAMSON

This essay, part of a book-length manuscript, "Hexagrams for My Chinese Daughter," is dedicated to my daughter, Bao, and my mother—and to Cecile Mactaggart, a generous mentor who knows the transformations of mothering, writing, travel and Chinese dragons. I've written, taught and rabble-roused at the University of Alberta since 1987. My splendid daughter (now eight) and I garden beautifully at latitude 53.

ACKNOWLEDGEMENTS

An anthology is a satisfying collaborative effort in every way, and I offer warm appreciation for the following contributions:

- Ann-Marie MacDonald for gracing the book with her writing talents and creative insights in the Introduction;
- All the women writers who had the courage and creativity to offer intimate glimpses of their lives in the form of proposals and essays. I am honoured to have been given the opportunity to read them all;
- Lorna Crozier, whose magic with words in the poem "To See Clearly" provided just the right image for our title;
- All those at Random House, especially Tanya, Marion and Anne, whose warmth and professional expertise have enhanced this anthology experience greatly;
- The memory of the wisdom and guiding light of my friend Carol;
- My brothers Jim and Fred, whose word wisdom I rely on, my sisters Sylvia and Louise whose enthusiasm for these anthologies has always

been there, and my new sister-in-law Grace who has joined the web of family writing-support services; and

- My husband, Gary, our four daughters and their families and all my wonderful women friends who stand beside me loyally during my project passions.